# BLOOM'S

# HOW TO WRITE ABOUT

# *Alice Walker*

## CHRISTINE KERR

BLOOM'S
LITERARY CRITICISM
*An imprint of Infobase Publishing*

**Bloom's How to Write about Alice Walker**

Copyright © 2009 by Christine Kerr

Bloom's Literary Criticism
An imprint of Infobase Publishing
132 West 31st Street
New York NY 10001

**Library of Congress Cataloging-in-Publication Data**

Kerr, Christine.
   Bloom's how to write about Alice Walker / Christine Kerr ; introduction by Harold Bloom.
      p. cm.—(Bloom's how to write about literature)
   Includes bibliographical references and index.
   ISBN 978-0-7910-9745-8 (acid-free paper) 1. Walker, Alice, 1944– Criticism and interpretation. 2. Criticism—Authorship. 3. Report writing. I. Bloom, Harold. II. Title. III. Title: How to write about Alice Walker. IV. Title: Alice Walker. V. Series.
   PS3573.A425Z74 2009
   813'.54—dc22                              2008005707

Bloom's Literary Criticism books are available at special discounts when purchased in bulk quantities for businesses, associations, institutions, or sales promotions. Please call our Special Sales Department in New York at (212) 967-8800 or (800) 322-8755.

You can find Bloom's Literary Criticism on the World Wide Web at
http://www.chelseahouse.com

Text design by Annie O'Donnell
Cover design by Ben Peterson

Printed in the United States of America

Bang MSRF 10 9 8 7 6 5 4 3 2 1

This book is printed on acid-free paper.

# CONTENTS

# SERIES
# INTRODUCTION

**B**LOOM's How to Write about Literature series is designed to inspire students to write fine essays on great writers and their works. Each volume in the series begins with an introduction by Harold Bloom, meditating on the challenges and rewards of writing about the volume's subject author. The first chapter then provides detailed instructions on how to write a good essay, including how to find a thesis; how to develop an outline; how to write a good introduction, body text, and conclusions; how to cite sources; and more. The second chapter provides a brief overview of the issues involved in writing about the subject author and then a number of suggestions for paper topics, with accompanying strategies for addressing each topic. Succeeding chapters cover the author's major works.

The paper topics suggested within this book are open ended, and the brief strategies provided are designed to give students a push forward on the writing process rather than a road map to success. The aim of the book is to pose questions, not answer them. Many different kinds of papers could result from each topic. As always, the success of each paper will depend completely on the writer's skill and imagination.

# HOW TO WRITE ABOUT ALICE WALKER: INTRODUCTION

*by Harold Bloom*

**B**IOGRAPHICAL AND social criticism are more suited to apprehending the varied works of Alice Walker than is the application of aesthetic and cognitive standards. My judgment in that sentence reflects the difficulties of being accurate in regard to so courageously fierce an ideologue as Walker. Her novels, widely influential, defend the rights of black women against everything that jeopardizes the potential wholeness of their lives.

Confronted by so worthy a cause, mere literary criticism is disarmed, though I wonder if even the best of Walker's novels, *Meridian* (1976) and *The Color Purple* (1983), are fated to be remembered only as period pieces.

The best counsel I can offer for writing usefully about Alice Walker is to juxtapose her with her chosen forerunner, Zora Neale Hurston (1891–1960), whose admirable novel *Their Eyes Were Watching God* (1937) has inspired much of Walker's work. Janie Crawford, heroine of Hurston's best book, clearly is the model for Celie in *The Color Purple*. The exuberantly heterosexual Hurston might have been disdainful of Celie's lesbian salvation and of her passive tendency to accept victimization, but those seem to me defensive swerves away from Hurston's overwhelming influence on Walker.

# HOW TO WRITE
# A GOOD ESSAY

WHILE THERE are many ways to write about literature, most assignments for high school and college English classes call for analytical papers. In these assignments, you are presenting your interpretation of a text to your reader. Your objective is to interpret the text's meaning in order to enhance your reader's understanding and enjoyment of the work. Without exception, strong papers about the meaning of a literary work are built upon a careful, close reading of the text or texts. Careful, analytical reading should always be the first step in your writing process. This volume provides models of such close, analytical reading, and these should help you develop your own skills as a reader and as a writer.

As the examples throughout this book demonstrate, attentive reading entails thinking about and evaluating the formal (textual) aspects of the author's works: theme, character, form, and language. In addition, when writing about a work, many readers choose to move beyond the text itself to consider the work's cultural context. In these instances, writers might explore the historical circumstances of the time period in which the work was written. Alternatively, they might examine the philosophies and ideas that a work addresses. Even in cases where writers explore a work's cultural context, though, papers must still address the more formal aspects of the work itself. A good interpretative essay that evaluates Charles Dickens's use of the philosophy of utilitarianism in his novel *Hard Times,* for example, cannot adequately address the author's treatment of the philosophy without firmly grounding this discussion in the book itself. In other words, any analytical paper about a text, even

1

one that seeks to evaluate the work's cultural context, must also have a firm handle on the work's themes, characters, and language. You must look for and evaluate these aspects of a work, then, as you read a text and as you prepare to write about it.

## WRITING ABOUT THEMES

Literary themes are more than just topics or subjects treated in a work; they are attitudes or points about these topics that often structure other elements in a work. Writing about theme therefore requires that you not just identify a topic that a literary work addresses but also discuss what that work says about that topic. For example, if you were writing about the culture of the American South in William Faulkner's famous story "A Rose for Emily," you would need to discuss what Faulkner says, argues, or implies about that culture and its passing.

When you prepare to write about thematic concerns in a work of literature, you will probably discover that, like most works of literature, your text touches upon other themes in addition to its central theme. These secondary themes also provide rich ground for paper topics. A thematic paper on "A Rose for Emily" might consider gender or race in the story. While neither of these could be said to be the central theme of the story, they are clearly related to the passing of the "old South" and could provide plenty of good material for papers.

As you prepare to write about themes in literature, you might find a number of strategies helpful. After you identify a theme or themes in the story, you should begin by evaluating how other elements of the story—such as character, point of view, imagery, and symbolism—help develop the theme. You might ask yourself what your own responses are to the author's treatment of the subject matter. Do not neglect the obvious, either: What expectations does the title set up? How does the title help develop thematic concerns? Clearly, the title "A Rose for Emily" says something about the narrator's attitude toward the title character, Emily Grierson, and all she represents.

## WRITING ABOUT CHARACTER

Generally, characters are essential components of fiction and drama. (This is not always the case, though; Ray Bradbury's "August 2026: There

Will Come Soft Rains" is technically a story without characters, at least any human characters.) Often, you can discuss character in poetry, as in T. S. Eliot's "The Love Song of J. Alfred Prufrock" or Robert Browning's "My Last Duchess." Many writers find that analyzing character is one of the most interesting and engaging ways to work with a piece of literature and to shape a paper. After all, characters generally are human, and we all know something about being human and living in the world. While it is always important to remember that these figures are not real people but creations of the writer's imagination, it can be fruitful to begin evaluating them as you might evaluate a real person. Often you can start with your own response to a character. Did you like or dislike the character? Did you sympathize with the character? Why or why not?

Keep in mind, though, that emotional responses like these are just starting places. To truly explore and evaluate literary characters, you need to return to the formal aspects of the text and evaluate how the author has drawn these characters. The 20th-century writer E. M. Forster coined the terms *flat* characters and *round* characters. Flat characters are static, one dimensional characters who frequently represent a particular concept or idea. In contrast, round characters are fully drawn and much more realistic characters who frequently change and develop over the course of a work. Are the characters you are studying flat or round? What elements of the characters lead you to this conclusion? Why might the author have drawn characters like this? How does their development affect the meaning of the work? Similarly, you should explore the techniques the author uses to develop characters. Do we hear a character's own words, or do we hear only other characters' assessments of him or her? Or, does the author use an omniscient or limited omniscient narrator to allow us access to the workings of the characters' minds? If so, how does that help develop the characterization? Often you can even evaluate the narrator as a character. How trustworthy are the opinions and assessments of the narrator? You should also think about characters' names. Do they mean anything? If you encounter a hero named Sophia or Sophie, you should probably think about her wisdom (or lack thereof), since *Sophia* means "wisdom" in Greek. Similarly, since the name *Sylvia* is derived from the word *sylvan,* meaning "of the wood," you might want to evaluate that character's relationship with nature. Once again, you might look to the title of the work. Does Herman Melville's "Bartleby, the Scrivener" signal anything about Bartleby himself? Is Bartleby adequately defined by his job as scrivener? Is this part of Melville's point? Pursuing questions like these can help you develop thorough papers about characters from psychological, sociological, or more formalistic perspectives.

## WRITING ABOUT FORM AND GENRE

*Genre,* a word derived from French, means "type" or "class." Literary genres are distinctive classes or categories of literary composition. On the most general level, literary works can be divided into the genres of drama, poetry, fiction, and essays, yet within those genres there are classifications that are also referred to as genres. Tragedy and comedy, for example, are genres of drama. Epic, lyric, and pastoral are genres of poetry. *Form,* on the other hand, generally refers to the shape or structure of a work. There are many clearly defined forms of poetry that follow specific patterns of meter, rhyme, and stanza. Sonnets, for example, are poems that follow a fixed form of 14 lines. Sonnets generally follow one of two basic sonnet forms, each with its own distinct rhyme scheme. Haiku is another example of poetic form, traditionally consisting of three unrhymed lines of five, seven, and five syllables.

While you might think that writing about form or genre might leave little room for argument, many of these forms and genres are very fluid. Remember that literature is evolving and ever changing, and so are its forms. As you study poetry, you may find that poets, especially more modern poets, play with traditional poetic forms, bringing about new effects. Similarly, dramatic tragedy was once quite narrowly defined, but over the centuries playwrights have broadened and challenged traditional definitions, changing the shape of tragedy. When Arthur Miller wrote *Death of a Salesman,* many critics challenged the idea that tragic drama could encompass a common man like Willy Loman.

Evaluating how a work of literature fits into or challenges the boundaries of its form or genre can provide you with fruitful avenues of investigation. You might find it helpful to ask why the work does or does not fit into traditional categories. Why might Miller have thought it fitting to write a tragedy of the common man? Similarly, you might compare the content or theme of a work with its form. How well do they work together? Many of Emily Dickinson's poems, for instance, follow the meter of traditional hymns. While some of her poems seem to express traditional religious doctrines, many seem to challenge or strain against traditional conceptions of God and theology. What is the effect, then, of her use of traditional hymn meter?

## WRITING ABOUT LANGUAGE, SYMBOLS, AND IMAGERY

No matter what the genre, writers use words as their most basic tool. Language is the most fundamental building block of literature. It is essential that you pay careful attention to the author's language and word choice as you read, reread, and analyze a text. Imagery is language that appeals to the senses. Most commonly, imagery appeals to our sense of vision, creating a mental picture, but authors also use language that appeals to our other senses. Images can be literal or figurative. Literal images use sensory language to describe an actual thing. In the broadest terms, figurative language uses one thing to speak about something else. For example, if I call my boss a snake, I am not saying that he is literally a reptile. Instead, I am using figurative language to communicate my opinions about him. Since we think of snakes as sneaky, slimy, and sinister, I am using the concrete image of a snake to communicate these abstract opinions and impressions.

The two most common figures of speech are similes and metaphors. Both are comparisons between two apparently dissimilar things. Similes are explicit comparisons using the words *like* or *as*; metaphors are implicit comparisons. To return to the previous example, if I say, "My boss, Bob, was waiting for me when I showed up to work five minutes late today—the snake!" I have constructed a metaphor. Writing about his experiences fighting in World War I, Wilfred Owen begins his poem "Dulce et Decorum Est" with a string of similes: "Bent double, like old beggars under sacks, / Knock-kneed, coughing like hags, we cursed through sludge." Owen's goal was to undercut clichéd notions that war and dying in battle were glorious. Certainly, comparing soldiers to coughing hags and to beggars underscores his point.

"Fog," a short poem by Carl Sandburg provides a clear example of a metaphor. Sandburg's poem reads:

> The fog comes
> on little cat feet.
>
> It sits looking
> over harbor and city
> on silent haunches
> and then moves on.

Notice how effectively Sandburg conveys surprising impressions of the fog by comparing two seemingly disparate things—the fog and a cat.

Symbols, by contrast, are things that stand for, or represent, other things. Often they represent something intangible, such as concepts or ideas. In everyday life we use and understand symbols easily. Babies at christenings and brides at weddings wear white to represent purity. Think, too, of a dollar bill. The paper itself has no value in and of itself. Instead, that paper bill is a symbol of something else, the precious metal in a nation's coffers. Symbols in literature work similarly. Authors use symbols to evoke more than a simple, straightforward, literal meaning. Characters, objects, and places can all function as symbols. Famous literary examples of symbols include Moby Dick, the white whale of Herman Melville's novel, and the scarlet *A* of Nathaniel Hawthorne's *The Scarlet Letter.* As both of these symbols suggest, a literary symbol cannot be adequately defined or explained by any one meaning. Hester Prynne's Puritan community clearly intends her scarlet *A* as a symbol of her adultery, but as the novel progresses, even her own community reads the letter as representing not just adultery, but able, angel, and a host of other meanings.

Writing about imagery and symbols requires close attention to the author's language. To prepare a paper on symbolism or imagery in a work, identify and trace the images and symbols and then try to draw some conclusions about how they function. Ask yourself how any symbols or images help contribute to the themes or meanings of the work. What connotations do they carry? How do they affect your reception of the work? Do they shed light on characters or settings? A strong paper on imagery or symbolism will thoroughly consider the use of figures in the text and will try to reach some conclusions about how or why the author uses them.

# WRITING ABOUT HISTORY AND CONTEXT

As noted above, it is possible to write an analytical paper that also considers the work's context. After all, the text was not created in a vacuum. The author lived and wrote in a specific time period and in a specific cultural context and, like all of us, was shaped by that environment. Learning more about the historical and cultural circumstances that surround the author and the work can help illuminate a text and provide you with productive material for a paper. Remember, though, that when you write analytical papers, you should use the context to illuminate the text. Do not lose sight of your goal—to interpret the meaning of the literary work. Use historical or philosophical research as a tool to develop your textual evaluation.

Thoughtful readers often consider how history and culture affected the author's choice and treatment of his or her subject matter. Investigations into the history and context of a work could examine the work's relation to specific historical events, such as the Salem witch trials in 17th-century Massachusetts or the restoration of Charles to the British throne in 1660. Bear in mind that historical context is not limited to politics and world events. While knowing about the Vietnam War is certainly helpful in interpreting much of Tim O'Brien's fiction, and some knowledge of the French Revolution clearly illuminates the dynamics of Charles Dickens's *A Tale of Two Cities,* historical context also entails the fabric of daily life. Examining a text in light of gender roles, race relations, class boundaries, or working conditions can give rise to thoughtful and compelling papers. Exploring the conditions of the working class in 19th-century England, for example, can provide a particularly effective avenue for writing about Dickens's *Hard Times.*

You can begin thinking about these issues by asking broad questions at first. What do you know about the time period and about the author? What does the editorial apparatus in your text tell you? These might be starting places. Similarly, when specific historical events or dynamics are particularly important to understanding a work but might be somewhat obscure to modern readers, textbooks usually provide notes to explain historical background. These are a good place to start. With this information, ask yourself how these historical facts and circumstances might have affected the author, the presentation of theme, and the presentation of character. How does knowing more about the work's specific historical context illuminate the work? To take a well-known example, understanding the complex attitudes toward slavery during the time Mark Twain wrote *Adventures of Huckleberry Finn* should help you begin to examine issues of race in the text. Additionally, you might compare these attitudes to those of the time in which the novel was set. How might this comparison affect your interpretation of a work written after the abolition of slavery but set before the Civil War?

## WRITING ABOUT PHILOSOPHY AND IDEAS

Philosophical concerns are closely related to both historical context and thematic issues. Like historical investigation, philosophical research can provide a useful tool as you analyze a text. For example, an investigation into the working class in Dickens's England might lead you to a topic on the philosophical doctrine of utilitarianism in *Hard Times*. Many other works explore philosophies and ideas quite explicitly. Mary Shelley's famous novel *Frankenstein*, for example, explores John Locke's tabula rasa theory of human knowledge as she portrays the intellectual and emotional development of Victor Frankenstein's creature. As this example indicates, philosophical issues are somewhat more abstract than investigations of theme or historical context. Some other examples of philosophical issues include human free will, the formation of human identity, the nature of sin, or questions of ethics.

Writing about philosophy and ideas might require some outside research, but usually the notes or other material in your text will provide you with basic information and often footnotes and bibliographies will suggest places you can go to read further about the subject. If you have identified a philosophical theme that runs through a text, you might ask yourself how the author develops this theme. Look at character development and the interactions of characters, for example. Similarly, you might examine whether the narrative voice in a work of fiction addresses the philosophical concerns of the text.

## WRITING COMPARISON AND CONTRAST ESSAYS

Finally, you might find that comparing and contrasting the works or techniques of an author provides a useful tool for literary analysis. A comparison and contrast essay might compare two characters or themes in a single work, or it might compare the author's treatment of a theme in two works. It might also contrast methods of character development or analyze an author's differing treatment of a philosophical concern in two works. Writing comparison and contrast essays, though, requires some special consideration. While they generally provide you with plenty of material to use, they also come with a built-in trap: the laundry list. These papers often become mere lists of connections between the works. As this chapter will discuss, a strong thesis must make an assertion that you want to prove or validate. A strong comparison/contrast thesis, then, needs to comment on the significance of the similarities and differences you observe. It is not enough merely to assert that the works contain similarities and differences. You might, for example, assert why the similarities and differences are important and explain how they illuminate the works' treatment of theme. Remember, too, that a thesis should not be a statement of the obvious. A comparison/contrast paper that focuses only on very obvious similarities or differences does little to illuminate the connections between the works. Often, an effective method of shaping a strong thesis and argument is to begin your paper by noting the similarities between the works but then to develop a thesis that asserts how these apparently similar elements are different. If, for example, you observe that Emily Dickinson wrote a number of poems about spiders, you might analyze how she uses spider imagery differently in two poems. Similarly, many scholars have noted that Hawthorne created many "mad scientist" characters, men who are so devoted to their science or their art that they lose perspective on all else. A good thesis comparing two of these characters—Aylmer of "The Birthmark" and Dr. Rappaccini of "Rappaccini's Daughter," for example—might initially identify both characters as examples of Hawthorne's mad scientist type but then argue that their motivations for scientific experimentation differ. If you strive to analyze the similarities or differences, discuss significances, and move beyond the obvious, your paper should move beyond the laundry list trap.

## PREPARING TO WRITE

Armed with a clear sense of your task—illuminating the text—and with an understanding of theme, character, language, history, and philosophy, you are ready to approach the writing process. Remember that good writing is grounded in good reading and that close reading takes time, attention, and more than one reading of your text. Read for comprehension first. As you go back and review the work, mark the text to chart the details of the work as well as your reactions. Highlight important passages, repeated words, and image patterns. "Converse" with the text through marginal notes. Mark turns in the plot, ask questions, and make observations about characters, themes, and language. If you are reading from a book that does not belong to you, keep a record of your reactions in a journal or notebook. If you have read a work of literature carefully, paying attention to both the text and the context of the work, you have a leg up on the writing process. Admittedly, at this point, your ideas are probably very broad and undefined, but you have taken an important first step toward writing a strong paper.

Your next step is to focus, to take a broad, perhaps fuzzy, topic and define it more clearly. Even a topic provided by your instructor will need to be focused appropriately. Remember that good writers make the topic their own. There are a number of strategies—often called "invention"—that you can use to develop your own focus. In one such strategy, called *freewriting*, you spend 10 minutes or so just writing about your topic without referring back to the text or your notes. Write whatever comes to mind; the important thing is that you just keep writing. Often this process allows you to develop fresh ideas or approaches to your subject matter. You could also try *brainstorming*: Write down your topic and then list all the related points or ideas you can think of. Include questions, comments, words, important passages or events, and anything else that comes to mind. Let one idea lead to another. In the related technique of *clustering*, or *mapping*, write your topic on a sheet of paper and write related ideas around it. Then list related subpoints under each of these main ideas. Many people then draw arrows to show connections between points. This technique helps you narrow your topic and can also help you organize your ideas. Similarly, asking journalistic questions—Who? What? Where? When? Why? and How?—can develop ideas for topic development.

## Thesis Statements

Once you have developed a focused topic, you can begin to think about your thesis statement, the main point or purpose of your paper. It is imperative that you craft a strong thesis; otherwise, your paper will likely be little more than random, disorganized observations about the text. Think of your thesis statement as a kind of road map for your paper. It tells your reader where you are going and how you are going to get there.

To craft a good thesis, you must keep a number of things in mind. First, as the title of this subsection indicates, your paper's thesis should be a statement, an assertion about the text that you want to prove or validate. Beginning writers often formulate a question that they attempt to use as a thesis. For example, a writer analyzing the functions of sewing in Walker's *The Color Purple* might ask: How does sewing help the characters develop and assert themselves? While a question like this is a good strategy to use in the invention process to help narrow your topic and find your thesis, it cannot serve as the thesis statement because it does not tell your reader what you want to prove about the activity of sewing. You might shape this question into a thesis by instead proposing an answer to that question: In *The Color Purple*, Alice Walker depicts sewing as an activity that characters use to express their emotions and satisfy creative impulses. Sewing can also foster unity among characters, function as an indicator of a character's emerging authentic self, and symbolize characters' defiance of traditional gender roles. Notice that this thesis provides an initial plan or structure for the rest of the paper, and notice, too, that the thesis statement does not necessarily have to fit into one sentence. After establishing why some characters are driven to take up sewing, you could examine the ways in which sewing leads to improved relationships with other characters, and then continue to show how these improved relationships help the characters to pursue self-realization. Finally, you could demonstrate that with a healthier sense of self, some characters are able to renounce the limiting gender roles imposed on them by society.

Second, remember that a good thesis makes an assertion that you need to support. In other words, a good thesis does not state the obvious. If you tried to formulate a thesis about *The Color Purple*'s use of sewing by saying, In Alice Walker's *The Color Purple*, sewing is an important motif, you have done nothing but state the obvious. Since Celie and the other characters are repeatedly described as engaged in the activity of sewing, there would be no point in using three to five pages to support that assertion. You might try to develop a thesis by asking yourself some further questions: Why does Celie first start sewing? What other characters sew with Celie? What do the different characters sew? How does sewing change Celie's life? When and why does Albert start sewing? Such a line of questioning might lead you to a more viable thesis, like the one in the preceding paragraph.

As the comparison with the road map also suggests, your thesis should appear near the beginning of the paper. In relatively short papers (three to six pages), the thesis almost always appears in the first paragraph. Some writers fall into the trap of saving their thesis for the end, trying to provide a surprise or a big moment of revelation, as if to say, "TA DA! I've just proved that the blend of different genres, the use of allusions, and the lack of final resolution in Alice Walker's "Advancing Luna—and Ida B. Wells" work together to illustrate how black women struggle to reconcile their conflicting responses to racism and sexism. Placing a thesis at the end of an essay can seriously mar the essay's effectiveness. If you fail to define your essay's point and purpose it clearly at the beginning, your reader will find it difficult to assess the clarity of your argument and understand the points you are making. When your argument comes as a surprise at the end, you force your reader to reread your essay in order to assess its logic and effectiveness.

Finally, you should avoid using the first person ("I") as you present your thesis. Though it is not strictly wrong to write in the first person, it is difficult to do so gracefully. While writing in the first person, beginning writers often fall into the trap of writing self-reflexive prose (writing *about* their paper *in* their paper). Often this leads to the most dreaded of opening lines: "In this paper I am going to discuss. . . ." Not only does this self-reflexive voice make for very awkward prose, it frequently allows writers to announce a topic boldly while completely avoiding a thesis statement. An example might be a paper that begins as follows: "In Search of Our Mothers' Gardens," one of Walker's most famous essays, describes the author's efforts to find her black female artistic heritage. As part of this quest, Walker refers to the work of many earlier writers. In this paper I am going to discuss the significance of Walker's use of allusion. The author of this paper has done little more than announce a topic for the paper (the significance of the use of allusion). While the last sentence might be intended as a thesis, the writer fails to present an opinion about the significance of the allusions. To improve this "thesis," the writer would need to back up a couple of steps. First, the writer should consider the various functions of the use of allusion in Walker's text. From here, she could select the function that seems most engaging and then begin to craft a specific thesis. A writer who chooses to explore Walker's use of allusion might, for example, craft a thesis that reads: Alice Walker's "In Search of Our Mothers' Gardens" uses allusion to emphasize the value of the past by showing how insights from the work of previous generations can illuminate the present. However, when searching for the legacy of black women, sources of inspiration must be sought in nontraditional places because of the historical context which, for centuries, denied black women the opportunity to express themselves through conventional art forms.

## Outlines

While developing a strong, thoughtful thesis early in your writing process should help focus your paper, outlining provides an essential tool for shaping that paper logically. A good outline helps you see—and develop—the relationships among the points in your argument and assures you that your paper flows logically and coherently. Outlining not only helps place your points in a logical order, but also helps you subordinate supporting points, weed out any irrelevant points, and decide if there are any necessary points that are missing from your argument. Most of us are familiar with formal outlines that use numerical and letter designations for each point. However, there are different types of outlines; you may find that an informal outline is a more useful tool for you. What is important, though, is that you spend the time to develop some sort of outline—formal or informal.

Remember that an outline is a tool to help you shape and write a strong paper. If you do not spend sufficient time planning your supporting points and shaping the arrangement of those points, you will most likely construct a vague, unfocused outline that provides little, if any, help with the writing of the paper. Consider the following example:

Thesis: Alice Walker's "In Search of Our Mothers' Gardens" uses allusion to emphasize the value of the past by showing how insights from the work of previous generations can illuminate the present. However, when searching for the legacy of black women, sources of inspiration must be sought in nontraditional places because of the historical context which, for centuries, denied black women the opportunity to express themselves through conventional art forms.

I. Introduction and thesis

II. Examples of black women's creativity
    A. Quilt in Smithsonian
    B. Storytelling
    C. Gardening
    D. "Contrary instincts"

III. Literary allusions
    A. Okot p'Bitek
    B. Virginia Woolf
    C. Jean Toomer
    D. Nella Larsen
    E. Zora Neale Hurston

IV. Phillis Wheatley
    A. Poem about liberty

V. Walker's mother

VI. Conclusion
    A. Walker uses a variety of different allusions to exemplify the value of a usable literary heritage and to recover the contribution made by black women to an American artistic legacy

This outline has a number of flaws. First, the major topics labeled with the Roman numerals are not arranged in a logical order. If the paper's aim is to show how Walker uses allusions to show the value of heritage and to reclaim the contribution made by black women, the essay writer should examine how Walker uses quotations from black males and white females before discussing the problems that have impeded black women's artistic production and led them to alternative creative outlets. Additionally, the writer includes Walker's mother as a major section of this outline. As a black woman whose creativity has inspired Walker considerably, the author's mother may well have a place in this paper, but the writer fails to provide details about her function in the argument. Third, the writer includes "contrary instincts" as one of the lettered items in section II. Letters A, B, and C are all concrete examples of nontraditional art forms where black women have expressed themselves creatively; "contrary instincts" do not belong in this list as a separate item. A fourth problem is the inclusion of a letter A in sections IV and VI. An outline should not include an A without a B, a 1 without a 2, and so forth. The final problem with this outline is the overall lack of detail. None of the sections provides much information about the content of the argument, and it seems likely that the writer has not given sufficient thought to the content of the paper.

A better start to this outline might be the following:

Thesis: Alice Walker's "In Search of Our Mothers' Gardens" uses allusion to emphasize the value of the past by showing how insights from the work of previous generations can illuminate the present. However, when searching for the legacy of black women, sources of inspiration must be sought in nontraditional places because of the historical context which, for centuries, denied black women the opportunity to express themselves through conventional art forms.

I. Introduction and thesis

II. The value of a usable literary heritage
    A. Okot p'Bitek

        B. Virginia Woolf
        C. Jean Toomer

    III. Obstacles for black women writers
        A. Phillis Wheatley—poem about liberty
        B. Nella Larsen—contrary instincts
        C. Zora Neale Hurston—autobiography

    IV. Black women's unconventional creativity
        A. Quilt in Smithsonian
        B. Oral storytelling
        C. Walker's mother's garden

    V. Conclusion

This new outline would prove much more helpful when it came time to write the paper.

    An outline like this could be shaped into an even more useful tool if the writer fleshed out the argument by providing specific examples from the text to support each point. Once you have listed your main point and your supporting ideas, develop this raw material by listing related supporting ideas and material under each of those main headings. From there, arrange the material in subsections and order the material logically. For example, you might begin with one of the theses cited above: In *The Color Purple*, Alice Walker depicts sewing as an activity that characters use to express their emotions and satisfy creative impulses. Sewing can also foster unity among characters, function as an indicator of a character's emerging authentic self, and symbolize characters' defiance of traditional gender roles. As noted above, this thesis already gives you the beginning of an organization: Start by proving the notion that characters take up sewing as an outlet for their emotions and as a way to express themselves creatively, move on to a discussion of how sewing brings characters together, and then explain how Walker shows the power of sewing to push characters toward self-realization, before finally examining the relationship between sewing and renouncing traditional gender roles. You might begin your outline, then, with four topic headings: 1) sewing: emotional and creative release; 2) sewing: unity among characters; 3) sewing: characters' struggle for self-realization; and 4) sewing: gender roles. Under each of those headings, you could then list ideas that support that particular point. Be sure to include references to parts of the text that help build your case.

An informal outline might look like this:

Thesis: In *The Color Purple*, Alice Walker depicts sewing as an activity that characters use to express their emotions and satisfy creative impulses. Sewing can also foster unity among characters, function as an indicator of a character's emerging authentic self, and symbolize characters' defiance of traditional gender roles.

1. Sewing: emotional and creative release
   - Celie embroiders Olivia's "daidies"
   - Shug encourages Celie to sew to divert her energy away from revenge on Mr. _____
   - In Shug's house, Celie experiments with all styles of pants
     - Importance of different styles of pants: reflect the characteristics of the wearer
     - Pants symbolize Celie's love for people— "Every stitch I sew will be a kiss"
2. Sewing: unity among characters
   - Sofia's offer to quilt after fight with Celie
   - Quilt symbolism: diverse pieces of material create a beautiful and useful whole
   - Shug participates in the quilt as she starts to appreciate Celie
   - Celie feels "just right" for the first time in her life when quilting
   - Quilting links women across cultures and across generations

3. Sewing: characters' struggle for self-realization
   - Celie and Shug wear matching homemade pants when they return to Celie's home to confront "Pa"
   - Celie turns sewing pants into thriving business where she employs two other women
     - Inherits store where she can sell pants
   - Pants symbolize hope—Sofia's purple and red pants will be worn "one day when she was jumping over the moon"
     - Symbolism of the color purple: "Womanist is to feminist as purple to lavender."
4. Sewing: gender roles
   - Since Celie ploughs the land—a traditional male job—she starts to wear pants to do it
   - Albert and Celie sew together on the porch
     - Albert remembers wanting to sew as a boy
     - Albert's learning to sew shows defiance of traditional masculinity and allows him to be authentic
   - Olinkan men
     - History of quilting derived from African male tradition
     - Olinkan men make quilts, sew, and wear "dresses"

Conclusion
   - Sewing:
     - Less relevant today than in Celie's time—meanings of sewing change with time
     - Promotes unity, which in turn promotes empowerment
     - Causes Celie's transformation
     - Its association with women in the USA is culturally and historically specific

○ Can unite women and men which leads to
stronger community

You would set about writing a formal outline with a similar process, though in the final stages you would label the headings differently. A formal outline for a paper that argues the thesis about "Advancing Luna—and Ida B. Wells" cited above—that the blend of different genres, the use of allusions, and the lack of final resolution in Alice Walker's "Advancing Luna—and Ida B. Wells" work together to illustrate how black women struggle to reconcile their conflicting responses to racism and sexism—might look like this:

Thesis: The blend of different genres, the use of allusions, and the lack of final resolution in Alice Walker's "Advancing Luna—and Ida B. Wells" work together to illustrate how black women struggle to reconcile their conflicting responses to racism and sexism.

I. Introduction and thesis

II. The mixture of genres reflects narrator's struggle on how to best approach a discussion of interracial rape
   A. Fictional short story
      1. First-person point of view creates distance from the difficult situations of the other characters
         a. Narrator's bias used to diminish and discredit Luna
         b. Not given insight into Luna's thoughts and feelings
         c. Narrator's naivety—has limited understanding until the end of the short story
         d. Emotional reaction to Luna's confession shuts down discussion of topic

    2. Historical context and setting
      a. Georgia, 1965—relationships between blacks and whites in the South
      b. History of lynching in the South
      c. Black women and rape
      d. New York, late '60s—Hispanic neighborhood leads to seeds of solidarity between black and white women

B. Essay
    1. Search for objectivity
    2. Use of facts moves issue from the hypothetical to the actual
    3. Essay's thesis
    4. Argument opens up dialogue between writer and reader

C. Autobiography
    1. Personalizes factual objectivity
    2. Shows long-term effect of issue on author's life
    3. Authenticates story and struggle—assigns truth and validity to rape issue

III. Conflicting opinions of allusions—reflect the conflicting viewpoints of black women
  A. Misogynist outlook
    1. Eldridge Cleaver—"practice on black women before moving onto white"
    2. Imamu Baraka—"Rape the white girls. Rape their fathers."
  B. Black women, history, and rape
    1. Emmett Till
    2. Ida B. Wells

     a. Black male "uncontrollable lust" for white women

     b. "Deny! Deny! Deny!"

     c. Silence equals loyalty

     d. Narrator/author's response to Wells's position

IV. Story's alternative endings reflect impossibility of easy solution

  A. The first ending

    1. Unanswered questions:

      a. What happened during Freddie Pye's visit?

      b. Why did the narrator not discuss the rape fully with Luna?

    2. Symbolism of Luna's pottery: "flaw improves the beauty and the fragility of the design"

    3. Narrator's explanation of "unresolved" ending—fear of repercussions on black community

  B. The second, "imaginary" ending

    1. "Discarded Notes"—positive reevaluation of Luna

    2. Luna afraid of Pye, but shows moral integrity and strength

    3. Pye disregarded by higher class blacks

    4. Narrator can only speculate whether Luna and Pye talk about the rape

  C. The third ending

    1. Cuba: revolutionary setting conducive to new political Interpretation

    2. Black men without a soul—kill and rape for money

      3. Evil of both black and white overrides racial and gendered divisions

V. Conclusion
    A. Narrator is torn between protecting black people from white aggression and protecting women from male (black or white) aggression
      1. "I had seen photographs of white folks standing in a circle roasting something that had talked to them in their own language before they tore out its tongue."
      2. "Some black men themselves do not seem to know what the meaning of raping someone is. . . . They have gloried in it."
    B. As a writer, author cannot remain quiet:
      1. Wants to find truth about this subject
      2. Wants to initiate dialogue between writer and reader
    C. The various endings show the author's battle to find a coherent resolution to the issue
    D. Lack of resolution shows that the debate is not over and that further discussion is needed

As with the previous example, the thesis provided the seeds of a structure, and the writer was careful to arrange the supporting points in a logical manner, showing the relationships among the ideas in the paper.

## Body Paragraphs

Once your outline is complete, you can begin drafting your paper. Paragraphs, units of related sentences, are the building blocks of a good paper, and as you draft you should keep in mind both the function and the qualities of good paragraphs. Paragraphs help you chart and control the shape and content of your essay, and they help the reader see your organization and your logic. You should begin a new paragraph whenever you move from one major point to another. In longer, more complex essays, you might use a group of related paragraphs to support major points. Remember that in addition to being adequately developed, a good paragraph is both unified and coherent.

## Unified Paragraphs

Each paragraph must be centered on one idea or point, and a unified paragraph carefully focuses on and develops this central idea without including extraneous ideas or tangents. For beginning writers, the best way to ensure that you are constructing unified paragraphs is to include a topic sentence in each paragraph. This topic sentence should convey the main point of the paragraph, and every sentence in the paragraph should relate to that topic sentence. Any sentence that strays from the central topic does not belong in the paragraph and needs to be revised or deleted. Consider the following paragraph which discusses an aspect of Walker's use of sewing as a motif in *The Color Purple.* Notice how the paragraph veers away from the main point, namely that the activity of sewing is a way for characters to express negative and positive emotions:

When Celie sees her daughter in a store, the memory that surfaces is that she embroidered her child's name, Olivia, in the seat of all her "daidies." Although this could be seen as practical, Celie also admits that she added a "lot of little stars and flowers too"(13). This decorative, but inessential, addition indicates Celie's love for her child, since she spent time and energy in making her child's clothing special. Later in the novel, when Celie learns that Mr. _____ has been hiding her sister's letters, her anger is so intense that she fantasizes about killing him. Mr. _____ has been blocking all communication between Celie and Nettie for years, although neither sister has been aware of his role in their failed correspondence. His vindictive behavior becomes a turning point for Shug because she realizes for the first time the depth of Mr. _____'s cruelty to others. Shug proposes that Celie start to make some pants, claiming that they would be practical to wear when working in the fields. Celie understands that Shug wants to deflect her energy and channel it into something productive, by putting "a needle and not a razor in [her] hand" (147). When Celie develops her hobby into a thriving pant-making business, her earliest samples are designed with specific friends and family in mind. She experiments with a multitude of colors, designs, and materials. Eventually, she produces a pair of pants that are uniquely crafted for Shug: comfortable, wrinkle-free, and styled to flatter her body. When the fame of her pants spreads, Celie decides to make a pair for her sister, Nettie, in Africa. Again, Celie takes into consideration Nettie's character and situation before designing a pair of pants specifically for her. In a letter where she tells Nettie about these pants, she explains that, "Every stitch I sew will be a kiss" (214). Thus, Celie uses sewing to express her positive emotions toward other people and as a productive way to harness the energy provoked by negative feelings.

The paragraph begins without a valid topic sentence, and only in the third sentence does it start to move toward the central argument of the paragraph. Later on, the author goes on a tangent. If the purpose of the paragraph is to demonstrate that the activity of sewing is an outlet for characters' negative and positive emotions, the sentences about Mr. _____'s cruel behavior in blocking Celie and Nettie's communication and Shug's reaction to this are tangential here. They may find a place somewhere else in the paper, but they should be deleted from this paragraph.

### Coherent Paragraphs

In addition to shaping unified paragraphs, you must also craft coherent paragraphs, paragraphs that develop their points logically with sentences that flow smoothly into one another. Coherence depends on the order of your sentences, but it is not strictly the order of the sentences that is important to paragraph coherence. You also need to craft your prose to help the reader see the relationship among the sentences.

Consider the following paragraph about Walker's use of the motif of sewing. Notice how the writer uses the same ideas as the paragraph above yet fails to help the reader see the relationships among the points:

> When Celie sees her daughter in a store, the memory that surfaces is that she embroidered her child's name, Olivia, in the seat of all her "daidies." Celie also admits that she added a "lot of little stars and flowers too" (13). When Celie learns that Mr. _____ has been hiding her sister's letters from her, her anger is so intense that she fantasizes about killing him. Shug proposes that Celie start to make some pants, claiming that they would be practical to wear when working in the fields. Shug puts "a needle and not a razor in [her] hand" (147). When Celie develops her hobby into a thriving pant-making business, her earliest samples are designed with specific friends and family in mind. She experiments with a multitude of colors, designs, and materials. Shug's pants are comfortable, wrinkle-free, and styled to flatter her body. Later, Celie decides to make a pair for her sister, Nettie, in Africa. In a letter where she tells Nettie about the pants, she explains that, "Every stitch I sew will be a kiss" (214).

This paragraph demonstrates that unity alone does not guarantee paragraph effectiveness. The argument is hard to follow because the author fails both to show connections between the sentences and to indicate how they work to support the overall point.

A number of techniques are available to aid paragraph coherence. Careful use of transitional words and phrases is essential. You can use transitional flags to introduce an example or an illustration (*for example, for instance*); to amplify a point or add another phase of the same idea (*additionally, furthermore, next, similarly, finally, then*); to indicate a conclusion or result (*therefore, as a result, thus, in other words*); to signal a contrast or a qualification (*on the other hand, nevertheless, despite this, on the contrary, still, however, conversely*); to signal a comparison (*likewise, in comparison, similarly*); and to indicate a movement in time (*afterward, earlier, eventually, finally, later, subsequently, until*).

In addition to transitional flags, careful use of pronouns aids coherence and flow. If you were writing about *The Wizard of Oz*, you would not want to keep repeating the phrase *the witch* or the name *Dorothy*. Careful substitution of the pronoun *she* in these instances can aid coherence. A word of warning, though: When you substitute pronouns for proper names, always be sure that your pronoun reference is clear. In a paragraph that discusses both Dorothy and the witch, substituting *she* could lead to confusion. Make sure that it is clear to whom the pronoun refers. Generally, the pronoun refers to the last proper noun you have used.

While repeating the same name over and over again can lead to awkward, boring prose, it is possible to use repetition to help your paragraph's coherence. Careful repetition of important words or phrases can lend coherence to your paragraph by reminding readers of your key points. Admittedly, it takes some practice to use this technique effectively. You may find that reading your prose aloud can help you develop an ear for effective use of repetition.

To see how helpful transitional aids are, compare the paragraph below to the preceding paragraph about Walker's use of the motif of sewing. Notice how the author works with the same ideas and quotations but shapes them into a much more coherent paragraph whose point is clearer and easier to follow:

> Sewing can serve as a release for creative impulses and a range of emotions. When Celie sees her daughter in a store, the memory that surfaces is that she embroidered her child's name, Olivia, in the seat of all her "daidies." Although this could be seen as practical, Celie also admits that she added a "lot of little stars and flowers too" (13). This decorative, but inessential, addition indicates Celie's love for her child, since she spent time and energy in making her child's clothing special. Later in the novel, when Celie learns that Mr. _____ has been hiding her sister's letters from her, her anger is so intense that she fantasizes about

killing him. Shug proposes that Celie start to make some pants, claiming that they would be practical to wear when working in the fields. Celie understands that Shug wants to deflect her rage and channel the energy into something productive by putting "a needle and not a razor in [her] hand" (147). When Celie develops her hobby into a thriving pant-making business, her earliest samples are designed with specific friends and family in mind. She experiments with a multitude of colors, designs, and materials. Eventually, she produces a pair of pants that are uniquely crafted for Shug: comfortable, wrinkle-free, and styled to flatter her body. Similarly, her positive feelings toward Jack (Sofia's brother-in-law) are projected into a pair of soft, strong camel pants. Their practical attributes—being washable, close fitting on the leg, and having lots of pockets—show Celie's respect, understanding, and warmth for this kind, family man. When the fame of her pants spreads, Celie decides to make a pair for her sister, Nettie, in Africa. Again, Celie takes into consideration Nettie's character and situation before designing a pair of pants specifically for her. In a letter where she tells Nettie about the pants, she explains that, "Every stitch I sew will be a kiss" (214). Thus, Celie uses sewing to express her positive emotions toward other people and as a productive way to harness the energy provoked by negative feelings.

Similarly, the following paragraph from a paper on the conflict of loyalties that black women face, as presented by Walker in "Advancing Luna—and Ida B. Wells," demonstrates both unity and coherence. In it, the author argues that the story's lack of final resolution reflects how black women struggle to reconcile their conflicting responses to racism and sexism:

The story's different endings reveal the narrator's divided loyalties and her inability to find definitive answers to the questions that Luna's confession of rape raises.

The first ending trails off unresolved. The narrator never discusses the significance of the rape with Luna, neither does she ask why Freddie Pye visited their New York apartment. The two women's friendship falters as a result of the inner conflict the narrator feels about interracial rape. Similarly to the piece of pottery that Luna brings to the narrator years later, friendship between American black women and white women is fragile and easily broken when loyalty to race precludes loyalty to gender. Given the history of race relations in the South, the story's first ending endorses Luna's decision not to scream when she was being raped. The narrator feels that Luna's silence was required to protect innocent black men from being lynched. Her negative portrayal of Luna's blindness to race and class privilege aids in helping to diminish sympathy for Luna's plight. Later, however, the narrator recognizes that she has "more than a little of Ida B. Wells' fear of probing the rape issue [. . .] running through [her]." Thus, her second ending attempts to redress her earlier failure to respond to Luna with more compassion. The "Discarded Notes" paint a better picture of Luna as the narrator now tries to uncover the truth. The reconstructed visit from Pye is imagined as one where Luna's integrity and decency allow her to help a man who had been used and discarded by the wealthy elite of his own black political movement. Despite the more positive reevaluation of Luna, the narrator still jumps to an exculpatory interpretation of Pye's visit, attributing a conscience to him through his recognition of Luna's strength in choosing not to scream when he raped her. The third ending shows the narrator move to a position where she now even doubts the nature of the real issue. The setting of Cuba serves as an appropriate backdrop to the revolutionary suggestion that Pye had been paid by the white government to rape. This version of events presents greed for money and power, not dysfunctional race relations, as being at

the root of the narrator's dilemma. This new scenario
questions the relevance of the narrator's conflict as
to whether her interests, as a black woman, are best
served by loyalty to race or by solidarity with women,
because it insinuates that racism and sexism can both
be offshoots of more insidious human forces at work in
society.

## Introductions

Introductions present particular challenges for writers. Generally, your
introduction should do two things: capture your reader's attention and
explain the main point of your essay. In other words, while your introduction should contain your thesis, it needs to do a bit more work than
that. You are likely to find that starting that first paragraph is one of
the most difficult parts of the paper. It is hard to face that blank page
or screen, and as a result, many beginning writers, in desperation to
start somewhere, start with overly broad, general statements. While it
is often a good strategy to start with more general subject matter and
narrow your focus, do not begin with broad sweeping statements such
as, Violence affects everyone, or Throughout the history
of literature, many authors have written about race
relations. Such sentences are nothing but empty filler. They begin
to fill the blank page, but they do nothing to advance your argument.
Instead, you might try to gain your reader's interest. Some writers like
to begin with a pertinent quotation or with a relevant question. Or, you
might begin with an introduction of the topic you will discuss. If you are
writing about Walker's discussion of racism and sexism in "Advancing
Luna—and Ida B. Wells," for instance, you might begin by talking about
the history of race relations in the South and how accusations of rape
have been manipulated for political ends. Another common trap to avoid
is depending on your title to introduce the author and the text you are
writing about. Always include the work's author and title in your opening paragraph.

Compare the effectiveness of the following introductions:

1)   Throughout the history of literature, many authors
     have written about race relations. The blend of

different genres, the use of allusions, and the lack of final resolution in Alice Walker's story work together to illustrate how black women struggle to reconcile their conflicting responses to racism and sexism.

2) During the post-Reconstruction era in the American South, the white population perpetuated an image of black men as savage rapists who were unable to control their lust for white women. Accusations of rape were often used to justify the lynching of black men; however, the lynchings were frequently politically motivated and had the goal of keeping the black population in thrall to the white. One legacy of this period of history has been the myth that black men find white women especially sexually desirable. Ida B. Wells was a prominent voice in the antilynching movement, and her research uncovered the truth that most of the black men killed for supposedly raping a white woman were innocent. Yet, if a white woman alleged that a rape had occurred, her word was rarely questioned and the repercussions on the black community were manifold. Consequently, a black woman was more likely to react to cries of rape with the goal of protecting her male family members than with empathy for the putative female victim. However, as the narrator in Alice Walker's "Advancing Luna—and Ida B. Wells" notes, black women were more likely to be the victims of rape in the context of the South; thus, sexual violence is a critical issue that cannot be ignored. The text's blend of different genres, its use of allusions, and the lack of final resolution work together to illustrate how black women struggle to reconcile their conflicting responses to racism and sexism.

The first introduction begins with a vague, overly broad sentence and then moves abruptly to the thesis. Notice, too, how a reader deprived of the paper's title does not know which story the paper will analyze. The second introduction works with the same material and thesis but provides more detail and is, consequently, much more interesting. It begins by discussing the history and dynamics of race and sex in the South and then speaks about the position of black women in the midst of these dynamics. The author and the title of the work to be discussed are woven in toward the end of the introduction. The paragraph ends with the thesis.

The paragraph below provides another example of an opening strategy. It begins by introducing the author and the text it will analyze, and then it moves on by briefly introducing relevant details of the story in order to set up its thesis:

In *The Color Purple,* many of Alice Walker's characters sew as part of their everyday activities. Early in the novel, for example, Celie makes Sofia some new curtains, and this exemplifies the utilitarian function of sewing. However, sewing often transcends its practical applications because sewers can express a creative vision through their work. Quilting is an example of how the practical and the aesthetic can come together. Quilting is a task that women can do alone; however, working on a pattern with other people creates chances for conversation along with the sharing of labor. Significantly, Celie and Sofia are able to repair their friendship by making a quilt together. Together or alone, through quilting or other forms of sewing, women can express themselves creatively, using color and design to signal their emotions. As a corollary, sewing can reflect a woman's sense of self at any given time, and a shift in a person's perception of her identity might be replicated in a change in the type of sewing that she produces. In Celie's case, she transforms her hobby of making pants for her friends and family into a lucrative business that enables her to compete in the male-dominated domain of enterprise. Likewise, when Albert admits to an interest in sewing and picks up a needle, he challenges conventional expectations of gender. Thus, the simple practice of sewing has multiple meanings. Walker depicts sewing as an activity that characters use to express their emotions and satisfy creative impulses. Sewing can also foster unity among characters, function as an indicator of a character's emerging authentic self, and symbolize characters' defiance of traditional gender roles.

## Conclusions

Conclusions present another series of challenges for writers. No doubt you have heard the old adage about writing papers: "Tell us what you are going to say, say it, and then tell us what you've said." While this formula does not necessarily result in bad papers, it does not necessarily result in good ones, either. It will almost certainly result in boring papers (especially boring conclusions). If you have done a good job establishing your points in the body of the paper, the reader already knows and understands your argument. There is no need to merely reiterate. Do not just summarize your main points in your conclusion. Such a boring and mechanical conclusion does nothing to advance your argument or interest your reader. Consider the following conclusion to the paper about black women's attitudes toward racism and sexism in "Advancing Luna—and Ida B. Wells":

> In conclusion, Walker shows that the issue of interracial rape is a complex one for black women. Through the contrasting perspectives presented through allusions and the alternative endings, Walker shows how black women struggle with divided loyalties because of a history that has left them with a deep-rooted mistrust of whites.

Besides starting with a mechanical and obvious transitional device, this conclusion does little more than summarize the main points of the outline (and it does not even touch on all of them). It is incomplete and uninteresting.

Instead, your conclusion should add something to your paper. A good tactic is to build upon the points you have been arguing. Asking "why?" often helps you draw further conclusions. For example, in the paper discussed above, you might explain how the conflict between race and gender has been portrayed elsewhere in Walker's work and why it is a subject that the writer returns to repeatedly. Another method of successfully concluding a paper is to speculate on other directions in which to take your topic, that is, by tying it into larger issues. You might do this by envisioning your paper as just one section of a larger paper. Having established your points in this paper, how would you build on this argument? Where would you go next? In the following conclusion to the paper on "Advancing Luna—and Ida B. Wells," the author briefly reiterates some of the main points of the paper but does so in order to amplify the discussion of the story's focus on the ways that, from a black woman's perspective, issues of race and gender can generate internal conflict. Notice, too, how the author moved some material from its original place in the outline. Instead of including the imaginary Wells's quotation, "Deny! Deny! Deny!," in a body paragraph, the writer moves that material to the conclusion, using it as transitional material:

Although "Advancing Luna—and Ida B. Wells" was published in 1981, Walker's earlier work such as *The Third Life of Grange Copeland* and later work such as *The Color Purple* have also urged the African-American community to examine black male attitudes and behavior critically, with a view to finding remedies. As a consequence of her mission of self-examination, however, Walker has been criticized for perpetuating negative portrayals of black men. The pressure to stay silent about black male aggression is still being demanded of black women. In 1991, when Anita Hill accused Supreme Court nominee Clarence Thomas of sexual harassment, she received outspoken criticism from segments of the black community who rebuked her for having shone a negative spotlight on an African-American man. Thus, although Walker's story revealed the need for greater discussion of the problems that arise for black women when the interests of race and gender clash, little headway has been made. Thomas's inflammatory claim that Hill's accusation was part of a "high-tech lynching" alluded to the appalling history of race relations in the South that Walker explores in her story. Ida B. Wells's fictional demand that women "Deny! Deny! Deny!" is seemingly still current, although Walker herself refuses to comply with that demand because she feels compelled as a writer to pursue truth. Through the use of other allusions, she countermands Wells's directive and openly critiques black male misogyny. However, although Walker presents the topic for debate, its lack of immediate solution is reinforced through the story's indefinite nature. The text's alternative endings and the instability of its genre contribute to showing the uncertainty that black women feel when their interests are compromised by the conflicting demands of racism and sexism.

Similarly, in the following conclusion to the paper on the motif of sewing in *The Color Purple*, the author draws a conclusion about the relevance of the topic to our world today, tying the paper's focus to larger issues.

Sewing is an activity that has declined in practice over time. People are less inclined to repair or make their own clothing since it is so readily available and affordable. Quilting has become more of an art form than a habitual and essential task. Thus, the meanings of sewing change over time. During the first half of the 20th century in rural Georgia, where the novel is set, the multiple meanings of sewing already indicate change and flux. Walker shows how sewing can effect unity. In the case of *The Color Purple*'s women characters, their unity empowers them and allows them to start making their own choices. Thus, sewing, an activity associated with female relegation to the domestic sphere, becomes a means of liberation and self-empowerment because making their own choices permits the women to abandon the lifestyle of dependence and domesticity that sewing formerly represented. Walker shows this development through Celie's transformation of sewing, taking it out of the home and into a commercial sphere to earn a living from it. Sewing also provides the opportunity for creative and emotive expression. By classifying sewing as a woman's activity, men cut themselves off from a possible outlet for expressing feelings or creativity. However, by stressing the cultural and historical specificity that labels sewing a woman's activity in the United States, Walker suggests that if sewing becomes an activity that is open to all, it could potentially contribute to the dismantling of limiting, traditional gender roles, which would strengthen understanding between men and women. Thus, the many meanings of sewing indicate Walker's hope for better personal opportunities and relationships, which would, in turn, lead to an improved sense of community.

# Citations and Formatting

## Using Primary Sources

As the examples included in this chapter indicate, strong papers on literary texts incorporate quotations from the text in order to support their points. It is not enough for you to assert your interpretation without providing support or evidence from the text. Without well-chosen quotations to support your argument, you are, in effect, saying to the reader, "Take my word for it." It is important to use quotations thoughtfully and selectively. Remember that the paper presents *your* argument, so choose quotations that support *your* assertions. Do not let the author's voice overwhelm your own. With that caution in mind, there are some guidelines you should follow to ensure that you use quotations clearly and effectively.

### Integrate Quotations

Quotations should always be integrated into your own prose. Do not just drop them into your paper without introduction or comment.

Otherwise, it is unlikely that your reader will see their function. You can integrate textual support easily and clearly with identifying tags, short phrases that identify the speaker. For example:

> The narrator describes Luna as a "very straight, clear-eyed, coolly observant young woman with no talent for existing outside her own skin."

While this tag appears before the quotation, you can also use tags after or in the middle of the quoted text, as the following examples demonstrate:

> "Your view of human weakness is too biblical," the narrator's acquaintance in Cuba tells her.

> "Even the name—Freddie Pye—was diminutive," the narrator thinks, "in an age of giants."

You can also use a colon to formally introduce a quotation:

> Nettie is appalled by the chauvinist behavior of Olinkan men: "They don't even look at women when women are speaking."

Longer quotations (more than four lines of prose) should be set off from the rest of your paper in a block quotation. Double space before you begin the passage, indent it to spaces from your left-hand margin, and double space the passage itself. Because the indentation signals the inclusion of a quotation, do not use quotation marks around the cited passage. Use a colon to introduce the passage:

> Shug explains the process of how she was able to replace the image of God as an old white man with a pantheistic vision:
>
>> My first step from the old white man was trees.
>> Then air. Then birds. Then other people. But one

day when I was sitting quiet and feeling like a
motherless child, which I was, it come to me: that
feeling of being part of everything, not separate
at all. I knew that if I cut a tree, my arm would
bleed. And I laughed and I cried and I run all
around the house.

Thus, according to Shug, the universe and its phenomena
are all manifestations of the divine.

It is also important to interpret quotations after you introduce
them and explain how they help advance your point. You cannot
assume that your reader will interpret the quotations the same way
that you do.

## Quote Accurately

Always quote accurately. Anything within quotation marks must be the
author's *exact* words. There are, however, some rules to follow if you need
to modify the quotation to fit into your prose.

1) Use brackets to indicate any material that might have been
   added to the author's exact wording. For example, if you need
   to add any words to the quotation or alter it grammatically
   to allow it to fit into your prose, indicate your changes in
   brackets:

   Once she starts living with Luna, the narrator
   explains how "[their] relationship, always
   marked by mutual respect, evolved into a warm
   and comfortable friendship which provided a
   stability and comfort [they] both needed at
   that time."

2) Conversely, if you choose to omit any words from the quotation, use ellipses (three spaced periods) to indicate missing
   words or phrases:

> Mr. _____ berates Celie, believing that she has
> no human value: "You black, you pore, you ugly,
> you a woman. Goddam . . . you nothing at all."

3) If you delete a sentence or more, use the ellipses after a
   period:

> Before she leaves with Shug, Celie curses
> Mr. _____: "Until you do right by me, everything
> you touch will crumble. . . . [E]verything you
> even dream about will fail."

## Punctuate Properly

Punctuation of quotations often causes more trouble than it should.
Once again, you just need to keep these simple rules in mind.

1) Periods and commas should be placed inside quotation marks,
   even if they are not part of the original quotation:

> Sofia asserts that a "girl child ain't safe in
> a family of men."

The only exception to this rule is when the quotation is followed by a
parenthetical reference. In this case, the period or comma goes after the
citation (more on these later in this chapter):

> Sofia asserts that a "girl child ain't safe in
> a family of men" (40).

2) Other marks of punctuation—colons, semicolons, question
   marks, and exclamation points—go outside the quotation
   marks unless they are part of the original quotation:

> Why does Tashi think that "because of the
> scarification marks on her cheeks Americans
> would look down on her as a savage"?

The narrator recalls that Freddie Pye was "among
the first persons to shout the slogan everyone
later attributed solely to Stokeley Carmichael—
Black Power!"

## *Documenting Primary Sources*

Unless you are instructed otherwise, you should provide sufficient information for your reader to locate material you quote. Generally, literature papers follow the rules set forth by the Modern Language Association (MLA). These can be found in the *MLA Handbook for Writers of Research Papers* (sixth edition). You should be able to find this book in the reference section of your library. Additionally, its rules for citing both primary and secondary sources are widely available from reputable online sources. One of these is the Online Writing Lab (OWL) at Purdue University. OWL's guide to MLA style is available at http://owl.english.purdue. edu/owl/resource/557/01/. The Modern Language Association also offers answers to frequently asked questions about MLA style on this helpful Web page: http://www.mla.org/style_faq. Generally, when you are citing from literary works in papers, you should keep a few guidelines in mind.

### Parenthetical Citations:

MLA asks for parenthetical references in your text after quotations. When you are working with prose (short stories, novels, or essays) include page numbers in the parentheses:

The narrator believes that "solidarity among black and
white women is only rarely likely to exist" (102).

### The Works Cited Page:

These parenthetical citations are linked to a separate works cited page at the end of the paper. The works cited page lists works alphabetically by the authors' last name. An entry for the above reference to Walker's "Advancing Luna—and Ida B. Wells" would read:

Walker, Alice. "Advancing Luna—and Ida B. Wells." *You
    Can't Keep a Good Woman Down.* New York: Harcourt
    Brace, 1981. 85-104.

The *MLA Handbook* includes a full listing of sample entries, as do many of the online explanations of MLA style.

## Documenting Secondary Sources

To ensure that your paper is built entirely upon your own ideas and analysis, instructors often ask that you write interpretative papers without any outside research. If, on the other hand, your paper requires research, you must document any secondary sources you use. You need to document direct quotations, summaries or paraphrases of others' ideas, and factual information that is not common knowledge. Follow the guidelines above for quoting primary sources when you use direct quotations from secondary sources. Keep in mind that MLA style also includes specific guidelines for citing electronic sources. OWL's Web site provides a good summary: http://owl.english.purdue.edu/owl/resource/557/09/.

### Parenthetical Citations:

As with the documentation of primary sources, described above, MLA guidelines require in-text parenthetical references to your secondary sources. Unlike the research papers you might write for a history class, literary research papers following MLA style do not use footnotes as a means of documenting sources. Instead, after a quotation, you should cite the author's last name and the page number:

> In many of her works, Alice Walker "uses the often unheralded heritage of black women, the creative sparks as well as the history of restrictions, as the foundation of her artistic vision" (Christian 52).

If you include the name of the author in your prose, then you would include only the page number in your citation. For example:

> According to Barbara Christian, Alice Walker "uses the often unheralded heritage of black women, the creative sparks as well as the history of restrictions, as the foundation of her artistic vision" (52).

If you are including more than one work by the same author, the parenthetical citation should include a shortened yet identifiable version of the title in order to indicate which of the author's works you cite. For example:

Barbara Christian argues that Meridian "is the median point of the circular patterns in the novel, for she has experienced sexism and racism, major obstacles to societal wholeness" (Novels 103).

Similarly, if you summarize or paraphrase the particular ideas of your source, you must provide documentation:

Walker's novels and stories can be described as literary "quilts" in the sense that she brings together plot elements, figurative language, and characters in an intricate and carefully constructed fashion that is never random and eventually reveals its grand design and coherent vision (Christian 50).

## Works Cited Page

Like the primary sources discussed above, the parenthetical references to secondary sources are keyed to a separate works cited page at the end of your paper. Here is an example of a works cited page that uses some of the examples cited above. Note that when two or more works by the same author are listed, you should use three hyphens followed by a period in the subsequent entries. You can find a complete list of sample entries in the *MLA Handbook* or from a reputable online summary of MLA style.

### WORKS CITED

Christian, Barbara. "Alice Walker: The Black Woman Artist as Wayward." *Black Feminist Criticism: Perspectives on Black Women Writers*. Ed. Barbara Christian. New York: Pergamon, 1985. 81–101.

——. "Novels for Everyday Use." *Alice Walker: Critical Perspectives Past and Present*. Eds. Henry Louis

Gates, Jr. and K. A. Appiah. New York: Amistad, 1993.
50–104.

White, Evelyn C. *Alice Walker: A Life.* New York: Norton,
2004.

## *Plagiarism*

Failure to document carefully and thoroughly can leave you open to charges of stealing the ideas of others, which is known as plagiarism, and this is a very serious matter. Remember that it is important to use quotation marks when you reproduce language used by your source, even if you use just one or two words. For example, if you wrote: Walker's novels can be described as complex quilts because she brings together plot elements, figurative language, and characters in an intricate and carefully constructed fashion that is never random and eventually reveals its grand design and coherent vision, you would be guilty of plagiarism, since you used Christian's distinct language without acknowledging her as the source. Instead, you should write: Walker's novels can be described as "complex quilts" because she brings together plot elements, figurative language, and characters in an intricate and carefully constructed fashion that is never random and eventually reveals its grand design and coherent vision (Christian 50). In this case, you have properly credited Christian.

Similarly, neither summarizing the ideas of an author nor changing or omitting just a few words means that you can omit a citation. Houston A. Baker, Jr. and Charlotte Pierce-Baker's essay "Patches: Quilts and Community in Alice Walker's 'Everyday Use'" contains the following passage which draws parallels between African-American women's quilt-making, Walker's short story, and jazz and blues:

> Quilts designed for everyday use, pieced wholes defying symmetry and pattern, are signs of the scarred generations of women who have always been alien to a world of literate words and stylish fantasies. The crafted fabric of Walker's story is the very weave of blues and jazz traditions in the Afro-American community,

daringly improvisational modes that confront breaks in the continuity of melody (or theme) by riffing. The asymmetrical quilts of southern black women are like the off-centered stomping of the jazz solo or the innovative musical showmanship of the blues interlude. They speak a world in which the deceptively shuffling Maggie is capable of a quick change into goddess, an unlikely holy figure whose dues are paid in full.

Below are two examples of plagiarized passages:

The quilts made by black southern women reflect the reality of black women's marginalized relationship with mainstream arts and culture. The quilts' nontraditional and unpredictable designs evoke the way that jazz and blues are often enhanced by creative deviations from the dominant tune. Similarly, in Walker's short story "Everyday Use," Maggie's transformation from self-effacing background figure to outspoken preserver of the family's heritage is unexpected.

Quilts made by black southern women defy symmetry and order in a way that is fitting for people who have long been outsiders when it comes to mainstream arts and culture. The quilts' asymmetrical designs are comparable to the musical traditions of jazz and blues where the main melody is broken by a daringly improvisational solo or interlude. Walker's short story, with Maggie's metamorphosis at the end, can also be considered as part of this African-American tradition of breaking with the predictable in the arts (Baker, Jr. and Pierce-Baker 315).

Although the first passage does not use the essay's exact language, it does borrow a main idea of the passage without citing the authors' work. Since comparing African-American women's quilt-making to the improvisational elements of jazz and blues is the authors' distinct idea, this constitutes plagiarism. The second passage has simplified the original, changed some wording, and included a citation, but some of the phrasing is the authors'. The first passage could be fixed with a parenthetical citation. Because some of the wording in the second passage remains the same, though, it would require the use of quotation marks in addition to a parenthetical citation. The passage below represents an honestly and adequately documented use of the original passage:

> According to Houston A. Baker, Jr. and Charlotte Pierce-Baker, black southern women's quilts are characterized by asymmetrical and unconventional designs that reflect their marginalization from mainstream artistic traditions. Walker's "Everyday Use" can also be considered as part of the African-American trend of innovation and unpredictability in the arts. Both the quilts and Walker's story are comparable to the African-American musical traditions of jazz and blues. Maggie's unanticipated transformation from humble, self-effacing background figure to the woman who will bear responsibility for the family's heritage evokes the "off-centered stomping of the jazz solo or the innovative musical showmanship of the blues interlude" (315).

This passage acknowledges that the idea of the parallels between quilting, writing, and music is derived from Baker, Jr. and Pierce-Baker, while appropriately using quotations to indicate their precise language.

While it is not necessary to document well-known facts, often referred to as "common knowledge," any ideas or language that you take from someone else must be properly documented. Common knowledge generally includes the birth and death dates of authors or other well-documented facts of their lives. An often-cited guideline is that if you can find the information in three sources, it is common knowledge. Despite this guideline, it is, admittedly, often difficult to know if the facts you uncover are common knowledge or not. When in doubt, document your source.

# Sample Essay

Jean-François Curiale
Ms. E. Zulu
English 103
December 11, 2008

**THE MULTIPLE MEANINGS OF SEWING IN *THE COLOR PURPLE***
In *The Color Purple,* many of Alice Walker's characters sew as part of their everyday activities. Early in the novel, for example, Celie makes Sofia some new curtains, and this exemplifies the utilitarian function of sewing. However, sewing often transcends its practical applications because sewers can express a creative vision through their work. Quilting is an example of how the practical and the aesthetic can come together. Quilting is a task that women can do alone; however, working on a pattern with other people creates chances for conversation along with the sharing of labor. Significantly, Celie and Sofia are able to repair their friendship by making a quilt together. Together or alone, through quilting or other forms of sewing, women can express themselves creatively, using color and design to signal their emotions. As a corollary, sewing can reflect a woman's sense of self at any given time, and a shift in a person's perception of her identity might be replicated in a change in the type of sewing that she produces. In Celie's case, she transforms her hobby of making pants for her friends and family into a lucrative business that enables her to compete in the male-dominated domain of enterprise. Likewise, when Albert admits to an interest in sewing and picks up a needle, he challenges conventional expectations of gender. Thus, the simple practice of sewing has multiple meanings. Walker depicts sewing as an activity that characters use to express their emotions and satisfy creative impulses. Sewing can also foster unity among

characters, function as an indicator of a character's emerging authentic self, and symbolize characters' defiance of traditional gender roles.

Sewing can serve as a release for creative impulses and a range of emotions. When Celie sees her daughter in a store, the memory that surfaces is that she embroidered her child's name, Olivia, in the seat of all her "daidies." Although this could be seen as practical, Celie also admits that she added a "lot of little stars and flowers too" (13). This decorative, but inessential, addition indicates Celie's love for her child, since she spent time and energy making her child's clothing special. Later in the novel, when Celie learns that Mr. _____ has been hiding her sister's letters from her, her anger is so intense that she fantasizes about killing him. Shug proposes that Celie start to make some pants, claiming that they would be practical to wear when working in the fields. Celie understands that Shug wants to deflect her rage and channel the energy into something productive by putting "a needle and not a razor in [her] hand" (147). When Celie develops her hobby into a thriving pant-making business, her earliest samples are designed with specific friends and family in mind. She experiments with a multitude of colors, designs, and materials. Eventually, she produces a pair of pants that are uniquely crafted for Shug: comfortable, wrinkle-free, and styled to flatter her body. Similarly, her positive feelings toward Jack (Sofia's brother-in-law) are projected into a pair of soft, strong camel pants. Their practical attributes— being washable, close fitting on the leg, and having lots of pockets—show Celie's respect, understanding, and warmth for this kind, family man. When the fame of her pants spreads, Celie decides to make a pair for her sister, Nettie, in Africa. Again, Celie takes into consideration Nettie's character and situation before designing a pair of pants specifically for her. In a letter where she tells Nettie about the pants, she explains that, "Every stitch I sew will be a kiss" (214). Thus, Celie uses sewing to express her positive emotions toward other people and as a productive way to harness the energy provoked by negative feelings.

Since sewing can be an outlet for emotions that link the sewer with the recipient of the sewn creation, sewing also promotes unity among people. When Harpo marries Sofia, Celie sews some curtains for their house. Later, out of jealousy at Sofia's self-assertiveness, Celie suggests to Harpo that he beat Sofia as a way to control her. Outraged that another woman would urge a man to oppress her, Sofia returns the curtains to Celie. During the heated conversation that ensues, Celie confesses her shame for having betrayed Sofia, especially given her own victimization at the hands of men. As Sofia grasps the depth of Celie's painful life, she proposes that the two women make a quilt out of the ruined curtains. The sewing of the quilt represents the solidarity of the two women and their realization that their life will be better served through unity rather than division. After a while, as Shug starts to appreciate Celie's worth, she offers to participate in the making of the quilt, even donating a yellow dress that becomes incorporated into it. The way that the distinct scraps of material are brought together in the quilt parallels the dynamics of the diverse people involved in its making. As critic Leder states, the "pieces of a quilt, like individuals in a pluralistic society, retain their original identities while functioning as parts of something else" (141). However much the pieces of material might appear like worthless, disconnected scraps, something beautiful and practical is created when they are joined together.

Sewing connects Celie to a feeling of power through unity with other women and this, in turn, allows her to grasp a sense of her own autonomy and selfhood, which is, likewise, expressed through sewing. When Celie starts to quilt with Sofia, she makes active choices for the first time in her life:

> Active creation replaces passive victimization as the two women, their sisterhood reaffirmed, set about constructing a pattern of their choice out of the fragments of their lives. Celie's decision to make the quilt is thus the turning point in her life because it is the first step to her empowerment via connection with other women. (Elsley 167)

As Celie starts to assert her own needs and desires, with Shug and Sofia's help, her emerging authentic self is revealed through changes in her sewing. Praised for her talent in making aesthetically pleasing pants, Celie takes her skill to a higher level and turns it into a lucrative business, where she employs two other women to help her sew. Her newfound sense of agency and self-confidence is indicated when she takes Shug to visit her former family home. For this visit, the two women wear matching "new blue flower pants," showing their united front against the man Celie believed was her father. Celie's behavior has changed significantly since the time of her marriage; she has evolved into someone who dares confront a man who raped her throughout her childhood. The blue color of the pants connotes this newfound energy and confidence. Similarly, Celie creates a pair of pants for Sofia, with one purple leg and one red leg. Celie envisions Sofia "jumping over the moon" in these pants. The pants contain Celie's hope that Sofia will regain her powerful sense of self that was stifled through years of imprisonment and domestic servitude. The color purple is not only associated with royalty but, for Walker, it is the color of black feminism. As she wrote in the epigraph to *In Search of Our Mothers' Gardens*, "Womanist is to feminist as purple to lavender." Sofia's purple pants look forward to a dream of black women one day being free of the damaging effects of racism and sexism. Only then can these women's emerging authentic selves be fully realized.

In order for black women's rights to be achieved, an important step is the dismantling of traditional gender roles that restrict choices and behavior. Once again, Walker uses the motif of sewing to show how these limiting roles can be challenged. When Shug first urges Celie to start sewing, she tells Celie to make herself a pair of work pants. As Shug points out, it is ludicrous that Celie is plowing the land all day wearing a dress. Drawing on the cliché that whoever wears the pants in a household is the dominant force there, Celie's making a pair of work pants confirms the reality that it is her labor that keeps the house running since Mr. _____ lounges around all day. Celie's realization that she can wear pants in her house, literally and figuratively, overturns the fictions that women are weak, passive, and incapable of hard labor. Celie is able to transform her pant-making into a business, another domain where women have traditionally been considered inept. However, sewing does not just illustrate women's defiance of traditional gender roles. Walker also uses sewing to show how proscriptive gender roles restrict men. When Celie and Albert start to talk honestly about their past, sewing together facilitates their reconciliation. In fact, Albert remembers wanting to sew as a boy, but everyone laughed at him, instilling enough shame in him to cause him to stop. By picking up the needle as an old man and sewing with Celie, Walker signals Albert's growth in awareness. His decision to sew illustrates that abandoning traditional gender roles is beneficial to everyone. Additionally, Walker underscores the cultural specificity of gender roles, thereby denying their universality, by having Celie explain to Albert that it is Olinkan men who have traditionally sewn and quilted. Ironically, African-American women's tradition of quilting probably has its roots in male practices. The implication of this is that to consider sewing as a woman's activity is not only limiting for those men who might want to express themselves through sewing, but is probably historically erroneous.

Sewing is an activity that has declined in practice over time. People are less inclined to repair or make their own clothing since it is so readily available and affordable. Quilting has become more of an art form than a habitual and essential task. Thus, the meanings of sewing change over time. During the first half of the 20th century in rural Georgia, where the novel is set, the multiple meanings of sewing already indicate change and flux. Walker shows how sewing can effect unity. In the case of *The Color Purple*'s women characters, their unity empowers them and allows them to start making their own choices. Thus, sewing, an activity associated with female relegation to the domestic sphere, becomes a means of liberation and self-empowerment because making their own choices permits the women to abandon the lifestyle of dependence and domesticity that sewing formerly represented. Walker shows this development through Celie's transformation of sewing, taking it out of the home and into the world to earn a living from it. Sewing also provides the opportunity for creative and emotive expression. By classifying sewing as a woman's activity, men cut themselves off from a possible outlet for expressing feelings or creativity. However, by stressing the cultural and historical specificity that labels sewing a woman's activity in the United States, Walker suggests that if sewing becomes an activity that is open to all, it could potentially contribute to the dismantling of limiting, traditional gender roles, which would strengthen understanding between men and women. Thus, the many meanings of sewing indicate Walker's hope for better personal opportunities and relationships, which would, in turn, lead to an improved sense of community.

## WORKS CITED

Dieke, Ikenna, ed. *Critical Essays on Alice Walker*. Westport, CT: Greenwood, 1999.

Elsley, Judy. " 'Nothing can be sole or whole that has not been rent': Fragmentation in the Quilt and *The Color Purple*." Dieke 163–170.

Leder, Priscilla. "Alice Walker's American Quilt: *The Color Purple* and American Literary Tradition." Dieke 141–151.

Walker, Alice. *In Search of Our Mothers' Gardens: Womanist Prose*. London: Women's Press, 1983.

——. *The Color Purple*. Orlando, FL: Harvest, 1982.

# HOW TO WRITE ABOUT
# ALICE WALKER

## AN OVERVIEW

**K**NOWLEDGE OF Alice Walker's biography will prove helpful in understanding some of the situations, themes, ideas, and characters that recur throughout her work. Not only does she draw on key, personal experiences and represent them in a fictional context, she also directly explores the significance of certain life events in her essays and poems. At different stages in her life, Walker's work often reflects the major concerns of the time and place in which she is living.

Walker was born in 1944 in the community of Eatonton, Georgia, to sharecropper parents, who had to work extremely hard to earn enough to meet the needs of their large family. The American South has been the birthplace for several of Walker's protagonists and provides the backdrop to various plot twists and turns. *The Third Life of Grange Copeland* graphically depicts the soul-destroying realities of the sharecropper system, detailing the corruption of men who get trapped into a system that exploits their labor and from which they often cannot escape. Black male violence against the women and children in their family is shown to be a consequence of the frustrations and bitterness that accompany this harsh life. The entrenched racism of the South is laid bare in novels such as *Meridian* and *The Color Purple,* with Walker's characters frequently feeling compelled to leave the South in order to carve out a life that allows them to pursue their dreams. Walker's ambivalence toward the South is articulated in her essay "The Black Writer and the Southern Experience," which would be a valuable place to start if you are writing on Walker's representation of the South. Although she depicts the South as racist, sexist, and impoverished, she also attributes positive qualities to the type of African-American community in which she was raised. Notably, there is a strong sense of community, with neighbors supporting one another in a cooperative and often selfless way. Stories such as "To Hell with Dying," which draws on events in Walker's life, show how involved the community can be in taking care of its own, even beyond the confines of immediate family. Walker's women characters, in particular, are portrayed as drawing on their inner strength and spirituality to withstand the challenges that they face living in the South. Walker writes about the innate wisdom, resilience, and vision of her black female ancestors in essays such as "In Search of Our Mothers' Gardens."

When she was eight, Walker was playing Cowboys and Indians with two of her brothers and she got shot in the eye with a BB pellet. Fearful of punishment from their parents, the brothers persuaded their younger sister to lie about the circumstances of this traumatic event, and she agreed to the fiction that a piece of wire had poked her in the eye. The essay, "Beauty: When the Other Dancer Is the Self," traces Walker's evolving emotions regarding this incident, showing how it affected her relationships with her family and friends, her personality, and her self-esteem for many years after the actual blinding. Writing poetry was an outlet that Walker used to explore and express emotions related to this life-changing experience.

In 1961, Walker was awarded a scholarship to Spelman College, a historically black liberal arts college for women in Atlanta. Given the time period of the early 1960s, Walker unsurprisingly became involved in the Civil Rights movement and started a long career as a political activist. Some of Walker's early novels and essays tackle issues that evolved out of her Civil Rights work, notably, black male sexism within the framework of fighting for racial equality. Since the unique concerns of black women had been sidelined by both white feminism and the Civil Rights movement, Walker formulated womanism as a response. The principles of womanism are personified in characters such as Celie and Meridian, who fight to redefine their relationships with the male characters and claim their rights as black women.

Walker found Spelman's goal of promoting ladylike behavior in its students (which she mocks in *Meridian*) ludicrous, and in conjunction with their lack of tolerance for her political work, Walker decided to finish her studies at Sarah Lawrence College in New York. This decision provided her with the opportunity to visit Uganda at the end of her junior year, which initiated a lasting interest in the continent of Africa. The short story, "Advancing Luna—and Ida B. Wells," which contains autobiographical elements, alludes to this trip to Africa and the welcome she received from the Ugandan people. The complex relationship between Africa, Africans, and African-Americans is a topic that Walker takes up in *The Color Purple, The Temple of My Familiar,* and *Possessing the Secret of Joy.* Ultimately, she became embroiled in accusations of cultural imperialism for speaking out against the practice of female genital cutting in Africa.

Another significant event that occurred during Walker's time at Sarah Lawrence was an unplanned pregnancy and her subsequent decision to have an abortion. The abortion resulted in a serious depression, triggering a range of emotions that, once again, Walker attempted to make sense of through writing poetry. Examples of these poems can be found in the collection *Once* (1968). The character Meridian also undergoes an abortion while at college, and her rejection of the maternal role is part of Walker's critique of society's promotion of motherhood as a sacred calling. Although she has written specifically about the concept of motherhood, the interaction between parents and children in general is a theme that Walker has probed throughout her writing career. *By the Light of My Father's Smile* (1998) offers an in-depth look at the way that parents can damage their children and the steps that could be taken to redress that hurt.

After graduation, Walker returned to the South both to write and participate in Civil Rights work, such as voter registration. During this time, she met Melvyn Leventhal, a law student who was helping draft lawsuits that were being filed against the state of Mississippi within the context of desegregation. Walker and Leventhal were married in New York in 1967 and, on their return to Mississippi, became the targets of racist vitriol. Walker discusses the intricacies of interracial relationships, particularly within the context of the history of the South, in several of her works. "Advancing Luna—and Ida B. Wells" and *Meridian,* for example, argue that the South's history of racism and sexism impedes the success of any interracial relationship, even in the case of friendship between black and white women. Walker's marriage ended in divorce in 1976, with one daughter born in 1969.

*The Third Life of Grange Copeland* was published in 1970, and with it Walker's writing career started to blossom, even though she was criticized in some quarters for portraying black men negatively in her work. However, many of Walker's black male characters, who are violent with their wives and children, experience redemption throughout the course of the novel and take corrective measures. Such is the case with Albert in *The Color Purple* or Grange Copeland. The black man who comes to understand that his violent behavior toward women and children has negative repercussions on the entire community is a recurring figure in Walker's work.

Throughout the 1970s, Walker continued to write and publish. She also actively promoted the work of black female writers, teaching a newly created course on African-American women writers at Wellesley College and uncovering and marking the gravesite of Zora Neale Hurston. Walker writes about her discovery of Hurston's work and the influence it had on her in several essays found in the collection *In Search of Our Mothers' Gardens.*

In 1979, Walker relocated to Northern California, and it is there that she started to write *The Color Purple,* the novel that brought her international acclaim and a Pulitzer Prize. Since the 1980s, Walker has continued to write in a variety of genres: children's books, essays, poetry, and novels. Her work from the late 1980s, such as *The Temple of My Familiar,* shows the influence of her chosen place of residence in Mendocino, because of its integration of new age ideas that were current at that time and place. In more recent work, the focus of her novels has moved away from the formerly dominant issues of race and gender to argue for concerns that have risen to prominence in the last couple of decades, such as protecting the environment, validating alternative belief systems and indigenous knowledge, exploring different forms of sexuality, and finding inner peace, healing, and self-acceptance.

As this brief overview of her life indicates, Alice Walker is, when compared to many public figures, an open book. She has talked and written about the women she has loved and her work has often included a loving, sexual relationship between two women. As someone who has experimented with a variety of genres, Walker's nonfiction often clarifies her position on issues that are raised in her fiction and poetry. Furthermore, she has always been transparent about her writing methods and influences, and some of her essays and interviews have outlined the process of bringing a particular work to fruition. For writers who want to explore links between Walker's biography and her work, it will be helpful to consult her numerous essays and interview transcripts, as well as analyze the primary texts themselves. With many writers, it is difficult to ascertain the extent of the connections between their life and work. With Alice Walker, her life and her work form a symbiosis. Additionally, her work engages themes and philosophical ideas that are reiterated throughout multiple texts, which provides a broader bank of commentary from which to assess her perspectives and attitudes.

## TOPICS AND STRATEGIES

This section will identify various topics for essays that could draw on multiple Walker works. The suggestions are intended to inspire your own ideas. Many of Walker's recurring themes, ideas, and characters find their inspiration in autobiographical incidents. However, the writer of an essay on Walker must be careful not to automatically assume the autobiographical nature of all her work, nor presuppose that plot details are always faithful re-creations of events in her life.

### Themes

Love manifests itself in a variety of ways throughout Walker's work: Men love their wives; wives love other women; parents love their children; and friends and family offer one another love and support. Love, thus, does not refer only to romantic or sexual love. Walker's concept of love is a force that can facilitate healing and provide strength for continued living. Receiving and giving love permits characters to transcend their anger toward the world and resentment toward other characters who treat them badly. Beyond operating on an individual level, love can aid psychologically damaged communities by uniting its members. A loving environment provides a more supportive milieu in which to raise families and diminishes the possibility of violence and exploitation. Although Walker's black communities cannot completely escape the racist violence directed at them by white populations, love and loving family relationships can help diminish its effect on each individual. Walker's novels and short stories depict both positive and negative family relationships, providing a contrast between those damaged by familial conflict and those empowered by understanding and love. In some cases, strong family ties are a deciding factor in how successfully characters survive the situations in which they find themselves. Many Walker characters are born into poverty and struggle with endemic violence and racism; however, Walker shows how some people are able to find the inner strength to overcome their circumstances and even encourage others to resist oppression. An important step in achieving resistance is for a character to find her or his voice and speak out. Both female and male characters must find the courage to resist being broken by the violent, sexist, exploitative, racist society in which they live. Love, violence, racism, spousal abuse, child abuse, family relationships, marriage, male-female relationships, survival, resistance, and finding one's voice: These themes recur throughout Walker's work, and their analysis could become the starting point for a variety of papers.

## Sample Topics:

1. **Love:** In Walker's works, how does the experience of love affect different characters? What are the different types of love that Walker presents in her novels, short stories, essays, and poems?

   An essay discussing Walker's use of the theme of love could analyze various texts to determine whether her view on love is strictly defined or whether it varies from text to text. What kinds of love does Walker portray in her works that challenge the conventional view of love as sexual/romantic interaction between a man and a woman? Another approach to this theme could consider what social, cultural, and political factors interfere with the possibility of love between characters. How do characters respond to these external forces in their pursuit of love? You could also investigate to what degree love has the power to transform lives. Additionally, several of Walker's works, *The Temple of My Familiar*, for example, propose a worldview that promotes the notion of universal love. How does a character's espousal of universal love transform the individual and the community? Examples of powerful love relationships are present in works such as *The Color Purple, The Third Life of Grange Copeland, By the Light of My Father's Smile,* and "To Hell with Dying."

2. **Family:** In what ways does Walker portray a negative image of the family unit? Conversely, Walker depicts the family as a source of support and love. How and why does she validate family relationships?

   In order to narrow your focus and make this topic easier to navigate, essays on this theme could start by looking at specific family relationships and choosing one or more types of relationship from the large spectrum found in Walker's writing. You could examine the bond between sisters or look at Walker's depiction of male-female or parent-child relationships. These papers could analyze Walker's representation of sibling, marriage, and parental relationships respectively. Some types of relationship provide characters with motivation to endure life's difficulties. Celie's and Nettie's sisterly love for each other in *The Color Purple* nourishes both characters at difficult moments in their lives. The sister relationship in *By the Light of My Father's Smile,* however, is portrayed as conflictual. Walker depicts other relationships, particularly between husbands and wives and between parents and children, as sources of absolute misery and suffering. A paper could evaluate Walker's objective in negatively foregrounding certain family relationships or assess why certain relationships become so beneficial to certain characters.

3. **Resistance:** Which characters in Walker's work feel driven to speak out against oppression? What personality traits and attitudes determine whether a character will stay cowed by society or voice his or her truth?

   This topic could be approached by analyzing different characters' movement from silence to speech. For example, Meridian, Celie, Tashi, and Ruth Copeland are all women who make a stand against forces, institutions, and people that oppress them. Other characters, however, such as Brownfield, Mrs. Hill, and Magdalena are crushed by their society's values and impositions. What social and personal forces determine whether a character will be silent and self-destructive or outspoken and self-assertive? Does gender play a role as to whether a character finds the will to speak his or her true thoughts? An angle that could be pursued is to assess to what extent the historical and social context influences women's and men's choices to be silent or to resist. Resistance can be considered both on an individual level and on a community level.

4. **Survival:** What tough choices do the characters have to make in order to meet the challenges they face in their lives? What different attitudes do the characters adopt that prove helpful in terms of their survival?

The theme of survival could be addressed by taking one of several approaches. It could be interpreted literally in the sense of the various activities characters perform in order to earn a living and take care of their families and themselves. How do these activities affect a character's relationships with others and their sense of self? Characters' dealings with others can also be understood as a form of survival; this is the case when characters deceive or use one another to get something. Different texts also show how some characters advocate attitudes they feel are necessary for survival, either on an individual or on a community level, and these attitudes can be either positive (e.g., love) or negative (e.g., hate). Works that engage the theme of survival include *The Color Purple, The Third Life of Grange Copeland, The Temple of My Familiar, By the Light of My Father's Smile,* and *Now Is the Time to Open Your Heart.*

## Character

Alice Walker has been criticized for rendering black men as violent, but such critiques fail to acknowledge the complexity of her characterization. In an interview with Claudia Tate published in *Black Women Writers at Work*, Walker addressed this criticism in the context of her portrayal of Brownfield in *The Third Life of Grange Copeland*: "I know many Brownfields, and it's a shame that I know so many. I will not ignore people like Brownfield. I want you to know I know they exist. I want to tell you about them, and there is no way you are going to avoid them. [ . . . ] I wish people would do that rather than tell me that this is not the right image. [ . . . ] The people who criticize me about Brownfield rarely even talk about Grange." Walker's portrayals of black men often show them as ineffectual, irresponsible, or abusive fathers. The effect that fathers can have on their children, intentionally or unintentionally, is a facet of parenthood that Walker returns to throughout her work. In *By the Light of My Father's Smile*, she proposes steps that black men can take in order to communicate more effectively with their daughters. Similarly, gulfs of understanding and a lack of compassion between mothers and daughters are shown to have long-lasting, detrimental effects on the child. However, Walker's work always stresses the social, political, and historical context that has contributed to these parents' dysfunction; they are not presented in a vacuum. As in the case of Grange Copeland, some characters are shown to follow a journey of self-awareness, and the new insights that they acquire compel these characters into performing actions intended to redress the damage they have done to others. The character on a journey of personal transformation, whether male or female, is a recurring type in Walker's work, although the nature of that transformation may vary depending on circumstances, gender, and context. Another recurring character is the figure of the wise woman. Many of Walker's texts depict a woman, perhaps having been formally educated or perhaps having innate wisdom, who is able to help steer other characters into seeing and understanding their world differently. Many of these wise women are significantly older than the characters with whom they interact, but in some cases, different life experiences may position them as voices of superior knowledge. Across Walker's work, different characters and their experiences share parallels and could become the focus of an essay synthesizing analysis of multiple texts.

## Sample Topics:

1. **Black men:** What causes Walker's black male characters to oppress their wives and families or act out violently against oth-

ers? What does Walker suggest that black men could do to redeem themselves in the eyes of their families and their communities?

Evaluating whether the criticisms of Walker's portrayal of black men have validity or not could be a starting point for an essay on her black male characters. You may want to look at characters such as Grange Copeland, Albert, or Mr. Robinson from *By the Light of My Father's Smile,* all black men who try to make amends for their destructive behavior. Alternatively, a paper could assess the process that Walker advocates for black men to reconnect to their authentic selves. How must black men change their perspectives on masculinity, women, and social roles in order for them to find self-fulfillment in a racist society?

2. **Mothers and fathers:** How do parents damage their children's sense of well-being throughout Walker's work? According to Walker, what makes an effective parent?

Many of Walker's mothers and fathers inflict such severe trauma on their children that it takes those children a lifetime to overcome that legacy. Additionally, parents can continue to harm their children even when they are adults. Walker often shows this brutal interaction stemming from the parents' own history of pain and suffering. An essay could analyze either mothers or fathers to assess why Walker repeatedly shows the destructive features of parent/child relationships. What is her goal in portraying these relationships as so influential and potentially damaging to children? What solutions does she propose for both parents and children to surmount the tension and problems that arise out of the parent/child relationship?

3. **Wise women:** How are Walker's wise women able to help others? Most of Walker's wise women instruct others how to live their lives more fruitfully. What are the tenets that other characters must learn in order to have better lives?

Shug in *The Color Purple* and in *The Temple of My Familiar,* Irene in *By the Light of My Father's Smile,* and Grandmother in *Now Is the Time to Open Your Heart* are all quintessential Walker wise women who have knowledge that allows them to live in harmony with themselves, with others, and with their environment. A paper could examine a selection of these wise women characters and analyze the sources, nature, and legacy of their wisdom. Another approach would be to look at Walker's wise male characters. They are usually men cast in a shamanistic role but also include characters such as Pierre in *Possessing the Secret of Joy* or Hal in *The Temple of My Familiar,* who have become wise by drawing on other sources of knowledge.

4. **Characters' journeys of personal transformation:** How do characters find their authentic selves? What obstacles must characters overcome in order to transform themselves and their relationships with others?

Both Walker's male and female characters struggle with the realization that they are not living their lives the way that would allow them to be true to their values or in harmony with the rest of the universe. An essay could be based on analysis of a selection of male characters (for example, Grange, Suwelo, and Truman) or a selection of female characters (for example, Meridian, Fanny, and Celie) to determine how they achieve their goals of living an authentic life. What principles must these characters adhere to in order to achieve self-fulfillment? What sacrifices do they make in order to accomplish their journeys?

## History and Context

The West is inclined to present Africa as a uniform country, with the notion that an African, for example, from Senegal has the same identity as someone from Zambia. This assumption ignores Africa's diversity and leads to generalizations about the continent that deny each country's and each population's specificity. Stereotypes attached to Africa and Africans have been taken as indisputable truths by many Westerners as a result of this distortion. Walker was condemned for her representation of Africa and Africans because her fictional Olinka was judged to typify this Western habit of discounting Africa's regional differences and her Olinkans were portrayed as needing to embrace American values in order to improve their lives. However, a close look at Walker's African settings and African characters reveals that, overall, there are arguments that can be used to attack and defend Walker's representations of Africa.

Another setting that recurs in Walker's work is the American South, and its presentation is usually tinged with ambivalence. Born and raised in Georgia, Walker has identified herself as a southern writer who has been inspired to write by events in her own life, such as growing up as the child of sharecroppers. Walker depicts this lifestyle as unrelenting, exacerbated by the racism of the white southern population and the violence that pervades such an environment. For Walker, the South is her birthplace; however, it is a birthplace that she felt compelled to leave in order to pursue the life that she wanted. Although the South can be so harmful to her black characters, Walker also repeatedly illustrates the positive elements of black southern community life. For example, in her essay "The Black Writer and the Southern Experience," Walker avers that black southern life has been characterized by centuries of "neighborly kindness and sustaining love."

Several of Walker's works grapple with issues that arose out of various social and political movements of the 1960s and 1970s. An important discourse that emerged in response to the white feminist movement and the Civil Rights movement addressed the status of black women. Second-wave white feminism of the 1960s and 1970s had made sweeping assertions about the needs and rights of women that overlooked the unique situation of black women who had to contend with racism and sexism. Alice Walker formulated the notion of womanism in *In Search of Our Mothers' Gardens: Womanist Prose* (1983). Its objective was to communicate the concerns of black women, taking into account the specificity of black female experience. This version of black feminism also tackled the sexism that women had encountered during their participation in the Civil Rights movement. Black women had increasingly been made aware that the Civil Rights movement universalized black male concerns and often perpetuated the oppression of black women.

Starting in the 1980s, Walker's interests, as reflected in her work, shifted emphasis from the political to the spiritual. *The Temple of My Familiar* is her first novel that strongly advocates new age and indigenous beliefs as a way to find one's authentic self. Walker presents these beliefs and practices as countercultural forces that can be life changing for those who approach them with an open mind. The spiritual practices that are explored in subsequent works are eclectic but are derived from multiple world religions such as Hinduism, Shamanism, and Buddhism and consider multiple alternative ideas such as reincarnation, astrology, and the power of crystals. Walker argues that indigenous knowledge has been rendered obsolete, not because of its lack of value, but because of the unfortunate ascendancy of white beliefs and way of life.

## Sample Topics:

1. **Representations of Africa:** How does Walker represent Africa and Africans in a positive light? What aspects of her portrayal of Africa and Africans could provide evidence to accuse Walker of cultural imperialism?

   Sometimes, Walker depicts Africa and Africans as helpless and uninformed; conversely, features of African life and its people are validated. An essay on her representation of Africa and Africans could examine how she depicts the relationships between Africa and African Americans and between Africa and white people. Examining the textual evidence in works such as *Possessing the Secret of Joy, The Temple of My Familiar,* and *The Color Purple* will lead you to draw conclusions that might critique, endorse, or be ambivalent about Walker's representation of Africa. An extension of this topic could compare her representation of Africa to her use of Latin America as a recurrent setting. How does Walker portray Latin America in works such as *Now Is the Time to Open Your Heart* or *The Temple of My Familiar*?

2. **Womanism as a response to the Civil Rights and Black Power movements:** How does Walker use references to historical events to demonstrate how black women characters

feel about some of the attitudes espoused by the Civil Rights movement? How does Walker demonstrate the effects of black male sexism on her black female characters? How does Walker show the influence of racism on black women in the past and in the present? Why do her black female characters adopt womanist ideology, and how is it reproduced in their behavior and actions?

An essay could focus on Meridian, Celie, Fanny, Tashi, or a selection of secondary characters and show how black women characters create a life for themselves that asserts their value as both black and female. Writers analyzing Walker's womanist philosophy will likely find it helpful to look at her definitions of womanism, which can be found in the essay collection *In Search of Our Mothers' Gardens: Womanist Prose.* With an understanding of the goals of womanism, another approach would be to identify and analyze womanist themes and concerns that Walker engages throughout her work. An alternative approach to this topic could pinpoint actual historical events that are directly mentioned, for example, Dr. Martin Luther King's funeral in *Meridian,* to consider the effect of history on women's changing consciousness in different time periods.

3. **The American South:** What are the positive aspects of life in black southern communities for Walker's characters? In what ways does Walker depict life in the American South as brutal?

A paper analyzing Walker's representation of the South could assess her contrasting attitudes toward her birthplace. Why do so many characters loathe life in the South and leave, yet keep finding themselves drawn back to it? Another approach could consider life in the South for male characters compared to that for female characters. What impedes the possibility of a good life for black women in the South? This topic could also be approached by comparing and contrasting life in the South with life in the North. Does Walker present the North as a

viable alternative for characters seeking to escape the problems associated with the South?

4. **New ageism and the value of indigenous beliefs:** What indigenous and nonmainstream spiritual practices and beliefs does
Walker incorporate into her work and to what aim? How does
Walker suggest that indigenous beliefs, customs, and traditions
offer a viable alternative to mainstream white beliefs, behavior,
and attitudes?

An essay investigating the influence of indigenous or new age
beliefs and practices on Walker's work could start by identifying the different examples that are incorporated into the plots of
her work. What does she show to be the societal and individual
benefits of being open to nonmainstream ideas and practices?
An extension of this topic could assess the validity of Walker's
argument that a reinstatement of these indigenous beliefs and
practices can benefit both indigenous populations and Westerners. How will these beliefs and practices help indigenous
populations, and how does this differ from the way they can
help Westerners?

## Philosophy and Ideas

An idea that is expounded in several of Walker works is the notion
of healing the body and mind. She advocates various techniques and
routes that people can follow in their quest to heal either on an individual level or at the community level. For example, the power of nature is
shown to be curative in *By the Light of My Father's Smile.* Tapping into
the creative spirit and reconnecting to ancestral traditions are depicted
as restorative in *The Temple of My Familiar* and *Now Is the Time to
Open Your Heart.* Not only can the topic of healing be the focus of an
essay, but also exploration of some of these associated ideas could form
the basis for a paper.

A source of strength that also facilitates healing can be found by
women joining together to support and uplift one another. Female solidarity takes a variety of forms throughout her work, but is shown to be
an invaluable component in defeating men's exploitation of and violence

toward women. In addition to transforming their personal lives, women can pursue political change when they are united. *Possessing the Secret of Joy* shows how a united front can challenge patriarchal structures and practices that are detrimental to them. Walker even suggests that women's solidarity is imperative in order for society's sexist and racist dictates to be resisted. In addition to joining forces with like-minded women, education and learning are both presented as useful for women in advancing their status and independence in society. Walker's work shows how a formal or informal education can be a means that both men and women employ to renounce the traditional gender roles that restrict their choices and to rise above the ignorance that might contribute to their limited worldview. On the other hand, Walker does not shy away from depicting the negative consequences of an education. In "Everyday Use" and "To My Sister Molly Who in the Fifties," Dee and Molly respectively feel the intellectual abyss that separates their families from themselves after they have been educated.

Many Walker characters must also come to terms with events in their past in order to function effectively in the present. Some characters struggle to overcome difficult legacies from their ancestors, their parents, and their childhoods. How characters deal with the past often depends on their individual strength and their desire to heal. Strong characters are not broken by the past, whereas others are shown to be so traumatized that they become self-destructive and live their lives inauthentically. A common thread that runs throughout Walker's work is the wisdom that can be harnessed by reconnecting to the past. Often, this wisdom can be learned from the older members of a society. Simply talking to elders can transform a character's perspective on life, as is the case with Suwelo after his conversations with Lissie and Hal. In particular, much of Walker's work advances the notion that populations whose pasts have been discredited by Europeans and their descendants, such as African Americans or Native Americans, have much to offer if their ideas and beliefs are approached with an open heart.

## Sample Topics:

1. **Healing:** How do Walker's characters become conscious that they are in need of physical, spiritual, and psychological

healing? What techniques does her work show that can facilitate the healing process?

An essay on this topic could look at the various measures that the characters take to promote their physical, mental, and spiritual well-being. What role do other people play in a character's healing? How can nature assist healing? Another approach to this topic could show how the healed individual becomes a benefit to the community. How does an individual's condition relate to the health of a community?

2. **The legacy of the past:** How do memories, dreams, or stories of the past affect the way various characters view their life? Which characters successfully break free from the past and which characters stay haunted by it? How does Walker establish the contribution and value of black women to an American heritage, artistic or otherwise?

If writing on this topic, you could consider the ways that Walker shows how being open to the lessons from the past can lead to gaining wisdom and strength. For example, how can knowledge of the wrong done to ancestors empower the living? Conversely, how can knowledge of wrong done to ancestors damage someone? Memory and the past influence the lives of many of Walker's main characters. A paper could investigate the legacy of the past as pertaining to a variety of characters. How does Walker validate memories and the wisdom of elders as viable sources of knowledge? An essay could also examine how Walker presents literary and artistic heritage in her work. How does she build on ideas from the past to make them relevant for the present?

3. **Female solidarity:** How does Walker's work emphasize the value of women's unity when fighting the political, social, and cultural status quo? How does her work show that women's mutual support in everyday life is essential to their interests? What situations does her work suggest might undercut women's unity?

This topic could be approached by analyzing Walker's perspective on the ways female solidarity benefits women. Such an essay could also assess how women's interests are jeopardized if women are antagonistic to one another. Mutual female support generates internal strength that allows some female characters to challenge the men who oppress them. An essay could chart specific characters' growth in understanding the benefits of women's solidarity. How do male characters react to the united front that the women establish and what are the women able to accomplish through unity?

4. **Education and learning:** What are the advantages and disadvantages of acquiring an education for Walker's African-American characters? If a character is unable to pursue a formal education, how else might he or she acquire learning and knowledge that will allow personal improvements?

A possible approach to this topic could consider how Walker shows that denying some people education can be used to foster inequalities, whether in the United States, Africa, or elsewhere. Another approach might look at the ways characters acquire learning despite a lack of formal education. How do characters acquire knowledge using alternative methods? How does Walker's work suggest an individual or a community can be transformed (either positively or negatively) when people become educated or knowledgeable?

## Form and Genre

Walker has worked in a variety of different forms and genres throughout her writing career, but whether the final product is a poem, an essay, or a short story, a common feature of her work is that it frequently does not adhere to usual genre conventions. Although "In Search of Our Mothers' Gardens" would normally be classified as an essay, it uses elements of other genres within that framework. Similarly, even though "Advancing Luna—and Ida B. Wells" is usually referred to as a short story, it contains components that are more usually associated with the essay or the autobiography. The function and effect of this blend of features from different genres could be explored in an essay. This confusion between the genres of the short story and the autobiography is sometimes encouraged by Walker's use of first-person narrators, where the voice of the narrator merges with the voice of the author. Some of Walker's short stories employ female first-person narrators, many of whom remain nameless, thereby making their identity open to question. Walker's use of first-person narration could be examined throughout her short stories, not only for its blurring of generic conventions, but also to show how she uses it to give voice to black women who have traditionally been silenced.

## Sample Topics:

1. **Breaking genre boundaries:** Why does Walker challenge form and genre conventions in her essays, short stories, novels, and poems? What is the effect of Walker's blurring of genre norms in her work?

Such an essay could analyze how Walker employs elements from different genres within her texts. How does the use of features from a mix of genres enhance a particular text's philosophical or thematic purposes? Walker often affirms her black female artistic heritage. Given the constraints put on black women to express themselves artistically throughout history, Walker's work has urged its audience to reconsider what constitutes art for black women, pointing to quilting, gardening, and oral storytelling as ways that were open to them to express a creative vision. Does Walker's breaking of genre conventions engage with her black female heritage in any way?

2. **Female first-person narrators:** Why does Walker frequently use the voice of either a named or a nameless black woman to tell her stories? How does the use of a first-person black woman narrator help Walker fulfill a text's philosophical and political goals?

"Advancing Luna—and Ida B. Wells," "To Hell with Dying," "Nineteen Fifty-five," and "Everyday Use" are examples of Walker's short stories that employ the device of a first-person black female narrator. Of two possible ways to approach a discussion of Walker's use of narrative point of view, the first could show how Walker articulates a specific perspective, that of the black woman whose opinions and attitudes have long been ignored by history and literature. How does expressing these previously overlooked perspectives promote the development of the themes and ideas that Walker explores in her work? The second approach could analyze the effects of her choice to leave some of her first-person narrators unnamed.

## Language, Symbols, and Imagery

Alice Walker has written about her own interest in quilting; thus, it is no surprise that she depicts some of her women characters as enjoying quilting or other forms of sewing. Sewing and quilting can have purely utilitarian goals. Characters such as Celie are shown making curtains or clothing for family members. However, in addition to that utilitarian function, sewing and quilting offer the opportunity for women to communicate creative visions. Such creativity has few other outlets within her female characters' daily routines of child-rearing, housework, and farming. Sewing can be done individually, but tasks like quilting are better tackled in the company of other women, an environment that also provides opportunities for companionship and communion. The sewn products can be for everyday use, but many of Walker's characters are such skilled sewers that their products can be considered art objects or worthy for sale. If sewing provides an opportunity for black women characters to come together, a recurring motif in Walker's work that shows the unity of both black women and men is music. Particularly in the context of church, singing together represents the fundamental unity of the characters even if, on the surface, their community seems fractured and troubled. In a story such as "Nineteen Fifty-five," Walker presents singing as an activity that has been used to voice the suffering of the African-American community. Music in all its forms offers the possibility for the expression of the true self, whether it is the blues of Gracie Mae Still or Carlotta's alternative bell music in *The Temple of My Familiar*. Similarly, nature is repeatedly shown to assuage the troubled spirits of some Walker characters. Trees, rivers, and animals all reappear in numerous texts to show that the human connection to nature is critical in order to find spiritual well-being, but that it is a connection that has come under threat as a result of the modern American lifestyle.

## Sample Topics:

1. **Sewing and quilting:** What are the functions of sewing and quilting in the black communities that Walker depicts? What does the making of a quilt symbolize? How do characters develop themselves through sewing?

   An essay could consider how Walker uses the symbolic meanings of quilting to enhance some of her key themes and ideas, such as the importance of female solidarity, the value of black women's artistic heritage, and the dismantling of restrictive gender roles. This topic could be extended to analyze the importance of all types of sewing and why sewing can be important to women, men, and the improvement of interpersonal relationships.

2. **Music and song:** How does Walker use music and singing to convey the heritage and history of some African-American southern characters? How does Walker depict the relationship among black women, music, and song?

   An essay could analyze Walker's perspective on the functions and significance of music for her African-American characters. While in church, Meridian grasps the importance of music to her community when she sees the stained-glass window of BB King. Gracie Mae Still's experience with music and the music industry shows it to be an arena where the differences between white and black Americans are accentuated. Carlotta discovers that composing music is an important component of her self-healing. Shug and Squeak realize that singing is a way for them to break free of society's restrictive expectations for women. Mr. Sweet expresses his pain through the blues, but brings joy to others. What does music mean to the different characters, and how has it influenced their responses to their different situations?

3. **The natural world:** How does Walker portray trees, plants, water, and animals in her work? How do characters respond to interaction with nature?

In the context of Walker's belief in universal connectedness, a paper could address her work's linking of nature to the divine. How do characters find redemption through interaction with nature? Another approach could discuss the symbolism of trees in a selection of her work. Trees are often shown to be crucial in a character's developing sense of self-awareness and self-understanding. The topic of trees could be extended to consider how other flowers and plants are given significance in her work. Water, especially in the form of rivers, is often shown to be important in helping characters reconnect to their authentic selves. What role does water play in helping characters understand themselves? Alternatively, an essay could examine the importance of references to animals and birds to Walker's overall thematic and philosophical goals.

## Compare and Contrast Essays

An essay that compares two or more characters is a potential place to start if assigned the task of writing a comparative paper. Many of Walker's male characters, for example, follow comparable paths; they lash out at those around them before realizing they must change in order to find peace, love, and self-acceptance. After they change, others in their lives become open to them, and they are able to establish loving relationships for the first time. A paper could compare and contrast two or more male characters and show how their behavior reflects their respective definitions of manhood and concretizes society's messages about masculinity. Each male character's understanding of what it means to be a man is shaped by the society in which he lives and by the way he perceives his role within society. As his understanding of his masculinity shifts, his relationships with his wife, his children, and his community is transformed. Comparison of some of Walker's female characters could also be the starting point for a paper. Many of Walker's female characters fight against the odds to free themselves from their brutal environments and relationships. In order to achieve a freer life, such women must often lead unconventional lives and challenge societal and gender norms. An essay could assess their various efforts to assert themselves with the men in their lives and within their communities. How do friendships with other women help or hinder them in their struggles? Another approach that could be used to compare female characters is to examine their respective attitudes toward men, love, or sexuality. Many of Walker's characters display unconventional attitudes toward sexual relationships or experience sexual difficulties because of society's repressive messages apropos female sexuality. Walker often shows male sexuality in her work to be exploitative and belittling when it comes to female partners. In response to this, some female characters stop being receptive to men sexually and turn to other women for love and sex, in search of intimacy free of sexual politics. Women may also feel it necessary to show the male characters alternative ways of relating to one another that would be as liberating for them as for the women. Whatever approach you take with your comparative essay, it is essential to remember that its focus must be analytical. Your essay should not merely identify a variety of similarities and differences between two or more characters. You must establish the significance of the comparisons you make.

## Sample Topics:

1. **Comparison of women and their struggles:** What different strategies do the female characters use to cope with the struggles they face? What societal attitudes and structures exacerbate the women's vulnerability as wives, mothers, and lovers?

   You could select two or more of Walker's female characters and compare and contrast their experience of being wives, lovers, mothers, or political and social rebels. Given that the social structures of the United States, particularly in the South but also elsewhere, can contribute to the suppression and exploitation of these women, how do the women overcome their situations to define themselves as women and work to improve the situation of all women? What are the differences between the struggles that Walker's black female characters face compared to those of her white female characters?

2. **Comparative masculinities:** How do Walker's black male characters assert themselves as men in a racist environment that negates their masculinity? What behavioral and attitude

changes must Walker's male characters make in order to feel a sense of self-worth and to receive love from others?

Walker's portrayals of black men have been condemned by some critics because black men are shown to be abusive, violent, exploitative, irresponsible, and in some cases, unredemptive. However, some of her male characters are dynamic, and their evolution to self-awareness and love for others is presented as hopeful. An essay could compare and contrast two or more male characters' transformations in awareness and their revolutions in attitudes and behavior. Another way to approach the male characters could be to compare and contrast a selection of secondary characters with the goal of examining Walker's perspective toward different masculinities. What types of masculine behavior does she endorse? A paper could also assess the degree to which Walker shows that societal structures and attitudes, such as racism, are responsible for the distortion of black masculinity.

3. **Comparing characters' attitudes toward sexuality:** What is the difference between male and female sexuality in Walker's work? Why do some characters have problems relating to the opposite sex and why? How do these characters surmount such problems?

The topic of sexuality can be approached in one of several ways. You could compare and contrast male and female attitudes toward sexuality. Another approach would be to examine different male, or different female, attitudes to sex, looking at how the politics of sexuality can shape sexual behavior and choices. An essay could also evaluate Walker's fictionalized solutions for bringing men and women together and allowing nonexploitative and noncontrolling expression of male and female sexuality.

## Bibliography and Online Sources

*Anniina's Alice Walker Page.* December 30, 2007. <http://www.luminarium.org/contemporary/alicew.htm>

Banks, Erma Davis, and Keith Byerman. *Alice Walker: An Annotated Bibliography 1968–1986.* New York: Garland, 1989.

Bates, Gerri. *Alice Walker: a Critical Companion.* Westport, CT: Greenwood Press, 2005.

Birch, Eva Lennox. "Alice Walker: The Spiritual Inheritance." *Black American Women's Writing: a Quilt of Many Colours.* New York: Harvester Wheatsheaf, 1994. 195–240.

Bloom, Harold, ed. *Alice Walker: Modern Critical Views.* New York: Chelsea House, 1989.

Christian, Barbara. "Alice Walker: The Black Woman Artist as Wayward." *Black Feminist Criticism: Perspectives on Black Women Writers.* Ed. Barbara Christian. New York: Pergamon, 1985. 81–101.

Dieke, Ikenna, ed. *Critical Essays on Alice Walker.* Westport, CT: Greenwood, 1999.

Gates, Jr., Henry Louis, and K. A. Appiah, eds. *Alice Walker: Critical Perspectives Past and Present.* New York: Amistad, 1993.

Lauret, Maria. *Modern Novelists: Alice Walker.* New York: St. Martin's, 2000.

Simcikova, Karla. *To Live Fully, Here and Now: The Healing Vision in the Works of Alice Walker.* Lanham, MD: Lexington, 2007.

Tate, Claudia, ed. "Alice Walker." *Black Women Writers at Work.* New York: Continuum, 1983. 175–187.

Walker, Alice. *Anything We Love Can Be Saved: a Writer's Activism.* New York: Random House, 1997.

———. *In Search of Our Mothers' Gardens: Womanist Prose.* London: Women's Press, 1983.

———. *Living By the Word: Selected Writings, 1973–1987.* San Diego, CA: Harcourt Brace Jovanovich, 1988.

———. *The Way Forward Is With a Broken Heart.* New York: Random House, 2000.

———. *We Are The Ones We Have Been Waiting For: Inner Light in a Time of Darkness: Meditations.* New York: New Press, 2006.

White, Evelyn C. *Alice Walker: A Life.* New York: Norton, 2004.

Winchell, Donna Haisty. *Alice Walker.* New York: Twayne, 1992.

# "EVERYDAY USE"

## READING TO WRITE

IN ALICE Walker's "Everyday Use," a mother narrates a story that dwells on the differences between her two daughters, Dee and Maggie. A character study of any of these three women, a comparative essay that considers the significance of the story's use of Dee and Maggie as foils, or a consideration of the relationships between the three women all offer possible topics for a paper. Family relationships can be complex, and sisters are not necessarily the best of friends. There can be multiple sources of tension that drive a wedge between siblings, even if they are raised in the same house and are treated similarly by their parents. The rift between Dee and Maggie has its roots in their childhood, but adulthood has not helped resolve their differences. As the excerpt shows, some of the sources of friction between the two women are their contrasting physical appearances, their divergent demeanors, their differing levels of education, and their conflicting attitudes toward their family's social class and status:

Dee is lighter than Maggie, with nicer hair and a fuller figure. She's a woman now, though sometimes I forget. How long ago was it that the other house burned? Ten, twelve years? Sometimes I can still hear the flames and feel Maggie's arms sticking to me, her hair smoking and her dress falling off her in little black papery flakes. Her eyes seemed stretched open, blazed open by the flames reflected in them. And Dee. I see her standing off under the sweet gum tree she used to dig gum out of; a look of concentration on her face as she watched the last dingy gray board of the house fall in toward the red-hot brick chimney. Why don't you do a dance around the ashes? I'd wanted to ask her. She had hated the house that much.

I used to think she hated Maggie, too. But that was before we raised money, the church and me, to send her to Augusta to school. She used to read to us without pity; forcing words, lies, other folks' habits, whole lives upon us two, sitting trapped and ignorant underneath her voice. She washed us in a river of make-believe, burned us with a lot of knowledge we didn't necessarily need to know. Pressed us to her with the serious way she read, to shove us away at just the moment, like dimwits, we seemed about to understand.

The first major difference between the two girls is that Dee is more physically prepossessing. Their mother describes Dee as "lighter" than her sister, with better hair and figure. The passage recounts the mother's memory of a fire that destroyed their house. The legacy of this blaze on Maggie is extensive scarring on her legs and arms. Maggie's physical inadequacy compared to her sister is reproduced in her belief in her psychological and intellectual inferiority. Her sister's arrival at the family home makes Maggie nervous. She feels as if Dee has always found life easier to handle than her. In the passage, their contrasting degrees of assuredness in the face of life's setbacks are brought out by their responses to the fire. While Maggie panics and, in terror, becomes a victim of the flames' fury, Dee stands coolly out in the yard, watching the conflagration with detachment. Significantly, she had somehow managed to escape the burning house unscathed, whereas Maggie's hair and clothing turned to ashes as her mother held her.

The fact that the mother is caught in the flames along with Maggie is also notable. As the excerpt suggests, Dee's setting herself apart from both her sister and her mother after she acquires an education, is foreshadowed by her distance from them during the fire. After she gets sent to school, Dee attempts to share some of her learning with her mother and Maggie. However, the mother's tone as she relates this part of their lives indicates that Dee's attempts were not well received. Whether mother and daughter fail to see the relevance to their lives of what Dee is telling them or whether they are unable to grasp the subject matter quickly are explanations the passage suggests may have contributed to the growing gap between Dee and her family. Dee's education exacerbates the feeling of distance that she had from her sister and her mother. Her mother feels that her daughter had always acted as if she were destined to something better than the social class into which she was born. Her disdain for her lowly origins is perceived by her mother even at the time of the fire. Her mother reads Dee's expression as she watches the house burn down as a longing for its destruction; Dee's hatred for the house and all that it represents is apparent.

The short story "Everyday Use" explores several themes that could become the focus of an essay. As the excerpt illustrates, topics such as family relationships, education, memory, and the past all offer ways to start thinking about writing on this text. The story is set probably in the 1960s or early 1970s, although it is not specified precisely. What makes this story worth reading today? Why is it still so widely anthologized?

## TOPICS AND STRATEGIES

The balance of this chapter will suggest topics related to "Everyday Use" and a variety of approaches that could be used to write essays on those topics. The suggested ideas should be used to help develop your own slant on these topics.

### Themes

Most people want their family unit to be a source of support and love. However, conflicts can develop when one family member has different values from everyone else. In "Everyday Use," Dee is described as being different even before she receives an education that takes her away from her family, literally and psychologically. Before Dee is educated, her mother believes that she felt hatred for her sister, Maggie. No explanation is offered why Dee would hate Maggie, but the story implies that Maggie's passive, unambitious, and self-effacing demeanor aggravates Dee. At the end of the story, Dee snaps at Maggie for not having adapted to the changing reality of their times. Dee also adopts a patronizing attitude toward her mother, assuming that her lack of education precludes her from seeing the value of their family heritage. Both Maggie and her mother experience conflict with Dee, but their relationship with each other is not straightforward either. Although they live together in relative harmony and cooperation, Maggie's imminent marriage means that her mother will soon live alone. When Mama thinks about this, her conclusion is that she will spend her free time singing church songs to herself—even though she cannot sing in tune. Thus, she clearly dreads having nothing to do and not being useful any longer. The story shows that a family with only three members can have complex dynamics. Maggie's desires have been overshadowed by her sister's for years because Dee is more self-assertive than her sibling. The mother-narrator reminisces how Dee always "wanted nice things" even as a teenager. Dee's friends were impressed by her, but nobody was able to get close to her because of her critical air. Maggie, on the other hand, tries to be invisible and never stands up to anyone because she has no expectations of anything positive happening to her in life. Mama demonstrates a blend of meekness and self-assertion. She does not challenge Dee's treatment of her initially, but refuses to yield when it comes to giving her the quilts. In fact, the mother's fighting spirit is indicated by her decision to walk a mile and a half just to see the black Muslim cattle farmers stand up to white racists who were trying to destroy their herd. Clearly, the mother is intrigued by the possibility of fighting back.

## Sample Topics:

1. **Family relationships:** How does Walker portray the interaction between the mother and her two daughters in the story? How does she present Maggie and Dee's relationship?

   There are a couple of possible approaches to writing an essay based on an examination of Walker's portrayal of family relationships. An essay could analyze the mother-daughter relationship, looking at both its negative and positive aspects. How well does the mother understand her two daughters? Does she ever show bias toward one daughter? A paper could also examine the sisterly relationship between Dee and Maggie. What are the sources of tension between them?

2. **Self-assertion:** How does Dee assert herself as a girl? What does Dee fight for as an adult? Why does the mother assert herself at the end of the story?

There are several instances of self-assertion described in the story. Dee, the mother, and the Muslim farmers are all depicted in a battle of wills with someone who wants to impose his or her will on others. An essay could analyze the different manifestations of self-assertion. What makes characters fight for what they believe in? What is the story's attitude toward self-assertion? Given the time and the place (the American South in the 1960s and 1970s), why might the story demonstrate sympathy for, and/or hesitancy toward, those who assert their rights?

## Character

Dee, Maggie, and Mama are all characters who could become the subject of a paper. Each woman is changed by the events that happen during Dee's visit to her family home. Maggie, who has always been self-effacing and unassuming, ends the story by giving a smile. Her mother explains how the smile is genuine and not marred by Maggie's usual fear of life and other people. At the beginning of the story, Dee is described as someone who acts as if "'no' is a word that the world never learned to say to her." Her mother ends the story by telling her daughter "no." Dee's reaction to being denied is petty, but this serves to prove that she is unaccustomed to not getting her own way. The mother has aided Dee in reaching her goals, even though it has caused friction between the two of them. Her fantasy of a reunion with Dee reveals the depth of her feelings of estrangement, commingled with a sense of pride in her daughter's achievements. Mama has enabled Dee to follow a path that would lead her out of the family's poverty and ignorance; however, she cannot condone Dee using her superior education and self-confidence to cheat Maggie out of the little inheritance that is hers. Thus, all three women are forced to reevaluate their relationships with one another and to reflect on the different ways that their family's history has left its legacy on each of them.

### Sample Topics:

1. **Dee/Wangero:** How does the story portray Dee before she makes her appearance at her mother's house? How effectively does the portrayal of Dee as a girl prepare the reader for her adult character? How does Dee's name change reflect her attitude toward the family items that she wants to take away with her?

An essay evaluating Dee could appraise her position on her family heritage or her relationship with her family. Although the story seems to endorse the mother and Maggie's attitude toward their belongings, is Dee's outlook presented sympathetically in any way? What details about Dee's adult life is the reader given? What critical information is missing about her life, and why do you think her mother does not provide this information? What kind of a relationship does Dee seem to have with Hakim? Does Dee change throughout the course of the story?

2. **Maggie:** Why does Maggie lack confidence and have so few expectations from life? How does Maggie react to Dee? What is Maggie's attitude toward things from the past?

More is said about Maggie by the other two characters than she says herself. This character is silent and self effacing and barely speaks to her mother, Dee, or Hakim-a-barber. What does Maggie's insecure behavior at her sister's arrival suggest about the sisters' relationship in the past and the present? Dee's formal education notwithstanding, what knowledge does Maggie possess that Dee lacks? An essay could analyze Maggie's behavior and outlook on life to determine why her mother decides that she deserves to inherit the family quilts.

3. **Mama:** What kind of life has Mama had? How does the story indicate some of her judgments and biases? Why did Alice Walker choose the mother to narrate this story?

An essay could discuss Mama as a character or as the narrator. As the mother looks back over her family's past, what realizations does she have about her two daughters and the way they have developed? She shares a fantasy wherein she has a television reunion with Dee. What does this fantasy reveal about Mama and her feelings toward Dee, Dee's life, and her own life? Why does she make her final decision to give the quilts to Maggie and not to Dee? If you consider Mama as narrator, why is it significant that Walker gave this character a voice? Since this is a first-person narrative, can Mama be considered unreliable or partial in any way? Does her lack of formal education influence her judgments?

# History and Context

"Everyday Use" is a short story that questions some trends in the Black Power movement of the 1960s and 1970s through the characters of Dee and Hakim-a-barber. The Black Power movement evolved out of the Civil Rights movement of the early 1960s, and one of its aims was to communicate a new racial consciousness among black people. The Black Power movement had a variety of foci that strove to promote racial pride, equality, and autonomy. To this end, some people sought to redefine black American identity, recognizing the importance of Africa as providing one strand of their heritage. For some people, this assertion of African heritage entailed a rejection of their American heritage because white names and culture had been imposed on Africans as a consequence of slavery. In the story, Dee changes her name, wears African clothing, and is with a man who identifies himself as a Black Muslim. She explains to her mother that she has discarded the name Dee because it is a slave name, whereas the new name, Wangero, reflects her decision to claim Africa as the only relevant strand of her cultural heritage. Her mother tries to point out that the name Dee, in fact, can be traced back several generations within their family. Big Dee had contributed to the making of the quilts that Dee is now attempting to claim. Mama feels that her daughter's rejection of her name is disrespectful to Big Dee and the other Dees who are her foremothers. This conflict between mother and daughter sets the stage for an examination of African-American identity and heritage.

## Sample Topics:

1. **The Black Power movement and Africa:** How does the story judge Dee's and Hakim's embracing of their African roots? What is the relevance of the story's inclusion of the anecdote about the Black Muslim farmers?

   An essay on this topic could evaluate how the story judges Dee's and Hakim's claiming of their African heritage. Look, for example, at Dee's ignorance about her own family heritage compared to Maggie's intimate knowledge of who made which item and when. Although the story is filtered through the point of view of the mother and is therefore subject to a certain bias because of her social status, education, and age, does the story provide any sympathy for Black Power attitudes and actions?

## Philosophy and Ideas

The main idea that this short story discusses is that of heritage. Walker uses her characters to debate the issue of where African Americans should look to for their cultural and personal identities. Dee and Hakim-a-barber are pitted against Maggie and the narrator, who argue for the African and the American strands of their heritage respectively. The relevance of the past is brought out by the narrator's memories, which are not simply stored in her mind. These memories are concretized in some of the family's belongings and brought to life by her own daily existence, which carries on traditions and skills passed down through the generations.

An important reason why Dee's outlook on her past differs so drastically from her mother's is because of the formal education she has received. This education has clearly allowed her a lifestyle that has more ease and comfort than her mother's. Dee's education makes her embarrassed of her family. She snobbishly informs her mother that she would never bring any friends to visit her family home, although she herself would continue to visit. This exemplifies her ambivalence toward her family: She cannot deny them but views them from a judgmental perspective. Depending on the changing fads of her middle-class world, her humble roots are a source of shame or a source of pride. Her education also makes her see the family's belongings from a different angle. She wants to preserve them for posterity as objets d'art, whereas her mother, as the title of the story reinforces, wants them to fulfill their utilitarian function. Thus, education has allowed Dee to escape a life of poverty, but it has caused a rupture between her and her family.

### Sample Topics:

1. **Heritage and the past:** How does the title of the short story underscore the family's conflicting attitudes toward heritage?

How does Walker use memories to trace the history of the differences between Dee and Mama that culminates in the fight over the quilts? How does each character understand the idea of memory and the past?

Conversation about specific objects and recollection of events from the past are used to build up the conflict over heritage that erupts between the characters at the end of the story. An essay could examine Walker's polemic on the meaning of heritage, looking at how she presents the arguments for claiming one's African roots as well as the reasons for not denying one's American heritage. What does the story suggest is the best way to view heritage?

2. **Education:** What are the advantages and disadvantages for Dee of acquiring an education? How does Dee's mother demonstrate ambivalence toward her daughter's education?

A possible approach to this topic would be to reflect on Dee's relationship with her family and her rural southern community as a result of being educated. Another approach might be to write about what different characters end up learning despite an absence of a formal education. What ways have characters acquired practical knowledge? Why does Mama have reservations about the knowledge learned through a formal education?

## Language, Symbols, and Imagery

The most important symbolic items in this story comment on the idea of heritage. The quilts that Dee wants to take away with her symbolize the conflict between preserving one's heritage in a museumlike way that stresses rupture between the past and the present or maintaining a living heritage that stresses continuity between the past and the present. Dee wishes to hang the quilts on her wall, while Maggie plans on using them on her marriage bed. Walker provides historical details of the family items—the quilts, the dasher, and the churn top that Dee wants—to highlight the differences in the way the characters view them.

These details could all provide material for an essay on Walker's use of symbolism.

## Sample Topics:

1. **The quilts, the churn top, and the dasher:** How does each of these objects represent the characters' different attitudes toward the past? How are these objects used to add to the characterizations of the three women?

   A quilt is made out of a variety of different fabric pieces, which sewn together in a creative pattern can produce an item that is both functional and aesthetically pleasing. The pieces of fabric are sometimes selected for the memories they evoke. What do the two quilts that Dee wants symbolize to the family? An essay could consider how Walker uses the quilts to add to the themes and ideas of the short story. This topic could be extended to analyze the meaning of other family belongings that bear the imprint of the family's history. A further extension to this topic could assess the symbolic significance of some of Dee's actions both in the past and the present, which shed light on her attitude to her family's past. For example, why does Dee take so many photographs of the house and why does she so carefully control what each photograph includes? How does Dee's behavior during the fire foreshadow her adult attitudes toward her family and her heritage?

## Compare and Contrast Essays

Owing to the brevity of this short story, there are a limited number of possible topics that could be used for a comparative essay; nevertheless, it would be feasible to compare and contrast the two sisters. Although this essay would likely find more elements to contrast, there are some broad similarities in the way the sisters treat each other and in their shared interest in the past. A contrast essay could focus on their dissimilar physical appearances, their different demeanors, their divergent levels of education, their conflicting attitudes toward their family's social class and status, and their opposing stances toward the past and its relevance. In a 1973 interview with Mary Helen Washington, Walker said that she saw the three female characters as different sides of one person:

". . . I really see ["Everyday Use"] as almost about one person, the old woman and two daughters being one person. The one who stays and sustains—this is the older woman—who has on one hand a daughter who is the same way, who stays and abides and loves, plus the part of them—*this autonomous person,* the part of them that also wants to go out into the world to see change and be changed. . . ."

Where does the story imply that Mama and Maggie have a side of them that might have wanted to go out in the world and have other life experiences?

## *Sample Topics:*

1. **Dee and Maggie:** Why does Walker establish the two sisters as foils of each other? What is the story's judgment of the two women?

   An essay on this topic could make an assessment of the way the two women differ in various areas of their lives, such as their attitudes and behavior. A comparative essay that also evaluates the story's judgment of the two women could look for evidence to show that there is some sympathy for Dee's perspective and some criticism of Maggie's ways.

### Bibliography and Online Sources

*Anniina's Alice Walker Page.* December 30, 2007. <http://www.luminarium.org/contemporary/alicew.htm>

Christian, Barbara T., ed. *Everyday Use: Women's Writers Texts and Contexts.* New Brunswick, NJ: Rutgers, 1994.

Cowart, David. "Heritage and Deracination in Walker's 'Everyday Use.'" *Critical Essays on Alice Walker.* Ed. Ikenna Dieke. Westport, CT: Greenwood, 1999. 21–32.

White, David. "'Everyday Use': Defining African-American Heritage." 2001. *Anniina's Alice Walker Page.* June 30, 2007. <http://www.luminarium.org/contemporary/alicew/davidwhite.htm>

Winchell, Donna Haisty. *Alice Walker.* New York: Twayne, 1992.

# "TO HELL
# WITH DYING"

## READING TO WRITE

REGARDLESS OF their family circumstances, children often retain a zest for life that is appealing to more jaded adults. Children's dearth of bitter life experience means that they are not yet cowed by lingering disappointments and sadness. The finality of death is also difficult for a child to grasp, so Mr. Sweet's repeated resurrections from his death-bed seem artless to the narrator when she is a child. However, as she matures, the narrator begins to have a clearer understanding of Mr. Sweet's moods that plunge him into deep depressions or prompt him to dance drunkenly around their yard. One way that the narrator learns about Mr. Sweet's troubled interior life is through the blues songs that he likes to play on his guitar:

> When he came to our house with his guitar the whole family would stop whatever they were doing to sit around him and listen to him play. He liked to play "Sweet Georgia Brown," that was what he called me some-times, and also he liked to play "Caldonia" and all sorts of sweet, sad, wonderful songs which he sometimes made up. It was from one of these songs that I learned that he had had to marry Miss Mary when he had in fact loved somebody else (now living in Chi-ca-go, or De-stroy, Michi-gan). He was not sure that Joe Lee, her "baby," was also his baby. Some-times he would cry and that was an indication that he was about to die again. And so we would all get prepared, for we were sure to be called upon.

Through song, Mr. Sweet discloses some of the reasons why he drinks so heavily. His disappointments in life are hard for him to bear. Growing up in a time when opportunities were extremely limited for black men, Mr. Sweet has had to set his career sights low. Disappointments in love and marriage also darken his view of his world. Mr. Sweet drinks to try and numb himself from the melancholy that envelops him. Analysis of the themes of disappointment and depression could become the starting point for an essay on "To Hell with Dying."

Mr. Sweet reacts to his feelings of disappointment by crying and taking to his bed. Although his situation is exacerbated by ill health, it seems that his depression makes him feel that life is not worth living and that he would be better off dead. The force that can drag him back into the land of living is love. The children's innocent belief that they have the power to revive an old dying man by tickling him and making him laugh reaffirms the value of life for Mr. Sweet. As the excerpt makes clear, the children know when they will be called upon to succor the dying man. Kisses and embraces from his neighbors' children offer Mr. Sweet a glimpse of hope, innocence, and warmth. Love is another theme that could be the focus of an analytical essay. Even as the narrator ages and her relationship with Mr. Sweet alters, her love for him does not waver. Additionally, the love shown by all his neighbors is a determining factor in Mr. Sweet's decisions whether to live or die. Although all the characters live in poverty, the sense of community when they rally around him during his crises offers emotional support to the troubled Mr. Sweet. Another potential essay topic is the dichotomy between life and death. Mr. Sweet's drunken life, his constant death wish, his near-death episodes, the narrator's powers of resurrection, and her ultimate failure to save him all destabilize the usually clear demarcation between the states of life and death. How does the story challenge conventional understandings of life and death?

Mr. Sweet has many qualities that make him a lovable character. Children love him for his kind and playful demeanor; he also has the ability to make a child feel special. Despite his excessive drunkenness, the narrator's mother does not fear that Mr. Sweet will endanger the safety of her children. However, his love for his neighbors' children stands in contrast to his feelings for the son he has raised. Doubtful even as to his paternity of Joe Lee, he condemns his son for being profligate and worthless. Even though his own family is fractured, Mr. Sweet's guitar-playing, as the passage shows, has the capacity to bring all his neighbors' family members together. Playing the guitar is the one thing that Mr. Sweet claims to do "extraordinarily well." Significantly, on his death, Mr. Sweet bequeaths his guitar to the narrator, who, on receiving it, plucks out the notes of "Sweet Georgia Brown" as a tribute to the old man. Why is this song special to the narrator? What does the guitar symbolize? An analysis of the complex character of Mr. Sweet would want to determine how Walker achieves sympathy for a man who is essentially an old drunk. What qualities redeem Mr. Sweet and make him such an endearing character?

## TOPICS AND STRATEGIES

The rest of this chapter will discuss topics for essays on "To Hell with Dying" and general approaches that could be used to develop those topics. This material should be used to help generate your own ideas.

### Themes

"To Hell with Dying" is a touching short story that relates the love shared between a family and their elderly neighbor. Mr. Sweet lacks love within his own family. He had been obliged to marry Miss Mary, even though he loved another woman. The emotions he feels toward the child Miss Mary claims is their son are not positive. In fact, he regards Joe Lee as "shiftless" and a spendthrift. Instead, Mr. Sweet receives love from his neighbors, particularly from the children who are oblivious of his age when he plays with them. When Mr. Sweet is overwhelmed by his feelings of disappointment and sadness, the entire community rallies around him, repeatedly proving their love for this emotional man. Over the years, the community becomes used to Mr. Sweet's desire to die. A diabetic alcoholic, Mr. Sweet makes no effort to promote longevity and health because his life has been a series of disappointments that have caused the depressed man to drink excessively. When drunk, his emotions spill out through tears, singing the blues, and episodes of "dying." The themes of love, disappointment, and community overlap in the context of the story, but they all could be explored independently in an analytical essay.

## Sample Topics:

1. **Love:** How does the love between Mr. Sweet and his neighbors manifest itself? Why does the narrator describe Mr. Sweet as her "first love"?

   An essay on the theme of love could analyze the different instances of love described in the story and show the power that love has to transform the characters. What different forms of love does the story depict? Consider the narrator's parents' love for Mr. Sweet, the children's love for Mr. Sweet, Mr. Sweet's love for the children, and the community's love for the elderly man. You could also think about how an absence of love within his immediate family affects Mr. Sweet and his relationships with other characters.

2. **Disappointment:** In what different ways does Mr. Sweet express his disappointments in life? How does the social and historical context of Mr. Sweet's life contribute to his sense of disappointment?

   Such an essay could examine the various sources of Mr. Sweet's sadness and depression. How did Mr. Sweet respond to professional and career disappointments? How has he reacted to personal disappointments? His age and race are factors that exacerbate his sense of disappointment: How have they contributed to his missing out on the opportunities that we see the narrator enjoy? Despite his own disappointments, why does Mr. Sweet never want to fail the neighbors' children in any way? Why does he rally from his deathbed when the children tickle and cuddle him?

3. **Community:** Why does the community protect and care for Mr. Sweet? How do the members of the southern community demonstrate their support for one another?

   The lives of the narrator's family and of all the neighbors are presented as lives of extreme poverty and hardship in material terms. An essay could look at the contrast between the economic poverty of the community and the spiritual wealth they share. What positive values do the community members demonstrate through their interaction with one another? For example, why are the narrator's parents tolerant of Mr. Sweet's alcoholism?

# Character

The short story develops only two characters in sufficient depth to make them the subjects of an essay based on characterization, Mr. Sweet and the narrator. Mr. Sweet is one of Walker's most endearing, albeit contradictory, male characters. On the negative side, he is an alcoholic who is on the verge of falling down drunk a lot of the time. He is a diabetic who makes no effort to minimize the impact of his illness by leading a healthy life. On the positive side, he is warm, loving, and considerate of children. He is an excellent guitar player who can draw people together to listen to his songs. Despite the difference in age between Mr. Sweet and the narrator, she describes Mr. Sweet as her "first love." The love she feels is essentially filial, but it transforms over the years. When she is a little girl, Mr. Sweet makes her feel like a "princess." She is convinced of her power to resurrect him from the dead through tickling and cuddling. A gift that Mr. Sweet gives the girl is the capacity to believe in herself. The story shows the narrator's maturation from little girl to doctorate student. However, even though she grows up, her love for Mr. Sweet never falters. Why is she so fond of the old man?

## Sample Topics:

1. **Mr. Sweet:** Why do all the neighbors love Mr. Sweet? What life events have caused Mr. Sweet to feel despair and sadness? What events in his life bring Mr. Sweet joy?

A character study of Mr. Sweet would want to examine his traits and behavior to show how he is struggling from internal conflicts that drive him to self-destructive acts. Even though Mr. Sweet is an emotional wreck, he still has qualities that draw people to him. What are his strengths as a friend and neighbor? Why does he inspire love and compassion in so many people?

2. **The narrator:** What is at the root of the narrator's special relationship with Mr. Sweet? As the narrator matures, how does her perception of Mr. Sweet change? Why does Walker use the girl's voice to tell this story?

There are two possible ways to approach a discussion of the narrator. The first approach could consider the girl's development throughout the story and analyze how her maturation contributes to her understanding of her community and Mr. Sweet's role within the community. How does her growing up affect her relationships with other characters? The second approach could analyze the story's use of a first-person point of view. How does using the girl's perspective on events facilitate the development of the themes and ideas that Walker explores in the story?

## Philosophy and Ideas

Why is Mr. Sweet seemingly ready to embrace death? If the old man's repeated deathbed experiences are understood as being at least partially self-willed, the main reason why Mr. Sweet welcomes such a fate is because of his dissatisfaction with life. For Mr. Sweet, life can be a kind of living death, but he can easily be reanimated from his deathlike condition. When he gives up on life or, in some instances, life may start to give up on him, the love of children and neighbors has the power to pull him back from the brink of death, with laughter acting as the antidote to his depressed state. Mr. Sweet's casual attitude toward death and dying is sustained by the innocence of children who do not fully grasp the finality of death. In fact, the narrator and her brother even believe in their own powers of resurrection. Strangely, after the children grow up and move away from home, Mr. Sweet does not appear to be in need of constant resurrection, until death finally does claim him because of his advanced age. His childlike need for reassurance of his worth and the value of his life is more likely to occur when there are children nearby to respond to his need. Thus, the old man is obliged to adapt his behavior as the children grow up and leave home. However, even though he no longer takes to his deathbed regularly, his sadness still lingers and this is signaled by his continued playing the blues on his old guitar.

## Sample Topics:

1. **Life and death:** Why does Mr. Sweet keep taking to his deathbed? What is Mr. Sweet's attitude toward life? How does the narrator view the relationship between life and death?

   An essay on this dichotomy could examine the different perspectives on life and death that the various characters demonstrate, perhaps commenting on Walker's blurring of the boundaries between the two states. Emotion adds an extra dimension to ideas of life and death. How do positive and negative feelings contribute to a character's attitude toward life and death? How does the narrator come to terms with Mr. Sweet's death at the end of the story? An important difference between Mr. Sweet and the narrator is the time period in which they are raised. How does the historical context affect the opportunities available to the two characters? How do the opportunities available to each character contribute to their perspectives on life and death?

2. **Aging:** Why do the children see Mr. Sweet as childlike when they are young? How does Mr. Sweet's behavior change as the children grow up?

   In some respects, Mr. Sweet acts like a child, whereas the children take on some adult responsibilities during the time that they all live as neighbors. An essay could examine the idea of aging, which is not straightforward in this story as the boundaries between childhood, adulthood, and old age are unstable. How do the children allow Mr. Sweet to forget, momentarily, the troubles of the world and have fun? How does the story show the parallel developments of the narrator and Mr. Sweet? How does the narrator's aging allow her to perceive Mr. Sweet more clearly? What are the similarities and differences between the child characters and the old characters?

## Language, Symbols, and Imagery

As a little girl, the two things that the narrator loves the most about Mr. Sweet are his hair and his guitar. When he cuts his white hair, the narrator remembers feeling sadness that she could not run her fingers through it. Knowing this, Mr. Sweet hides his head from her after a haircut. As he ages, Mr. Sweet grows a long white beard and mustache, which the narrator enjoys combing and braiding. Another item that the narrator identifies with Mr. Sweet throughout his life is his guitar. He claims that playing the guitar is the only thing he does well, and all the neighbors gather around when he starts to sing the blues. The narrator is deeply moved when she is given Mr. Sweet's guitar after his death. When she plays the notes of "Sweet Georgia Brown," she feels that the "magic of Mr. Sweet lingered still in the cool steel box." Receiving Mr. Sweet's guitar is akin to receiving the seed of his musical talents. Items connected to Mr. Sweet could become an essay topic, but you will probably need to combine analysis of more than one item in order to have sufficient material for a well-developed essay.

### Sample Topics:

1. **Mr. Sweet's hair and guitar:** What does the guitar symbolize? Why does the narrator love Mr. Sweet's hair so much?

   An essay analyzing Mr. Sweet's guitar and his hair would need to consider why these items have such an effect on the narrator. How does Mr. Sweet use his guitar to express some of the realities of his life? Why does the narrator's brother pretend to play the guitar during Mr. Sweet's numerous death episodes? Why does Mr. Sweet bequeath the guitar to the narrator, and what effect does this have on her? Why is Mr. Sweet's hair so important to the narrator? How does his hair create a bond between the two characters?

## Bibliography

Petry, Alice Hall. "Walker: The Achievement of the Short Fiction." *Alice Walker: Critical Perspectives Past and Present.* Eds. Henry Louis Gates, Jr. and K. A. Appiah. New York: Amistad, 1993. 193–210.

Winchell, Donna Haisty. *Alice Walker.* New York: Twayne, 1992.

# "NINETEEN FIFTY-FIVE"

## READING TO WRITE

"NINETEEN FIFTY-FIVE" is narrated by Gracie Mae Still, a blues singer who has struggled for years to make a decent living out of her powerful voice. As she explains in the excerpt, her life on the road was not lucrative because she sang in small, black-only "jooks" that paid no more than 10 dollars a night and were often dangerous. An important factor that has aggravated her lack of success is the historical context of the segregated southeastern United States in 1955, which denied black singers the same opportunities as white. An essay could focus on the disproportionately favorable treatment received by Traynor as a singer in comparison to Gracie Mae, simply because he is a white man in a business riddled with racism and sexism. When Traynor's manager (the deacon) knocks on her door to try and buy the rights to her songs for a pitiful sum, Gracie Mae has no illusions about his intention to swindle her if she lets him. She tries to make the best deal that she can under the circumstances:

> I had done unlocked the screen when I saw I could get some more money out of him. Now I held it wide open while he squeezed through the opening between me and the door. He whipped out another piece of paper and I signed it.
>
> He sort of trotted out to the car and slid in beside Traynor, whose head was back against the seat. They swung around in a u-turn in front of the house and then they was gone.

> J. T. was putting his shirt on when I got back to the bedroom. Yankees beat the Orioles 10—6, he said. I believe I'll drive out to Paschal's pond and go fishing. Wanta go?
>
> While I was putting on my pants J. T. was holding the two checks.
>
> I'm real proud of a woman that can make cash money without leavin' home, he said. And I said *Umph*. Because we met on the road with me singing in first one little low-life jook after another, making ten dollars a night for myself if I was lucky, and sometimes bringin' home nothing but my life.

The use of contrast permeates the entire short story, and analysis of its function and effects would make a viable essay topic. For example, contrast is used effectively to highlight the differences between Gracie Mae and Traynor. Although Gracie is much older than Traynor and has experienced more disappointments, the character that seems to have given up on life is the younger Traynor, notwithstanding that he is fêted as a superstar wherever he goes. As the imagery in the passage shows, Traynor moves through life with no energy or passion, like one of the living dead. His head is slumped back against the car seat, emitting no enthusiasm for the fact that his manager has just purchased the rights to a song he will record. Gracie, on the other hand, displays a more sanguine approach to her life. Even though she has just been exploited by the white music business, she tries to focus on the gains she has made. In this case, she was able to obtain an amount of money which she considers better than nothing. In fact, she is immediately able to put the exploitation behind her and gets ready to join her husband on a fishing trip. The contrast between the apathetic Traynor being driven off in his red convertible with Gracie Mae pulling on some old pants to go fishing underscores the difference in their attitudes toward life. While Gracie Mae is active and gets on with her life, ironically, the unresponsive Traynor cannot even get excited about his impending fame and celebrity.

Many themes are touched on through Walker's use of contrast. The theme of exploitation is explored throughout the story, particularly in the context of white exploitation of black artists. However, as the passage illustrates, Gracie Mae's husband also has a conveniently limited view of his wife's past efforts to achieve success through her singing. Gracie Mae's response to her husband's joke, however, is revelatory of her characterization: *"Umph."* She does not waste any energy on reminding him of the past because she is confident in herself and knows what is important in life for her. She deals with the issue of career success or failure phlegmatically. Traynor, too, demonstrates carelessness toward wealth, celebrity, and success; however, the explanation for his lack of interest contrasts with Gracie Mae's. Whereas Gracie Mae does not attribute much importance to the trappings of wealth because she feels that she has everything that she wants, Traynor cannot enjoy his celebrity because he knows that his singing lacks authenticity. He suspects that he is a fake. The themes of wealth, celebrity, success, failure, and authenticity could all become the focus of a thematic analysis.

Walker provides clues to the reader as to how to approach this short story through the dedication and title of the story collection, *You Can't Keep a Good Woman Down,* in which it is included. The dedication invokes blues singers such as Ma Rainey and Bessie Smith who "insist[ed] on the value and beauty of the authentic." The quasi-fictional Gracie Mae Still clearly fits in this tradition of authenticity, in contrast to the inauthentic Traynor. The dedication and title raise some questions that you might consider as you start to write on this story: In what ways can Gracie Mae be considered authentic? How does Walker define authenticity through her characters? How does the notion of beauty link to that of authenticity? How does the absence or presence of authenticity link to spiritual emptiness and fullness? How does the notion of spiritual fullness or emptiness determine the characterizations of Gracie Mae and Traynor? How does Gracie Mae demonstrate the value of the authentic?

## TOPICS AND STRATEGIES

Further topics for essays on "Nineteen Fifty-five" will be discussed in the remainder of this chapter. Some general approaches that could be used to write about those topics will also be proposed. These topics and approaches should be used as a resource to help generate your own essay titles.

### Themes

In the United States, success tends to be defined by a person's property acquisition and demonstrative wealth. However, extreme wealth, which allows Traynor to buy whatever he wants, bring him success only in the eyes of others. He is dogged by a sense that something is missing from his life, something ineffable, which he suspects Gracie Mae might possess despite her obvious lack of material wealth and celebrity. Thus, success and failure cannot always be measured by the amount of money in someone's bank account or by his or her degree of popular acclaim. The ways that success and failure are measured often differ on personal and societal levels. A quality that Gracie Mae has in abundance, which Traynor lacks, and that contributes to her solid sense of worth is resilience. Although Traynor's quality of life drastically improves according to society's values, he feels like an outsider in his new world. He is nonplussed by Gracie Mae's refusal of his gift of a mansion to her because he believes that everyone must want an enormous house. On the other hand, when Gracie Mae points out that she does not want to end up cleaning such a house and that she does not want to live around crowds of people she does not know, Traynor interjects that he is surrounded by strangers, including his own wife. Gracie Mae knows what she wants from her life and adapts to the conditions that she finds herself in, whereas Traynor fails to adjust and is left feeling alienated, unfulfilled, and alone. Overall, his world of fabulous wealth and adoring fans leaves him feeling empty, whereas Gracie Mae is mostly satisfied with what she has, even though her living conditions are not as grandiose as Traynor's and she is loved by only a few people.

## Sample Topics:

1. **Success and failure:** How does Traynor measure success? In what ways can Traynor be considered a failure? How can Gracie Mae be judged a success despite her commercial failure as a singer?

   An essay on this topic could analyze how judgments of success and/or failure could be leveled at Gracie Mae and/or Traynor. How do the characters' personal opinions on success and failure clash with societal definitions? How do the characters respond to societal opinions concerning their respective success or failure?

2. **Emptiness:** Why does Traynor constantly feel spiritually empty? How does he try to address his feelings of emptiness? What prevents Gracie Mae from feeling empty despite the hardships in her life?

   Traynor repeatedly complains of an inner emptiness because he is unable to grasp the soul of the songs that he sings. When he sings, he asserts that his fans are "getting the flavor of something but they ain't getting the thing itself." An essay could evaluate why Traynor feels so empty in comparison to Gracie Mae. What does he lack? How does he try to counteract that lack in himself?

3. **Resiliency:** How is Gracie Mae's strength revealed in the story? What qualities allow her to triumph in her life despite the economic, personal, and societal obstacles she faces?

   Most readers might expect Gracie Mae to be affected by resentment or jealousy for the way that Traynor carves out a successful career, using her song-writing skills. Gracie Mae, however, remains dispassionate throughout her relationship with the rock star. She never loses sight of what is meaningful and what is chimerical in her life. If writing on the theme of resiliency, you could consider how Gracie Mae's personal qualities and outlook allow her to make the most of her life despite the social and historical contexts that limit opportunities for black women.

## Character

Critics have noted parallels between the two main characters of this short story and actual singers from the 1950s. Walker uses many aspects of Traynor's characterization to evoke Elvis Presley, from his black hair, the "nasty little jerk" he does "from the waist down," and the plantation-style house he lives in, which brings Graceland to mind. However, Traynor does not correspond to Elvis entirely, and you should not lose sight of the fact that he is a fictional character whose behavior and attitudes can supply material for an analysis without taking Elvis Presley into consideration. On the other hand, another possible approach to writing about Traynor would be to do some research on the life of Elvis Presley and determine to what extent the character resembles the man. Similarly, Gracie Mae "Little Mama" Still bears a strong, intentional resemblance to Willie Mae "Big Mama" Thornton (1926–84), a blues and rock singer who performed during the same time period as Elvis. However, Walker does take creative liberties with Thornton's life. Maria Johnson's article (see bibliography for details) identifies many of Gracie Mae's similarities to Willie Mae Thornton and also comments on the elements that have been invented or altered by Walker. Thus, as with Traynor, essays on Gracie Mae Still could consider her purely as a fictional character or compare and contrast her with the woman on whom she is based.

### Sample Topics:

1. **Traynor:** Why is Traynor dissatisfied with his celebrity? Why does Traynor pursue friendship with Gracie Mae?

   A character analysis of Traynor could examine the sources of his dissatisfaction in life and the reasons behind his apparent spiritual emptiness. How does his excessive lifestyle contrast with his inner world? What does Gracie Mae represent to Traynor? Why does Traynor encourage Gracie Mae to appear on the Johnny Carson show with him? Why does their appearance on the show leave Traynor feeling "whipped"? An alternative approach to Traynor would be to compare him to Elvis Presley. How has Walker made aspects of her fictional character deviate from the Elvis legend, and what is her purpose in making those changes?

2. **Gracie Mae Still:** Why does Walker use the voice of Gracie Mae Still to narrate this story? Which of Gracie Mae's characteristics are placed in juxtaposition with some of Traynor's traits and to what effect?

   This short story has parallels with "Everyday Use" in the sense that Walker gives a voice to a woman who has been virtually silenced by her historical and social context. Gracie Mae's records languish unbought, and her name is unrecognized by the general music-listening public. An essay could analyze Walker's choice of a first-person narrative that uses Gracie Mae's perspective. How does the point of view affect the way the reader understands the story? How does the point of view help to communicate the author's themes and central ideas? Another approach to Gracie Mae could consider her strengths and weaknesses. How does she manage to survive her changing fortunes? Why does neither poverty nor wealth affect her core values? Finally, an essay could compare the fictional character to the blues singer Willie Mae Thornton. How does the character resemble the woman? Why has Walker made significant changes to events in Thornton's life for the sake of the story?

## History and Context

The events of the story span the years from 1955 to 1977 and unfold in the American South. The story exposes the dire realities of race relations of the particular time and place. When Traynor and his manager first drive up to Gracie Mae's house, one of the first things she notes is their whiteness, which makes her "wonder what in the world they doing in this neighborhood." In the segregated South, white men who wander into a black neighborhood want something; it is just a matter of what. In the context of the music business, white business moguls routinely exploited black musicians as exemplified by the deacon's purchase of Gracie Mae's songs for a paltry sum. White singers could make more profit out of black songs than the original black artists because of the racial prejudice of the 1950s. Traynor mentions that he is making $40,000 a day from Gracie Mae's song, for which she was paid a total of $1,000. Gracie Mae retains an ironic detachment to her own exploitation and to Traynor's successful career as a result of her song, which he even sings replicating her style. Gracie Mae's awareness of the effects of unequal race relations is shown throughout the story. In 1968, for example, when Traynor and an entourage of white men visit her house, she mentions that, with hoods, the men could pass for Klansmen. At the end of the story, Gracie Mae's observation that one day, the United States will be a "pitiful country," stands as an indictment of her racist society. This short story is intricately tied to its historical and social context and could be approached from this perspective.

*Sample Topics:*

1. **The American South 1955–77:** How does the time period govern aspects of Gracie Mae's and Traynor's lives and careers? How does Walker use Gracie Mae's tone and attitudes to critique white exploitation of blacks?

Throughout the story, the passing of time is reinforced through brief references to historical events that are happening offstage. For instance, Grace Mae refers to the deaths of Malcolm X and Martin Luther King, Jr. Allusions to popular culture icons such as Johnny Carson and Ed Sullivan also give the story a sense of historical grounding. An essay could consider how Walker uses the historical and social context to critique race relations in the South during the 1950s, 1960s, and 1970s, particularly in the music industry.

## Philosophy and Ideas

Elvis Presley was one of the earliest rock superstars who enjoyed exceptional celebrity status that continues even after his death. Similarly, Traynor is shown to have legions of adoring female fans who scream every time he performs his "nasty little jerk" below the waist. As a result of his celebrity, Traynor amasses a fortune that allows him to build a vast southern plantation-style house and give away lavish gifts to friends and family, with the same generosity for which Elvis has been credited. Attaining the American Dream does not, unfortunately, bring Traynor happiness. Ironically, the much poorer and less famous Gracie Mae finds greater satisfaction with her life than the rock star. Most Americans would suppose that wealth and celebrity are preferable to poverty and obscurity; however, "Nineteen Fifty-five" draws a different conclusion. Gracie Mae's state of contentment and acceptance of her life emanates from a sense that she lives authentically. She does not have to do what other people tell her to do, she does not have to listen to other people's constant lies, and she is able to enjoy close relationships with loved ones. All of these seemingly simple facets of her existence are denied Traynor, who is being controlled and manipulated by music industry moguls. Even his relationship with his wife is distant, and Traynor describes his marriage as comparable to "singing someone else's record." Traynor feels as if every aspect of his life lacks authenticity, whereas Gracie Mae goes through life singing her own songs, literally and figuratively.

## Sample Topics:

1. **The American Dream:** How does Traynor react to his wealth and celebrity? What is Gracie Mae's attitude toward her lack of fame? How does Gracie Mae respond to Traynor's expensive gifts to her?

   An essay on this topic could investigate the story's stance toward wealth and celebrity. How does Walker critique Traynor's fabulously wealthy lifestyle? Take a look, for example, at the portrayals of people in his entourage, such as his manager. How does Gracie Mae's description of Traynor's mansion create a bleak picture? What values in life does the story suggest have greater meaning than money and fame?

2. **Authenticity:** What personal qualities allow Gracie Mae to live authentically? What are the causes of Traynor's lack of authenticity?

   The story implies that it is impossible for Traynor to replicate the spirit and soul of black blues singers and their music because of his different upbringing and cultural influences. However, Traynor's white audience is unable to detect the lack of substance in their icon's singing, leaving Traynor disturbed by their essential dishonesty. An essay could consider why Gracie Mae lives her life "singing [her] own song, [her] own way," despite the historical and social context that strives to diminish her. Additionally, Traynor's battle, and ultimate failure, to live authentically could be analyzed.

## Language, Symbols, and Imagery

Walker uses the two characters' fluctuating weight to symbolize their contrasting experiences of life. For the most part, Gracie Mae carries her enormous girth unashamedly and accommodates it with specially made dresses. However, for health reasons, she regularly tries to lose a few pounds. By the end of the story, she acknowledges that her weight is a problem that she must address. Not only does her obesity compromise her health, but she also realizes that her weight problem is a physical manifestation of psychological problems. She has been eating to mask pain that she has felt all her life. Traynor, in contrast, squeezes his excess weight into corsets in a pathetic attempt to conceal it. When Gracie Mae observes Traynor walking toward her house one day, she realizes that he never has to fret about his weight because his wealth raises him above mundane concerns. Nonetheless, it is likely that Traynor's weight also reflects his ongoing unhappiness. In a similar fashion, the song that both Gracie Mae and Traynor sing is used in the story to highlight differences between the two characters' approach to life. Critics, such as Johnson, widely believe that the song Walker alludes to, but never names, is Elvis's big hit "Hound Dog," which he recorded in 1956. However, Walker has changed many historical details to fit the needs of her story, because Willie Mae Thornton did not write "Hound Dog" and its lyrics are not so complex that Traynor would be brooding on their meaning for years. Nevertheless, both Willie Mae Thornton and Elvis recorded versions of "Hound Dog," with Elvis's version being far more commercially successful. In the story, the unnamed song highlights the gap between Traynor and Gracie Mae in terms of life experience.

### Sample Topics:

1. **Weight:** What does Gracie Mae's and Traynor's excess weight reveal about their respective psychological states? How do their different responses to their weight problems disclose crucial differences between the two characters?

   An essay writer analyzing the symbolism of weight could start by looking at the significant meeting between Gracie Mae and Traynor on the Johnny Carson show. How does Walker use their weight to hint at society's racism, the impossibility of Traynor ever getting close to Gracie Mae emotionally and spiritually, and both characters' psychological struggles? How does weight become an important factor at the end of the story in both characters' lives?

2. **The song:** Why is Traynor so preoccupied with grasping the true meaning of the song? How does Walker use their singing of the song on the Johnny Carson show to critique white society's appropriation of black music?

Although the story focuses only on a single blues song that when sung by a white boy becomes a massive commercial hit, the song's appropriation typifies the experience of many black musicians in this time period. An essay could analyze Walker's perspective on the white music industry's relationship with black musicians and music. Alternatively, a paper could focus on the importance of the song to the two principal characters and what it represents to each of them.

## Compare and Contrast Essays

The story is structured around a series of contrasts between Traynor and Gracie Mae and, at first glance, they seem to have little in common. They differ in terms of race, gender, and age. Traynor is always described as being half-asleep, whereas Gracie Mae is active and alert. Although Traynor is extremely wealthy, he is plagued by a sense of failure and emptiness. Gracie Mae, on the other hand, lives modestly but her life is filled with love. Although the characters seem poles apart, they do share some similarities. For example, they both have weight problems—although they respond to them differently. They are both singers who sing the same songs in the same way—although Traynor is celebrated for his performances while Gracie Mae is ignored. They both battle with psychological problems— although the nature of those problems bears no similarity. Overall, the two characters provide ample material for a comparative essay.

### Sample Topics:

1. **Gracie Mae and Traynor:** By placing the two characters in contrast to each other, what themes and ideas does this allow Walker to accentuate? How do the two characters differ and what do they have in common?

An essay comparing and contrasting these two characters could discuss how their differences allow Walker to explore key themes and concerns. How does their contrast create a commentary on racism, exploitation, and authenticity? Additionally, the characters have some traits and attitudes that are similar. How do these similarities elaborate Walker's exploration of the themes of emptiness, fullness, success, failure, and resilience?

## Bibliography and Online Sources

*Anniina's Alice Walker Page.* December 30, 2007. <http://www.luminarium.org/contemporary/alicew.htm>

Johnson, Maria V. "'You Just Can't Keep a Good Woman Down': Alice Walker Sings the Blues." *African American Review.* Summer 1996.FindArticles.com. 04 Sep. 2007. http://www.findarticles.com/p/articles/mi_m2838/is_n2_v30/ai_18571821

Mickelsen, David J. "'You Ain't Never Caught a Rabbit': Covering and Signifyin' in Alice Walker's 'Nineteen Fifty-Five.'" *Southern Quarterly.* Spring 2004. FindArticles.com. 06 Sep. 2007. http://www.findarticles.com/p/articles/mi_qa4074/is_200404/ai_n9385213

Petry, Alice Hall. "Walker: The Achievement of the Short Fiction." *Alice Walker: Critical Perspectives Past and Present.* Eds. Henry Louis Gates, Jr. and K. A. Appiah. New York: Amistad, 1993. 193–210.

Winchell, Donna Haisty. *Alice Walker.* New York: Twayne, 1992.

# "ADVANCING LUNA— AND IDA B. WELLS"

## READING TO WRITE

FOR A friendship to develop, people are ideally open and honest with each other. But what happens if someone shares a secret with a friend that has the capacity to rupture that friendship? Would it have been better to keep silent? There are some truths that are hard to hear because they destroy an image or memory of the past and force an alternative reading of events that once seemed clear and incontestable. In "Advancing Luna—and Ida B. Wells," Walker presents a problematical truth. A white woman tells her black female friend that during their time together in the South registering voters for the Civil Rights movement, she was raped by a black man. As the excerpt shows, the narrator's reaction to Luna's secret is complex, but her anger reveals her wish that that she had been left in blissful ignorance:

> "What did you do?"
>
> "Nothing that required making a noise."
>
> "Why didn't you scream?" I felt I would have screamed my head off.
>
> "You know why."
>
> I did. I had seen a photograph of Emmett Till's body just after it was pulled from the river. I had seen photographs of white folks standing in a circle roasting something that had talked to them in their own language before they tore out its tongue. I knew why, all right.
>
> "What was he trying to prove?"
>
> "I don't know. Do you?"

"Maybe you filled him with unendurable lust," I said.

"I don't think so," she said.

Suddenly I was embarrassed. Then angry. Very, very angry. How *dare she tell me this!* I thought.

This passage touches on a variety of themes that could become the focus of an essay. First, the theme of friendship is explored by Walker in a provocative way. Luna's confession to the narrator is logical in the framework of friendship. A rape is a violation that affects every area of a woman's subsequent life. It is natural that Luna would want to communicate this to someone whom she believes is becoming a close friend. Friendship, however, is a dynamic relationship that often cannot survive changes to its initial context. The theme of emotions is explored in the story through the narrator's array of feelings as she contemplates what Luna has told her. Her naiveté is shattered by the devastating realization that her time working for Civil Rights was not the idealistic, fun, coming-together of like-minded people that she remembers. The excerpt indicates that she resents Luna's decision to speak out. The themes of silence or speaking out resonate for the narrator beyond the specific situation of Luna's confession. Although Luna has spoken the truth to the narrator, she did not make a sound at the time of the rape. When the narrator asks Luna why she did not scream, Luna explains that given the historical context of interracial rape in the South, she did not feel that it was an option because the repercussions would have been out of proportion to the crime. The narrator then conjures up images of black men who were tortured and lynched because of accusations, usually false, of raping white women. As the narrator dwells on the possible consequences of Luna speaking out at that time, she recalls the words of activist Ida B. Wells, who spent her life defending black men from trumped-up charges of interracial rape. The narrator imagines that Wells would urge silence on her to protect the black community from white aggression. The short story's interplay between silence and speaking out could make an interesting topic for a paper.

The conflict between loyalty to her race and loyalty to her gender is at the heart of the narrator's dilemma. White society has long overvalued white femininity, arguing that black men find white women so sexually desirable that they cannot control themselves around them. The narrator sarcastically alludes to this overvaluation of white femininity when she suggests that Luna's rapist was overwhelmed by lust in her presence. Thus, the narrator's response to Luna as another woman is in conflict with her response to white Luna as a black woman. The Civil Rights time period is the perfect setting for such ambivalence to play itself out. Some of Walker's other works, such as *Meridian* or *In Search of Our Mothers' Gardens,* have exposed the failure of the Civil Rights movement and white feminist groups to take into account the specificity of black women's position at the junction of racism and sexism. Essays exploring the story's historical context, analyzing the theme of loyalty, or comparing "Advancing Luna—and Ida B. Wells" with other works that address the conflict black women feel when faced with white female racism or black male misogyny would all be germane.

The narrator's complex emotional reaction to Luna both in terms of what constitutes the truth and whether silence or speaking out is the correct choice are ultimately unresolvable. The impossibility of a solution to the narrator's mental impasse is reinforced by the structure of the story. Walker provides alternative endings and hypotheses as the narrator tries to establish a firm foundation from which to respond to the issue of interracial rape. Essays on this short story will have to accept that it does not provide precise answers and that it raises more questions than it answers.

## TOPICS AND STRATEGIES

This section will discuss various topics for essays on "Advancing Luna—and Ida B. Wells" and will suggest different approaches to those topics. The topic suggestions are meant as a starting place to help stimulate your own ideas and ultimately to generate your own topic for your essay. The material should be used as a resource to help prompt your own ideas related to the topic, not as a blueprint for a perfect essay.

## Themes

What would make a woman stay silent as she is being raped? Her silence might be provoked by fear or terror. Maybe the aggressor is threatening the woman to stay quiet; screaming for help might bring worse consequences. The narrator assumes that she would have shouted out if she were the victim of sexual violence. However, Luna's silence transcends her individual situation and is indicative of her strength of character.

She knows that her screams might elicit a murderous backlash against other black men, effectively undermining the Civil Rights work that she believes in. History silences Luna. Much later, she chooses to tell the narrator, now a woman she considers a close friend, the truth about her rape. The weight of the confession leads the narrator to experience a gamut of emotions, but, overall, she resents Luna's decision to tell her the truth. Luna's choice to speak out ironically places the narrator in a comparable quandary—she must decide whether to stay silent or speak about the issue of interracial rape. Luna's confession of rape ultimately fractures her friendship with the narrator. Many friendships are circumstantial and cannot survive a change in situation or context. An interracial friendship faces unique challenges in a racist society that has validated white femininity above that of other women. If the narrator chooses loyalty to Luna, then she fears she may betray her race. If she stays silent about Luna's story, then she will be condoning violence against women. Friendship, silence, speaking out, emotions, and loyalty are just some of the important themes that this short story engages and that could become the basis for an analysis.

## Sample Topics:

1. **Friendship:** What is the basis of the friendship between Luna and the narrator? What issues cause the friendship to founder?

   What is the basis of friendship? There must be some common ground between two people in order for a relationship to be established. When the basis of that friendship is destabilized, the nature of the friendship may alter. How do racism, race, and sexuality destabilize the friendship between Luna and the narrator? An essay analyzing this topic would need to scrutinize the key friendship in the story. What brings these two people together, and what keeps them together initially? How and why is the narrator's perception of Luna continually tinged with negativity? Why is the friendship rocked by Luna's confession?

2. **Silence and speaking out:** In what different ways are the characters faced with the decision to be silent or speak out? How do

history and the past affect whether a character stays silent or speaks out?

Each specific situation determines whether silence or speaking out is the most appropriate response. Silence can be indicative of either weakness or strength. One approach to this topic would be to write a paper on the interplay between speaking out and silence, but the two themes could also be tackled independently of each other. Both themes can be linked to an analysis of resistance and/or power. The effect of historical and social context on the characters' decisions whether to be silent or speak out is also an angle that could be investigated.

3. **Emotions:** What range of emotions does the narrator pass through as a result of her friendship with Luna? How does each emotional stage affect the narrator's interaction with Luna?

An essay discussing the theme of emotions could start by listing all the different feelings and states that the narrator experiences throughout the story, from her time with Luna in the South until her final discussion about Freddie Pye in Cuba. What prompts each emotion? How does each emotion reflect her degree of awareness on race and human relations in the United States? How is Luna's confession of rape a turning point for the narrator?

4. **Loyalty:** How is the narrator's loyalty to her race pitted against her loyalty to her gender?

If loyalty is a component of friendship, the narrator's loyalty toward Luna is tested when the issue of interracial rape comes between the two women. An essay could address how the narrator tries to resolve her conflicting loyalties. Why does the narrator struggle with the idea of loyalty to Ida B. Wells? Does the narrator set race above gender, or are women's issues more important to her? To answer these questions, consider her response to Luna, her act of writing Luna's story, and the story's multiple endings.

# Character

Successful papers on character often focus on interpretations of changes in a character throughout a text. The behavior of both the narrator and Luna changes, but the reader only has access to the thoughts of the narrator. Luna's attitudes and motivations are elusive, filtered as they are through the perspective of the narrator. After Luna confides in the narrator about the rape, the narrator admits that she failed to ask Luna pertinent questions about her feelings on the episode. Thus, critical information is lacking in Luna's responses to various events, such as the rape and Freddie Pye's visit. The narrator is distanced from Luna and, as a consequence, so is the reader. The narrator's maturation and personality will be easier to write on than Luna's; nevertheless, Luna could still be the focus of an essay, using her character to explore some of the story's themes and ideas.

## Sample Topics:

1. **The nameless narrator:** What does the narrator learn about herself as a result of her reaction to Luna's rape? How does the story conflate the narrator with the author?

   Written from a first-person perspective, the narrator's passage from idealist to cynic is explored through the complex prism of race relations in the United States. The narrator changes from idealistic Civil Rights worker to angry and resentful friend but, by the end of the story, she explains how she wrote Luna's story and read it to an audience of artists. An essay could consider how the narrator develops as a friend, as an activist, or as a writer.

2. **Luna:** Which of Luna's traits does the narrator ridicule? Which of Luna's qualities eventually lead to her becoming friends with the narrator?

   An essay on this character must note that all information about her is filtered through the point of view of the narrator. Despite this bias, what qualities does Luna demonstrate during her time working in the South? Why do Luna and the narrator become close friends in New York? What does Luna's reaction to her rape indicate about her character? A paper could explore Luna's traits and show how they are used to illuminate themes and ideas, such as friendship, interracial stereotypes, silence, and speaking out.

# History and Context

"Advancing Luna—and Ida B. Wells" is one of Walker's texts that use the backdrop of the Civil Rights and Black Power movements of the 1960s and 1970s to articulate the complexity of black women's placement at the intersection of racism and sexism. In the early years, the Civil Rights movement advocated tactics such as mass voter registration, as is illustrated by the work of Luna and the narrator, to change the white-controlled political structures of the South. When the Black Power movement evolved out of the Civil Rights movement, some of its spokesmen were blindly misogynist as part of their insurrectionary stance. Walker exemplifies this violent misogyny through the story's allusions to Eldridge Cleaver and Amiri (Imamu) Baraka, who suggested raping white women as a means to diminish white men. Similar to *Meridian*, "Advancing Luna—and Ida B. Wells" focuses on the interracial relationships of Civil Rights workers that had to negotiate attitudes such as Cleaver's and Baraka's. The narrator is influenced by the words of Ida B. Wells (1862–1931), a militant antilynching crusader and women's rights activist, for guidance on how to react to a white woman's claim of rape by a black man. However, changing historical contexts shape black women's responses to the issue of rape. The narrator ponders whether Wells's advocacy of silence is the appropriate response 50 years later.

## Sample Topics:

1. **The Civil Rights and Black Power movements:** How does Walker use allusions to highlight the conflict the narrator feels towards some of the Black Power movement's methods and attitudes? How does Walker use the story's setting to enhance themes, philosophical ideas, and characterization?

"Advancing Luna—and Ida B. Wells" depicts the interplay between the political and the personal in the lives of black and white Civil Rights workers. An essay could look at the historical figures that are alluded to, for example, Ida B. Wells or Eldridge Cleaver, to examine how the burden of history affects women's personal choices and way of thinking. Reading Walker's essay "The Civil Rights Movement: What Good Was It?" might give you some insight into this topic. The narrator also mentions that she had read Ida B. Wells's *Crusade for Justice* (1928), and this autobiography could also prove helpful in understanding the mind-set of black female activists in the post-Reconstruction period.

## Philosophy and Ideas

Black women are impeded from viewing black man/white woman sexual relationships neutrally because of white America's historical overvaluation of white womanhood. Historically, interracial sex has been tainted by false accusations of rape, lynchings, and sexual exploitation of black women. Myths of black men's uncontrollable appetite for white women have been propagated and used to control and intimidate. Discourses surrounding such stereotypes have influenced the thinking of black and white Americans to the point that the narrator has come to believe, supported by her reading of Ida B. Wells, that no white woman was ever actually raped by a black man. Luna's story shatters this illusion. The narrator feels compelled to pursue the facts of the matter as a writer but comes up against various contesting truths. The notion of truth in connection with interracial sex is unstable. Lies and distortions have regularly been used to influence the mindset of different segments of the population. Thus, white America comes to believe that black men want to violate their wives and daughters, whereas black America disavows interracial rape as being a figment of the white imagination concocted as a weapon of political and social control. The narrator tries to negotiate all the stereotypes, misrepresentations, and lies to find answers for black women, whose own sexuality and femininity are compromised by the fiction of black male lust for white women.

### Sample Topics:

1. **Interracial interaction:** How do history and racial stereotypes in the South affect the narrator's response to Luna's story? How does the history of interracial rape in the South affect what hap-

pens between Luna and Freddie Pye? How does the history of interracial interaction in the United States complicate friendship between Luna and the narrator?

In the context of the United States, interracial sex is judged through the lens of politics and history. An essay could look at the important interracial relationships—the narrator/Luna and Luna/Freddie Pye—and consider how each interaction is affected by history, by stereotypes, by race, and by gender.

2. **The instability of truth:** How do perceptions of truth have an effect on Luna and the narrator's behavior? How does the narrator negotiate her inner conflict that arises out of hearing differing versions of the truth?

An essay on the topic of truth could examine the instances in the story where the narrator is confronted by doubts as to the nature of truth. How does she attempt to pursue the truth? How does the history of white America's lying about rape affect the narrator's perception of the truth? Such an essay could also connect to an exploration of the form and genre of the story. The text's unusual mix of genres and alternative endings also raise questions on the notions of truth and fiction. See the "Form and Genre" section below for more information.

## Form and Genre

Even though "Advancing Luna—and Ida B. Wells" is usually referred to as a short story, its genre is actually more complicated. At its start, it has all the trademark components of a short story, such as characters, plot, and a narrator. However, as the story progresses, the characters and the narrator are described as "still alive"; thus, the plot breaks down because the actual endings of these people's lives have not happened and so cannot happen in the story either. Furthermore, the narrator's voice mutates into a voice that appears to be that of Walker. As a result of these shifts, it becomes unclear whether "Advancing Luna—and Ida B. Wells" is a short story, an autobiographical excerpt, or an essay. The function and effect of this mixture of elements from different genres could be explored in an essay. Another unusual feature of this text is the selection of alternative endings that Walker provides. These endings link to the fact that the narrative voice does not know how the "story" finishes. It can only speculate, hypothesize, and present alternatives. The multiple endings and the ambiguous genre of the text create a dialogue between the writer and the reader, as we are obliged to negotiate the interplay between fact and fiction and truth and lies.

### Sample Topics:

1. **The instability of form and genre:** Why does Walker include alternative endings? Why does Walker confuse the boundaries between the genres of the short story, the autobiography, and the essay in "Advancing Luna—and Ida B. Wells"?

   Writing about the text's multiple endings could consider why the narrator finds it impossible to provide a definitive resolution. This essay could also include analysis of the different types of genre that the text incorporates. How does the use of conventions from different genres enhance the text's philosophical and thematic goals?

## Compare and Contrast Essays

Some of the issues and themes that the story engages with are also explored in the novel *Meridian*. The novel and this short story deal with racial and sexual politics arising out of the Civil Rights and Black Power movements and address how black women are affected by the sometimes conflicting concerns of racism and sexism. However, *Meridian* is a novel and incorporates a more comprehensive range of themes, and its characterization is developed with greater complexity. Consequently, if comparing these two texts, you should select your topics for comparison carefully because you will need to have a balanced selection of textual evidence from the two texts to support any argument.

### Sample Topics:

1. *Meridian* **and "Advancing Luna—and Ida B. Wells":** How do the two texts present friendship between a black woman and a white woman? How do the two texts present black male rape of

a white woman? How do the black female protagonists negoti- ate their feelings concerning their conflict over loyalty to race and their own self-interests as women?

A comparison of these two texts could take one of several approaches. One focus could be to compare and contrast the way that Walker presents the friendship between a black woman and a white woman and the political and histori- cal impediments to that friendship. Meridian struggles with comparable emotions to the narrator of "Luna" when faced with a white friend's interaction with a black male. Another approach would be to examine how both main characters articulate black women's concerns and interests, which have often been overlooked in movements that battle against rac- ism or sexism.

## Bibliography

McKay, Nellie Y. "Alice Walker's 'Advancing Luna—and Ida B. Wells': A Strug- gle Toward Sisterhood." *Rape and Representation.* Eds. Lynn Higgins and Brenda Silver. New York: Columbia UP, 1991.

Petry, Alice Hall. "Walker: The Achievement of the Short Fiction." *Alice Walker: Critical Perspectives Past and Present.* Eds. Henry Louis Gates, Jr. and K. A. Appiah. New York: Amistad, 1993. 193–210.

Walker, Alice. "The Civil Rights Movement: What Good Was It?" (1967). *In Search of Our Mothers' Gardens: Womanist Prose.* London: Women's Press, 1983. 119–129.

# THE THIRD LIFE OF GRANGE COPELAND

## READING TO WRITE

**I**N THE pre–Civil Rights era when Grange and Brownfield are toiling on the land, a sharecropper's life in the southeastern United States was an endless cycle of backbreaking physical labor that led only to escalating debt to the landlord. The balance of power in the relationship between landlord and worker is described in the following excerpt where Grange and the other sharecroppers wait while the landlord collects the cotton crop:

> While the truck stood backed up in the field the workers held their breath. A family of five or six workers would wonder uneasily if they would take home, together, a whole dollar. Some of the workers laughed and joked with the man who drove the truck, but they looked at his shoes and at his pants legs or at his hands, never into his eyes, and their looks were a combination of small sly smiles and cowed, embarrassed desperation.
>
> Brownfield's father had no smiles about him at all. He merely froze; his movements when he had to move to place sacks on the truck were rigid as a machine's. At first Brownfield thought his father was turned to stone by the truck itself. The truck was big and noisy and coldly, militarily gray. Its big wheels flattened the cotton stalks and made deep ruts in the soft dirt of the field. But after watching the loading of the truck for several weeks he realized it was the man who drove the truck who caused his father to don a mask that was more impenetrable than his usual silence. Brownfield looked closely at the man and made a startling discovery; the man was a man, but entirely different from his own father.

When he noticed this difference, one of odor and sound and movement and laughter, as well as of color, he wondered how he had not seen it before. But as a small child all men had seemed to merge into one.

The sharecroppers avoid making eye contact with Mr. Shipley. They do not articulate their frustrations and anger with him out of fear of the power he wields over them. He controls their lives by taking the majority of the profit from their labor. In return for their labor, he provides them with the absolute bare minimum to allow them to exist and continue working. The cost of the sharecroppers' living expenses was advanced as credit, which had to be paid off when the crop was finally sold. This is why Grange is in debt to Mr. Shipley to the tune of $1,200 (according to Brownfield's cousins)—a massive sum for the time. Since the landlord sold the cotton and the workers were all mostly illiterate, the opportunities for exploitation were rife. The only way that Grange can see to break free from his debt is for his wife to prostitute herself. An essay drawing on the historical and social context of this novel could explore the personal and social repercussions of the sharecropping system as portrayed by Walker. The system torments the workers psychologically because they perceive the futility of their work. However, the iniquities and inequities of this lifestyle affect relationships within the entire family, and analysis of these deleterious family dynamics provides a way to begin composing a paper on this novel.

The almost certain failure of the black laborers to pay off their debt to their white landlords also ensures that the status quo in terms of racial relationships is maintained to the benefit of the whites. Unsurprisingly, given the setting of 1930s Georgia, Brownfield determines that Mr. Shipley is of a different species than his father. Although he recognizes that both are men, Mr. Shipley is distinct from Grange by more than just by color. Brownfield notices that Shipley's movements, smells, and sounds differentiate him from his father. However, Brownfield is already 10 by the time he perceives this difference. As a small child, he had seen all men as the same. Thus, he has learned to differentiate his father and himself from Mr. Shipley; his recognition of racial differences is not innate. *The Third Life of Grange Copeland* raises many questions about racial difference, showing how judgments each race makes of others often act as justification for appalling treatment of someone from a different race. An essay could appraise the novel's spotlight on racial difference. Does Walker argue for intrinsic racial difference, or does she present perception of racial difference as a reflection of the power structures of a particular community?

If Brownfield grasps the nature of the unbridgeable chasm between blacks and whites from his father's frozen response to Mr. Shipley, what else might a child learn from a father? A boy's first understanding of what it means to be a man is usually learned from watching his father relate to others and to his community. In Brownfield's case, his father's silence, as illustrated in the excerpt, is typical of his normal level of communication with his son. Thus, Brownfield's initiation into masculinity is achieved through observation and emulation. An essay comparing father and son is a potential essay topic. How responsible is Grange for Brownfield's adult cruelty? Alternatively, a paper could explore the novel's position on personal accountability for one's own behavior and attitudes.

The dismal monotony of a sharecropper's existence is reinforced through Walker's use of bleak imagery. In the passage, Mr. Shipley's truck is described as "militarily gray." Its wheels make "deep ruts" in the fields, suggesting its immense power that can crush the "soft dirt" of the laborers' place of work. Brownfield is named after the flat, brownish, Georgia cotton fields. On the day his mother and father name him, the drab imagery associated with Brownfield's birth reinforces the depression his parents feel, knowing that he is condemned to a life as miserable as theirs. They feel that the unexciting routine of their life will never change; Grange even wonders whether the entire universe is colored brownish. Ultimately, against all odds, Grange achieves personal transformation—the silent, hostile, enraged man seen in the excerpt becomes a man capable of sacrificing himself so that his granddaughter might live. This transformation could form the focus of an essay that would get to the very heart of the novel.

## TOPICS AND STRATEGIES

The remainder of this chapter will present possible topics for essays on *The Third Life of Grange Copeland*. The suggested approaches should inspire you to develop novel ways to write about a topic.

# Themes

The sharecropping life of Grange and Brownfield is soul-destroying. Their endless and backbreaking toil leads them only further into debt to their landlords. Their standard of living is pitiful since good food is scarce and their homes are falling down. Turning to alcohol or chasing after women and sex are two options for these men to try to blot out the misery of existence. Another way that a man can make himself feel powerful and in control is to assert himself over his wife. The male-female relationships in this novel are violent and degrading to both the women and the men. A woman's belief in love and family and the lack of economic opportunities that society offers her conspire together to oblige her to stay with a man who makes her life even more cheerless than his own. The novel condemns this brutish treatment of women by the very men they look to for support and love. Brownfield wants to blame all of his negative behavior and attitudes on whites. He is even able to attribute his murder of his wife to white people's malevolent influence. In an argument, Grange urges his son to take accountability for his own actions. He contends that however inhuman the white people's treatment of blacks may be, each man must make humane life decisions for himself and his family because, otherwise, he is giving up all his power as a man to whites. Hatred for whites is simply one component of a world filled with hatred. Before his epiphany on accountability, Grange tries to teach his granddaughter about the necessity of hatred in order to survive. Grange believes that Ruth must learn to hate white people; otherwise, she runs the risk of being destroyed by the reality of race relations later in life. For him, hatred facilitates survival in a racist environment. The novel shows the different struggles of the characters as they try to survive in a racist, violent, and exploitative world. From sharecropping to prostitution to theft, *The Third Life of Grange Copeland* illustrates the lengths that people are forced to go simply to feed themselves and their families.

## *Sample Topics:*

1. **Male-female relationships:** How is marriage portrayed in the novel? Why do women stay with violent men in loveless relationships?

An essay examining the topic of male-female relationships could start by looking at the principal couples in the novel: Grange and Margaret, Grange and Josie, Brownfield and Mem, and Brownfield and Josie. What does each man and woman initially find attractive in each other, and what breaks them apart? A paper could analyze the characteristics of the novel's male-female relationships and how they change over time. Why do the male-female relationships in the novel tend to deteriorate the longer the couple stays together?

2. **Accountability:** As an old man, how does Grange try to redeem himself and to make amends for his youthful violent and irresponsible behavior? What does the novel suggest is the global effect on the black community of men not taking accountability for their actions?

An essay on this topic might begin by closely examining Grange's metamorphosis from irresponsible, selfish husband/lover to caring and loving grandfather. What causes him to reform himself? With regard to other male characters, how does their refusal to be answerable for their misdeeds allow violence and abuse to be perpetuated within the black community? How does a lack of accountability ironically empower the whites to exercise even greater control over the lives of black male characters?

3. **Hatred:** How does the novel represent and evaluate the effect of hatred on individual characters? Does the effect of hatred differ between black and white characters and between male and female characters?

The black characters mostly hate white people. The white characters hate black people. However, each group is obliged to interact with the other. An essay could consider the way that the black characters manage their hatred of whites and the way whites demonstrate their hatred of blacks. Another approach would be to apply the theme of hatred to male-female relationships and show how hatred is a key factor in the way men and women treat one another. What is the role of self-hatred in the lives of the characters? Additionally, an essay could discuss the effects of love as a counterforce to hatred. How do love and hatred contribute to Grange's various transformations?

4. **Survival:** What different jobs do the characters do as a means to survive? What different activities do the characters indulge in as a way to survive their miserable lives? What different attitudes do the characters adopt as an aid to survival?

An essay on the topic of survival could take one of several approaches. First, the theme of survival could be tackled in the sense of the different jobs and activities characters pursue in order to make a living. How do these jobs affect a character's interpersonal relationships and sense of self? Second, the way characters interact with one another could also be considered a form of survival, particularly in cases where characters manipulate or exploit one another to get something they want. Analysis of this type of interaction could provide the basis for an essay. Finally, the novel shows how some characters promote certain attitudes they feel are essential for survival in their world. What attitudes does the novel endorse as crucial for, or detrimental to, the survival of the African-American community?

# Character

The popular cliché states that blood is thicker than water; this assertion promotes the idea that family relationships are more important than any other tie. Family members are supposed to offer love and support to one of their own during difficult times. Whereas friends come and go, family will always be there. For many people, however, this is a myth. Family is the source of most of their interpersonal problems, and some family members may threaten their safety and security. Alice Walker depicts this reality through her portrayal of the dysfunctional relationships within the Copeland family. When Grange abandons his family, his son, Brownfield, is left to fend for himself after his mother's suicide. Father and son do not know each other. The father has shown Brownfield a negative model of what it means to be a husband and father. Brownfield repeats much of Grange's negative behavior with his own wife, Mem, and children. When Grange reforms in later life, he is not able to reconnect with his son, who still harbors resentment and anger toward his father. The only way that Grange can alter the pattern of dysfunction within the family is to rescue Ruth, one of his grandchildren, after Brownfield murders Mem, is imprisoned, and leaves the children parentless. As a consequence of Grange's support, Ruth is able to retain an open spirit and to view the world as a place of possibility. Like her biblical namesake, Ruth transmits a message that selfless love may demand sacrifice. On the other hand, genuine love and compassionate sacrifice will be rewarded. In the Bible's Book of Ruth, Ruth's loving sacrifice results in her becoming one of Christ's ancestors. How does Grange sacrifice himself for Ruth, and what is his reward for doing this? Grange, Brownfield, Mem, and Ruth: Any one of these characters is sufficiently well-developed in the novel to provide ample material for an essay organized around character analysis.

## Sample Topics:

1. **Brownfield:** Why is Brownfield constantly so angry? Why does he blame all of his shortcomings on white people? Does he have any redeeming characteristics?

   Brownfield's name seems to set him up for a life of drudgery and ugliness. Born into a situation of violence, unhappiness, and neglect, his life is doomed before it really starts. An essay analyzing this character's negative interaction with other characters could show how his life experiences cause him to lose hope and trust and descend into barely repressed rage. Why is he unable to rise above his unfortunate fate in life? Which emotions and needs drive this character?

2. **The three lives of Grange Copeland:** How have the different phases of Grange's life shaped him into the man he finally becomes? What makes Grange reevaluate his life choices in his search for a sense of worth? What is the ultimate sacrifice Grange makes?

First he is an abusive husband and father, then he becomes a violent criminal, before finally transforming himself into a protector and caretaker of a young girl. An essay could explore how in each life stage, Grange tries to find ways that he can take pride in himself as a man. Only in his third life does he come to understand the harm he has done to others in his first two lives. This prompts him to work toward redeeming himself in his own eyes and achieving some form of self-empowerment. Analysis of Grange's transformations and rebirth can be linked to consideration of the themes of accountability, hatred and love, and family relationships, or it could connect to the ideas of cycles of violence and racial difference.

3. **The Book of Ruth:** How does Ruth embody a message of love and sacrifice? How does Ruth represent hope for future generations of black women?

As a young girl, Ruth suffers extreme violence at the hands of her father, and she also witnesses his murder of her mother. When her grandfather takes custody of her after this event, her life is changed. His selfless love for her allows her to grow up and be educated without the helplessness and terror that have marked the two previous generations of women in her family. An essay could evaluate the gift of hope and possibility that her grandfather bestows upon her. How does Grange save Ruth from the family's cycles of violence and powerlessness? Another approach to Ruth would be to analyze her for her symbolic function as an embodiment of unconditional love that has the power to transform. This essay could make parallels with the biblical Ruth (to whom Walker alludes in the novel).

4. *La même*—**Mem:** What does Mem symbolize? Which of her traits contribute to her destruction by Brownfield?

Alice Walker explains in the novel's "Afterword" that Mem's name is derived from the French word *la même* which means the same. Walker makes Mem's fate as abused and murdered wife represent the fate of so many black women brutalized by male violence. A popular French expression states, *Plus ça change, plus c'est la même chose.* This saying suggests that history repeats itself and that nothing ever really changes. An essay could explore how Mem's tragic life and death symbolize the novel's notion of history repeating itself, in the sense that generations of black women have ended up paying the price for black men's emasculation by systemic racism. Alternatively, Mem could be analyzed as a woman who was destroyed by her own trust and goodness. Which other traits or social contexts contribute to Mem's decline and demise?

## History and Context

In *The Third Life of Grange Copeland,* Walker's portrayal of the American South is multivalent. Walker has identified herself in several of her essays as a southern writer who draws upon her experience of growing up in a sharecropper family in Georgia. Despite the hard grind of the sharecropper life and despite the profound impact of white southern racism, Walker claims the South as her homeland, albeit a homeland that obliged her to leave. Many of her feelings toward the South are articulated in her essay "The Black Writer and the Southern Experience" in *In Search of Our Mothers' Gardens,* which would be a place to start when thinking about writing on Walker's vision of the South.

Through the character development of Brownfield, Walker showcases the worst that the South can do to a black man. He is destroyed by his circumstances before he even reaches manhood. As he ages, he ekes out an existence through sharecropping, but the rewards of his labor are not enough to provide his family with an acceptable standard of living. The main causes of his degradation are the pervasive racism in the South, the violence in his family, and his own lack of education. As a young man, Grange's experience of the South is comparable to his son's. However, unlike Brownfield, he travels to the North, establishing a distance that permits him a fresh perspective on his place of birth. His return to Georgia reveals the possibilities of life in the South. Removed from the worst of white racism on a plot of his own land, he strives to make the farm a loving home by teaching his granddaughter to embrace the positive aspects of black southern life and educating her on how to survive the world beyond the farm's confines. In "The Black Writer and the Southern Experience," Walker describes black southern heritage as:

> a compassion for the earth, a trust in humanity beyond our knowledge of evil, and an abiding love of justice. We inherit a great responsibility as well, for we must give voice to centuries not only of silent bitterness and hate but also of neighborly kindness and sustaining love. (21)

## *Sample Topics:*

1. **The American South:** In what ways does Walker show life in the South to be harsh and unforgiving? What are the positive features of life in the South for Walker's black characters? How does the novel end on a note of hope for social change in the South?

   Deeply racist, violent, bleak: These are the dominant attributes of the South for a character like Brownfield. However, Grange feels that his hatred for Georgia notwithstanding, any other place is "foreign." The South, by default, is home. An essay analyzing Walker's representation of the South could consider her different perspectives on the South. How can a place be home, yet so many characters are desperate to leave it? What aspects of black southern life are validated in the novel? How does the sharecropping existence break the spirit of both Grange and Brownfield? What is the quality of life like for black women in the South? This topic could be expanded by comparing and contrasting the portrayal of the South with the North. How does Grange feel during his stay in the North? Why is the North not a straightforward alternative for Grange and other characters seeking to escape the South's racism?

## Philosophy and Ideas

"The Tree of the Family of Man," which Ruth discovers in a new history textbook given to her at school, depicts the hierarchy of the races as perceived by the book's authors: white, yellow, red and, last, black. Ruth's outrage spills out into vitriolic abuse of her teacher for using such a text as a mode of instruction. The book explains how white people have taught the lower races how to be civilized, although the implication of the illustrations shows that black people are ranked so far below the other races that they are not even a direct outgrowth of the family tree of humanity. Instead, they are joined to the other races only by a "rootless branch." The representative picture of the black man shows a grinning male in a grass skirt waiting by a boiling pot of water. The intent of the image is to associate black people with a sort of crass primitiveness and cannibalism. *The Third Life of Grange Copeland* examines other instances of the possibility of inherent racial difference. As Grange watches the pregnant white northerner, he is amazed by her fortitude in face of her desertion. He associates her repression of emotion with white Americans, noting that such comportment would never lead to the singing of blues. However, in watching her misery, Grange perceives that white people undergo pain and experience emotion the same as the rest of humankind. Thus, he toys with the idea that white and black people share some fundamental emotional similarities. However, later, when the pregnant woman rejects his offer of help and taunts him for his blackness, which in her mindset makes him lesser than she, Grange reverts to distancing himself from all whites, loathing their constant need to assert themselves over other races.

By giving into his hatred, Grange becomes part of ongoing cycles of violence between different races. Social and personal transformations are required for relationships to ever change among human beings. Grange comes to understand this, not only in terms of his attitude toward white people, but also in terms of relationships among people in the black community. Violence and hatred perpetuate violence and hatred. The novel's ending contains scenes depicting people involved in the Civil Rights movement. A carload of young black and white people arrive at Grange's farm to persuade him of the value of voting. This implies that political transformation can change the racial status quo by all people working together. Grange's personal transformation, in a sense, is harder to accomplish because it is a journey he must make alone. Ultimately, his individual transformation starts to effect change within the wider community, as is symbolized by Ruth's refusal to give up her sense of identity and be seen as Brownfield's property. The novel suggests she will make her own choices in life, receive an education, and will probably leave the South. Her path will differ drastically from her mother's and her grandmother's. Cycles of oppression and violence can be broken at both the individual and community levels. In fact, the novel presents personal and social transformation as two sides of the same coin.

## Sample Topics:

1. **Racial difference:** Does the novel argue for or against the idea of intrinsic racial difference? According to the novel, how does a perception of racial difference affect behavior so far as interaction between the races is concerned?

   An essay on the topic of racial difference would start by analyzing the incidents of Ruth reading her history book and Grange confronting the white woman in Central Park. If racial difference is indeed a reality, how does the novel suggest that black and white people may differ? How do other races fit in America's and Grange's racial schema? Look, for example, at Grange's story to Ruth about how Native Americans became the blood brothers of African Americans. How does Ruth respond to this story? An essay could evaluate the novel's debate on racial difference.

2. **Cycles of violence:** According to the novel, what social and personal forces work together to perpetuate cycles of violence within the black community and within the larger community of blacks and whites?

   Like father, like son. Like mother, like daughter. Regardless of the dreams and aspirations of each character when they are younger, the novel shows each generation replicating the violent behavior patterns of the previous generation. An essay could explore how the cycles of violence are passed from generation to generation. In both black and white families in the novel, how is the son's behavior often shown to be even more violent and oppressive than that of the father? Such an analysis could consider how women and children are usually the people who suffer the most in terms of violence within the black community. Appraisal of the violent attitudes and behavior of whites in the South and the North could also form the basis of a paper, showing how violent white behavior affects the quality of life and the psychology of the blacks in their own community.

3. **Political and personal transformation:** How does Grange manage to re-create himself through his relationship with Ruth? How can his personal transformation lead to transformation on a wider scale?

In the "Afterword," Walker refers to Grange and Ruth as the novel's "soul survivors." By this, she means that they have not compromised their humanity in reaction to society's racism. Their soul remains inviolate. An essay could show how Walker's novel argues that personal transformation can be the starting point for political and social transformation. The oppression of a wife by her husband goes hand in hand with the oppression of blacks by whites.

## Language, Symbols, and Imagery

One definition of the word *grange* is an outlying farm. A grange incorporates not just the farm, but also the farmhouse and other buildings on the land. Walker signals the importance of Grange Copeland's farm by the character's name. Grange is able to "cope" on his "land." It is the one place where he is able to create a sense of belonging and worth for himself and to protect his granddaughter from the ravages of the Copeland family's cycles of violence. He erects a fence around his property to try and establish a feeling of security. However, Grange often fears that white people want to steal his land or violate his sanctuary in some way. He tells Ruth that she needs to learn how to shoot a gun in case the time comes when she must fight to retain control of the farm and the freedom it symbolizes. In Ruth's log cabin playhouse on the farm's land, Grange and Ruth sing and dance. They brew homemade wines and explore the surrounding woodlands. Nonetheless, Ruth does not envisage her future hidden behind the fences of the farm. She feels that she must venture out into the world rather than accept the type of jobs that are available to black women in the South.

The reason why Ruth and her grandfather view the sanctity of the farm differently is because of Grange's past of which Ruth is ignorant. Grange decides not to tell Ruth about his hate-filled and violent past because he does not want to shatter her optimism and her openness to life. However, he carries a dark secret past of murder, robbery, and hatred of white people. One of his more powerful memories is of his role in the death of a pregnant white woman. He espies this woman in Central Park and witnesses her betrayal by her married boyfriend. In the ensuing drama, Grange contributes to her drowning in a pond, although her revulsion for black people also means that she spurns the little help he does offer her. His interaction with the woman is a defining moment in his life because he knows that he would have saved anyone else who had not demonstrated such utter contempt for him, even if that person were racist. This participation in death liberates Grange to give full voice to his hatred of white people. The pregnant white woman's death also means that the child in her womb does not survive. Thus, she symbolizes many things to Grange both in her life and her death.

## Sample Topics:

1. **Grange's farm:** What does Grange's farm mean to him, to Ruth, and to Josie? What positive and what negative values are associated with the farm?

   The farm is the place where Grange lives out his third and final stage of life. An essay exploring the symbolic meanings of the farm could look at the activities that are carried out on the farm and the way that relationships develop on the farm. When the voter registration people arrive at the farm to talk to Grange and Ruth, how do Ruth and Grange both react to this visit? How does the farm serve as a source of education to everyone who lives there?

2. **The pregnant white woman:** How does the woman both challenge and reinforce Grange's perception of white people? How

is the episode with the pregnant woman a defining moment in Grange's life?

A paper analyzing the symbolism of the pregnant white woman could ascertain the changing responses she provokes in Grange as he watches her drama with the soldier unfold. What is his initial response to her demonstration of emotion? How does this reaction shift dramatically when he tries to interact with her after the soldier's departure? How does her death shape Grange's subsequent life decisions?

## Compare and Contrast Essays

*The Third Life of Grange Copeland* describes the situations of different couples. Walker's narrative presents the details of the interaction between each couple's man and woman and between the parents and the children being raised in the household. These relationships offer fertile ground for devising comparative essays. One approach would be to compare and contrast the two principal male characters and the way their behavior reflects their respective definitions of manhood and masculinity. Their definition is influenced by the society in which they live at any given time and by the way they perceive their role within that society. In each case, their shifting understanding of their manhood has a corresponding effect on the women and the children with whom they live. Comparison of these women, too, could make a feasible paper.

### *Sample Topics:*

1. **Comparative masculinities:** How do Grange and Brownfield strive to define themselves as men in the racist world that diminishes their manhood? How do their definitions of manhood evolve throughout the novel?

   Brownfield learns most of what it means to be a man from his father. He learns what it means to be a black man from the racist milieu of Georgia where he lives and works. As young men, Grange and Brownfield share many similarities in their respective passages from hope to disappointment. What do the two men have in common? How do they differ in the ways

they view their work, treat their wives and children, and interact with their racist environment?

2. **Comparison of women's struggles:** How do the main female
   characters deal with the struggles they face? What social forces
   contribute to the women's vulnerability as wives, mothers, and
   lovers? How do the women treat their children?

To write on this topic, you could select two or three of the
main female characters and compare and contrast their
experience of being wives, lovers, and mothers. Given that
the social structures of rural Georgia contrive to silence and
exploit these women, how do the women attempt to find happiness and define themselves as women? How is their contrasting treatment of their children a consequence of their
own specific situations? What message does Walker want to
give the reader through her portrayal of these women's lives
and deaths?

## Bibliography and Online Sources

*Anniina's Alice Walker Page.* December 30, 2007. <http://www.luminarium.org/
contemporary/alicew.htm>.

Christian, Barbara. "Novels for Everyday Use." *Alice Walker: Critical Perspectives Past and Present.* Eds. Henry Louis Gates, Jr. and K. A. Appiah. New
York: Amistad, 1993. 50–104.

Hogue, W. Lawrence. "Discourse of the Other: *The Third Life of Grange Copeland.*" *Alice Walker: Modern Critical Views.* Ed. Harold Bloom. New York:
Chelsea House, 1989. 97–114.

Lauret, Maria. "The Third Life of Grange Copeland." *Modern Novelists: Alice
Walker.* New York: St. Martin's, 2000. 30–59.

Walker, Alice. "The Black Writer and the Southern Experience." *In Search of Our
Mothers' Gardens: Womanist Prose.* London: Women's Press, 1983. 15–21.

Winchell, Donna Haisty. "The Burden of Responsibility, the Flaw of Unforgive-
ness: *The Third Life of Grange Copeland.*" *Alice Walker.* New York: Twayne,
1992. 43–56.

# MERIDIAN

## READING TO WRITE

THE WORD *meridian* has a multitude of meanings and can operate as a noun or an adjective. Alice Walker begins her novel *Meridian* with a listing of 12 definitions. Definition number 6(b) explains that a meridian is a "distinctive character." What makes the character Meridian distinctive?

Early in the novel, the eponymous protagonist finds herself among a group of self-proclaimed revolutionaries, unwilling to voice her readiness to kill a human being as a means to foster social change. As Meridian struggles internally with the issue of whether killing can ever be justified, her mind wanders to another incident where silence had, similarly, been her rejoinder because she had felt averse to lying simply to conform to the majority viewpoint. The second episode of silence occurs in church and is seminal in determining the relationship between Meridian and her mother. Meridian refuses to affirm a belief in God as her Master and meets with rejection from her mother as a consequence. What could have been a transcendent moment where she embraces God and is thereby embraced by her mother instead descends into a moment of despair where she denies God and so is denied her mother's love. The two instances of willful silence merge in the narrative as Meridian dwells on the revolutionaries, as well as the estrangement between her mother and herself:

> They were waiting for her to speak. But what could she say? Saying nothing, she remembered her mother and the day she lost her. She was thirteen, sitting next to her mother in church, drunk as usual with the

wonderful music, the voices themselves almost making the words of songs meaningless; the girls, the women, the stalwart fathers singing

> The day is past and gone
> The evening shade appear
> Oh may we all remember well
> The night of death draw near

Sniffling, her heart breaking with love, it was her father's voice, discerned in clarity from all the others, that she heard. It enveloped her in an anguish for that part of him that was herself—how could he be so resigned to death, she thought. But how sweet his voice! It was her mother, however, whom she heeded, while trying not to: "Say it now. Meridian, and be saved. All He asks is that we acknowledge Him as our Master. Say you believe in Him." Looking at her daughter's tears: "Don't go against you heart!" But she had sat mute, watching her friends walking past her bench, accepting Christ, acknowledging God as their Master, Jesus their Savior, and her heart fluttered like that of a small bird about to be stoned.

The theme of silence is pivotal in the novel, and its analysis would make a valid topic for an essay. *Meridian* recounts anecdotes where black women have literally been silenced throughout history by violence or intimidation. However, silence may become a choice if the truth goes against the grain of popular belief; moreover, it can assume the status of action when it defies. In both of the instances mentioned in the excerpt, Meridian's silence acts as a kind of resistance. She is resisting conformity, social norms, peer pressure, a debasement of her values, and parental expectations. An essay could chart the development of the theme of resistance in the novel, and one option would be to analyze the incongruous symbiosis between silence and resistance. The incongruity is that resistance is usually associated with speaking out and speaking one's mind. Meridian belies this perception of resistance through her relative reticence throughout the novel; her resistance manifests itself predominantly through action. However, she comes to value the power of voice later on when she argues with a man that if he registers to vote, it could be "the beginning of the use of [his] voice." The man believes that "speaking out" will only bring him trouble in the form of retribution from white people. A paper could examine the concept of voice—in the sense of voice as a medium or a tool for self-expression—as used by Walker in the novel. In the excerpt, Meridian discerns the sweetness of her father's singing voice. In the framework of the novel, the purity and beauty of song in church is a manifestation of the purity and beauty of the souls of the people singing. Writing on the topic of voice could also be expanded to explore the idea of voice in the context of music and song, notable motifs in *Meridian.*

The contrast in the use of their voices in the passage calls attention to fundamental differences between Meridian's mother and father. A comparative study of Mr. and Mrs. Hill, not only with reference to their respective voices, but also as measured by their divergent attitudes toward the past and toward their daughter would make a compelling paper. Her father sees the African American situation as having parallels with the Native American experience. Her mother, in contrast, disavows the relevance of the past and lives her life as a "willing know-nothing," putting all her faith in the omnipotent, punitive God to whom she urges Meridian to submit. Another essay topic that emerges from a close reading of the excerpt is a consideration of the nature of the relationship between Mrs. Hill and her daughter. At the time of her mother's rebuff in church, Meridian is 13. This is a formative time in a girl's development because she is approaching the threshold of womanhood. A girl might normally model herself after her mother. However, the rupture between mother and daughter leaves Meridian in the position of having to find her own path to womanhood. The disparities between mother and daughter could also be examined through the prism of a social and historical standpoint. Later on in the novel, the narrator observes that Gertrude Hill's purity of existence was "compelled by necessity," because she did not live in an "age of choice." Meridian is forced to consider the degree to which her mother's time and place in history may have helped shape who she became.

There are many other topics that the passage touches on and that could become the starting point for an essay. For example, the importance of churchgoing is highlighted, and the novel pursues an examination of the role and function of the church in African-American communities. The excerpt laces the past and the present together through its flashbacks and digressions. Through these textual juxtapositions, the novel poses critical questions about human existence that transcend specific historical situations. Thinking about these questions may steer you toward a potential thesis: Is violence ever justified? What other forms of resistance might be more constructive than violence? How can humans learn from the past without being controlled by its legacy?

## TOPICS AND STRATEGIES

This section of the chapter will discuss possible topics for essays on *Meridian* and various approaches that could be used to write about those topics. This material should be used to help you formulate your own original essay theses.

## Themes

Silence can be a reaction to many different emotional states, such as anger, disinterest, uncertainty, fear, or hostility. Silence can be the consequence of the pain caused by overwhelming memories and the burden of the past. Silence can be forced on someone by a controlling person or power. A silent response is often assumed to be indicative of passivity and inferiority. With this way of thinking, the silent person seems to lack sufficient conviction or understanding to make a valid contribution to a dialogue. Paradoxically, silence can signal courage and strength of character. When Meridian refuses to tell other people what they want to hear, she accepts the inevitability of retribution. Meridian will not mindlessly parrot other people's beliefs because she is searching for her own authentic voice. In this way, silence can be a tactic that is used to resist what is being said or done by others. Throughout history, there have been people who have advocated nonviolent resistance. *Meridian* depicts a society in turmoil as it rises up to oppose the discrimination and violence meted out to black Americans by the white majority. One central question the novel raises is whether violence can ever be justified if it has the objective of revolutionary or corrective social transformation. Meridian fears that goals achieved through violence will incorporate the structures of oppression that the revolutionaries seek to overturn. Killing can lead to retaliatory killing but does not teach new values or lead to transformed interpersonal relationships. If violence is reviled as a revolutionary tactic, what other methods can be deployed to change society? Meridian's behavior points toward an answer to this question: self-directed, grassroots activism, inducing change small step by small step. However, her stance against bloodshed shifts toward the end of the novel when an epiphany about her connection to all black people and their struggles prompts her to reevaluate the necessity of violence.

Another powerful concept with which Meridian has to contend is guilt. Individual guilt is a state in which someone experiences conflict at having done something he or she is aware should not have been done. In Meridian's case, her mother makes her daughter bear the guilt for her having been born. Motherhood effectively ended Mrs. Hill's chance at an exciting or interesting life. The premise of collective guilt is that a group of humans or an institution is responsible as a unit for something that has been done/not done contrary to the norms of moral rightness. *Meridian* hypothesizes whether whites can be held collectively responsible for the inhuman treatment of African slaves and their American-born descendants. The possibility of collective white guilt has repercussions on many of *Meridian*'s characters, both black and white, and impinges on their interactions with one another.

### Sample Topics:

1. **Silence and speaking out:** How is Meridian paradoxically both a relatively silent character and a spokesperson for various black communities? Which other characters in *Meridian* have been compelled to be silent or felt compelled to speak out?

   Each specific situation determines whether silence or speaking out is the most appropriate response. Silence can be indicative of either weakness or strength. Louvinie's legend provides an extreme example of how black women have been silenced throughout history. However, Louvinie buried her tongue where The Sojourner now grows. The allusions to Sojourner Truth illustrate how Louvinie's spirit endured because The Sojourner evokes a woman who felt driven against all odds to speak out. Thus, speaking out can result in silencing, and silencing can induce speaking out. One approach to this topic would be to write on the interplay between speaking out and silence. An essay could also tackle the three themes of silence, speaking out, or finding one's voice independently. All of these themes can be linked to analysis of resistance and/or power. The effect of historical and social context on the exercise of black women's voices is also an angle that could be investigated.

2. **Resistance:** What are the different forms of resistance that *Meridian* depicts through its characters? What conclusions does the novel reach on violent versus nonviolent resistance?

*Meridian* describes many forms of passive and active resistance to social institutions and political systems. An essay could examine types of resistance and determine what characteristics Walker shows are necessary for a person to challenge oppression successfully. One approach to this topic would be to analyze the position on resistance Walker inclines toward. How does she portray standard revolutionary behavior (violence, strong leadership, marches, etc.) compared to Meridian's long-term, low-key presence in oppressed communities? A variation of this topic could look at why certain characters are antipathetic to change. What traits predominate in these characters? What causes characters to resist resistance?

3. **Violence:** How is violence used by people in power in *Meridian* to keep other people in a state of subjection? How does *Meridian* depict history as repetitive cycles of violence?

*Meridian* recounts incidents of rape, murder, massacre, colonization, discrimination, and child abuse among other types of violent behavior. An essay could investigate the novel's various examples of violence and their impetus. According to *Meridian,* violence begets violence and history can be described as cycles of violence against different populations. Why does Walker include so many accounts of murdered and abused children in the novel? What does Meridian come to understand about violence and her own relationship to it? Does *Meridian* suggest that it is possible to break free from cycles of violence? Answering these questions could lead you to devise a variety of theses derived from analysis of the theme of violence.

4. **Guilt:** Why is Meridian haunted by a sense of guilt? Is she able to overcome it by the end of the novel? In terms of collective guilt, can Lynne be held responsible for the racist crimes committed by other white people?

There are two main avenues into this topic: individual guilt and collective guilt. An essay analyzing individual guilt could investigate the source of Meridian's guilt and her efforts to transcend it. Truman also battles with the concept of guilt on an individual level. Ironically, his individual guilt is prompted by consideration of the possibility of collective guilt. Since his wife is white, he grapples with the legitimacy of feelings of resentment toward her for being white. Another essay could consider the notion of collective guilt and Truman's and/or Lynne's reactions to the assumptions made about her as a consequence of her whiteness.

## Character

The three main characters of this novel—Meridian, Truman and Lynne—all present a challenge to the essay writer because they are multifaceted and complex. In the chapter "Release," Truman tells Meridian, "Your ambivalence will always be deplored by people who consider themselves revolutionists, and your unorthodox behavior will cause traditionalists to gnash their teeth." In other words, Meridian is a character who has carved out her own route in life. She never received guidance from her family or her community that made sense to her, and she is not willing to follow the paths created by other people simply because they are well-trodden. Her unpredictable behavior and refusal to act like a "lady" or even a "woman," according to the values of her time and place, make her character difficult to define. Her conflicts rage internally since she rarely confides in other characters. Nonetheless, the other characters are drawn to her because she projects a sense of purpose, forbearance, and wisdom.

Truman, in particular, pursues Meridian. He is not prepared to lose her from his life even when he is married to another woman. However, Truman is more than a womanizer and a betrayer, buoyed by his own sense of male supremacy, even though that is how Meridian views him when he is young. The "conquering prince" makes a significant transition throughout the course of the novel and repeatedly ponders issues of race and sexuality that show him to be in pursuit of understanding. At the end of *Meridian,* he is described at the point of being reborn, ready to follow Meridian's example as to how to lead a meaningful life.

Lynne is similarly a dynamic character. Judged by others to be representative of the white race, she is ironically Jewish and thus is part of a group of people who have historically been ostracized by other white populations. Nevertheless, on the basis of skin color and her youthful ignorant comments, she is seen as embodying racist ideas and consequently provokes many negative responses in the black people with whom she interacts. She turns to Meridian when her interracial marriage with Truman fails. The two women arrive at a level of rapprochement based on their shared experience of gender, even though their racial difference and sexual histories with Truman create division and hostility. By the end of the novel, Lynne has declined psychologically and physically, a decline exacerbated by the murder of her child.

Meridian's mother, Gertrude Hill, is an important minor character because she is critical in instigating profound conflicts within her daughter. She is a woman who has shut herself down to much of the outside world and self-righteously fulfills what she believes is her Christian duty. Her dislike of motherhood instills a sense of guilt and sadness in Meridian, who is unable to escape her mother's resentment at the way life has turned out. However, Mrs. Hill's frustration and bitterness are tempered by the narrative's inclusion of descriptions of her life before motherhood and by Meridian's coming to terms with her mother's anger.

## *Sample Topics:*

1. **Meridian:** How do the 12 definitions of the word *meridian* at the start of the novel relate to the characterization of the eponymous character? What does the character Meridian symbolize? Why are other characters, such as Truman, Lynne, and Anne-Marion, drawn to Meridian?

There are several possible approaches that an essay analyzing Meridian could take. First, her transition throughout the novel can be examined. What allows her to find her sense of self by the end of the novel? What problems must she overcome? (For more information on this topic, see the "Form and Genre" section of this chapter.) Second, consider the significance of the 12 definitions of the word *meridian* to the actual character. How does Walker's choice of her name symbolize the trajectory of the character's life? Meridian's ambivalence and complexity could also be discussed. Why has Walker chosen to make her character elude straightforward classification or positioning? Third, investigate what Meridian brings to the other characters. Why are they compelled to keep in touch with her even though she does not encourage them to do so?

2. **Truman:** Why does the novel condemn Truman as a "conquering prince"? How does Truman evolve throughout the novel? What is the role of art in Truman's life?

Truman is another character who defies easy labeling and definition. One way to approach this character is to consider the key questions that he struggles with regarding race, sexuality, and gender. What is his position at the start of the novel concerning these issues, and how does his viewpoint shift by the end of the novel? Another essay topic could look at his role in the Civil Rights movement and his connection to black culture. Why does he speak French so often? Why is he attracted to white women? How do the ideals of the Black Power movement affect his attitudes? An essay could look at the influences in his life that Truman has to address in order to establish an identity for himself as a black man with self-worth. A completely different approach could examine the function of art in his life. How does his changing role as an artist reflect the evolution of his character?

3. **Lynne:** How does Lynne's race affect her involvement in the Civil Rights movement? Why is Lynne attracted to Truman? As

a student, how does Lynne perceive black life in the South? How does Lynne's thinking about race change throughout the course of the novel?

As a student, Lynne has a reductionist attitude to black people and black culture, aestheticizing them as exotic art. An essay could chart how her perception and understanding of black people changes as a consequence of her time spent in the South. How does Lynne adjust to the reality of how her whiteness is perceived in the South? A paper could examine how her whiteness shapes the reality of both her life and the black characters whose lives intersect with hers. An alternative approach to Lynne would be to examine her degeneration throughout the novel. What social and personal forces contribute to her decline? Meridian states that she has made an effort "not to hate" Lynne. An essay could consider the relationship between Lynne and Meridian to ascertain why Meridian allows Lynne to have a role in her life or why Lynne turns to Meridian in times of crisis.

4. **Mrs. Gertrude Hill:** Why is Mrs. Hill's relationship with her daughter so fraught with conflict? What role does Christianity play in Mrs. Hill's life? Why does Mrs. Hill dismiss the past as irrelevant?

On one level, Mrs. Hill is the quintessential bitter mother who should have never had children. Her resentment at the limits that motherhood has placed on the unfolding of her own life is projected onto Meridian. An essay could analyze why Mrs. Hill has retreated into a docile relationship with Christianity as a result of her life experiences. Another approach to this secondary character could consider the influence of the past on her present life. Why does she declare that the past says nothing to her? Given her personal history, why does Mrs. Hill fail to instruct her daughter on the realities of sexuality and pregnancy? This essay would likely assess the effect of her historical and social context on decisions and choices that she has made.

## History and Context

The story of Native Americans is a facet of America's past that tends to get obscured in accounts of the antagonistic history of black and white America. Meridian's father becomes fascinated by Native American history and fills a room with maps, photographs, and books that document the violence that Native Americans endured at the hands of whites. Mr. Hill learns that a part of the land he farms was originally a sacred burial site. His study of history informs him that black soldiers sometimes participated in white men's battles against Native Americans for control of the land. By giving back the deed to his land to Walter Longknife, Meridian's father hopes to expiate his sense of guilt and historical complicity in the brutality of white colonization. Mr. Hill believes that the lesson of the past, made clear by his study of Native Americans, is that comparable legacies of violence and oppression establish connectedness between African Americans and Native Americans. The history of the United States has been marked by cycles of violence that have been targeted against other population groups as well as African Americans. Mrs. Hill, on the other hand, disavows any responsibility ("I wasn't even born"). Through this exchange of opinions, Walker implicitly broaches the issue of whether white America should redress, through some form of compensation, the hurt done to black Americans.

*Meridian* deals with questions raised by the Civil Rights and Black Power movements of the 1960s and 1970s. Meridian's political awareness is created when a neighboring house, which was planned to be a base for a voter registration drive in her southern hometown, is fire-bombed in April 1960. In 1960, the Civil Rights movement was primarily using tactics such as mass resistance, nonviolent civil disobedience, and litigation to challenge the segregated and discriminatory social and political structures of the United States. *Meridian,* however, does not provide many details of specific historic events despite allusions to freedom marches or the voter registration process. Rather, *Meridian* focuses on the relationships of specific Civil Rights workers and the issues that grew out of their work. However, the historical is more than a mere backdrop to the personal. As the ideals of the Black Power movement supersede the original integrationist and nonviolent ethos of the Civil Rights movement, these ideological shifts are reproduced in the lives of, and interaction among, *Meridian*'s characters.

A key discourse that grew out of the Civil Rights period concerned the rights of black women. White feminism of the 1960s and 1970s had made broad sweeping assertions about the nature of femininity and womanhood that did not correspond with the experiences of black women. For example, the issue of the right to work emphasized the gap between black and white women's histories. Middle-class white women were fighting for the right to work outside the home. This was a ludicrous debate for black women, who had habitually been obliged to work outside their homes. Meridian contemplates this discrepant aspect of their female experience when pondering why Truman would be interested in a white woman. She thinks how black women had long escaped "to become something unheard of," while white women were passively accepting their roles as wives and mothers. Black feminism also addressed the sexism that women had encountered during their participation in the Civil Rights movement. Notably, the first question that Meridian is asked by the two male Civil Rights workers when she volunteers to join them is, "Can you type?" Black women increasingly realized that the Civil Rights movement universalized black male concerns, which sometimes perpetuated the oppression of black women. Black women's positioning at the nexus of racism and sexism produced unique concerns that both white feminism and the Civil Rights movement overlooked. To address this problem, Alice Walker promulgated "Womanism" in *In Search of Our Mothers' Gardens: Womanist Prose* (1983). Womanism's goal was to communicate the specific concerns of black women.

## Sample Topics:

1. **Native Americans and the history of the United States:** What is the symbolic significance of the Sacred Serpent? What are the attitudes of Meridian, Mr. Hill, and Mrs. Hill toward Native Americans? Why does Walker use a quotation from Black Elk as her epigraph to the novel?

   The placement of an epigraph at the beginning of a novel highlights its common function as an indicator of theme for the story that follows. Walker's choice to quote Black Elk signals the thematic importance of the violence and loss of hope that Native Americans suffered as a result of the European conquest of the Americas. An essay could examine how the Black Elk epigraph is significant for the rest of the novel. (For an idea of how to get started with this topic, look at the "Language, Symbols, and Imagery" section of this chapter under the topic "The Motif of Trees.") The massacre that Black Elk describes evokes the Sacred Serpent burial site. The chapter "Indians and Ecstasy" details different responses and usages of the Sacred Serpent burial ground. A paper could analyze the symbolic importance of the Sacred Serpent, perhaps even specifically looking at how it relates to Meridian throughout the novel. Another approach to this topic could compare the different attitudes toward Native Americans that the Hill family members express. How do the different attitudes toward this past affect the characters' lives in the present?

2. **The Civil Rights movement:** How are the changing conditions and beliefs of the Civil Rights movements, as it moves from the 1960s to the 1970s, reproduced in the lives and attitudes of the main characters? How does Walker use allusions to actual historical events to highlight the ambivalence Meridian feels towards some of the Civil Rights movement's methods and attitudes?

*Meridian* exposes the reciprocity between the political and the personal in the lives of the Civil Rights workers. An essay could focus on Meridian, Truman, Lynne or a selection of secondary characters and show how the shift from the nonviolent, integrationist civil resistance of the early 1960s to the Black Power self-reliant racial consciousness of the mid-60s affects each character and his or her activities as a Civil Rights worker. Another essay could look at the historical events that are directly mentioned, for example, Dr. Martin Luther King's funeral, to examine how Walker creates parallels between events and people in the past and events and people in the present. Walker's essay "The Civil Rights Movement: What Good Was It?" might be helpful for this topic.

3. **Womanism:** How does Walker demonstrate the effects of sexism on the female characters when they interact with male Civil Rights workers? How does Walker show the effect of racism on black women in the past and in the present? Why does Meridian adopt womanist principles, and how are they reflected in her behavior and actions?

Before starting an essay drawing on Walker's womanist philosophy, it will be helpful to read her definitions of womanism that can be found at the start of the essay collection *In Search of Our Mothers' Gardens: Womanist Prose.* With a grasp of the meaning and scope of womanism, one approach would be to identify and analyze womanist themes and concerns that Walker engages in *Meridian.* Additionally, an examination of how Meridian carves out a life for herself that allows her to retain her integrity as both black and a woman becomes viable. From the standpoint of the 21st century, are Walker's solutions for Meridian tenable?

## Philosophy and Ideas

The concept of motherhood is a sacred cow in the United States, and it has affected both black and white women to some degree. Under the romanticized version of motherhood, women should be hard-working, caring, and self-sacrificing when it comes to raising their children. Furthermore, because of its elevated position as a noble ideal, motherhood is presented as the ultimate calling of all women. Within this schema, there is no place for a childless woman, above all for a woman who chooses to be childless. The myth of motherhood demonizes women who declare themselves ill-suited to be mothers or who find the experience of child-rearing to be unfulfilling. However, the harm caused by resentful mothers fulfilling their social obligations as women is brought home through the relationship between Meridian and her mother. In being a mother, it is assumed to be a woman's duty to sacrifice her own desires and only put energy into pursuing the needs of her children and, to a lesser extent, the father of the children. The choices Meridian makes concerning motherhood, namely adoption, abortion, and sterilization, are extreme, but they serve the purpose of showing how not all women can be unquestionably classified as maternal.

As Meridian shows, choosing to be a mother or not is a condition that is closely bound to a woman's sexual choices. Kate Millet's *Sexual Politics* (1969), a highly influential book in the 1970s, proposed that since the United States was a patriarchal society, with women having little representation in the power structures of that society, sexual relationships were also tainted by positions of male dominance and female subordination. The politics of sexuality are reinforced throughout *Meridian* with incidents such as Eddie instructing his wife to demonstrate enjoyment of his sexual activity with her—with no suggestion that he could make any effort to actually help her enjoy it. In one of the more repellent scenes, the doctor aborting Meridian's fetus observes that he could help sterilize her if she includes him in some of her "extracurricular activity." Sexual politics are further exacerbated when race is factored in. Meridian's shock when Truman chases after Lynne is compounded by a genuine feeling of betrayal. White America's overvaluation of white femininity prevented black women from viewing black man/white woman sexual relationships dispassionately. The black/white relationships portrayed in the novel are all overlaid with historical and cultural constructs of black and white and male and female sexuality.

## Sample Topics:

1. **Motherhood:** What are the values associated with motherhood that cause Meridian to reject being a mother? Does Meridian demonstrate any maternal inclinations? How does the romanticized concept of motherhood affect the lives of the characters in the novel?

   One possible essay on this subject would be to examine the qualities in a woman assumed by mainstream black society in the 1970s to be essential for effective mothering and discuss how Walker dismantles those assumptions through the characters of Meridian and Mrs. Hill. Another angle to this topic could scrutinize Meridian's experiences of pregnancy and motherhood in order to assess the reproductive decisions that she makes. Minor characters' responses to being mothers and pregnant could also provide a broader picture of Walker's critique of society's overarching model of motherhood. What positive images of motherhood does Walker include in the novel?

2. **Sexual politics:** In what ways do sexual dynamics affect Meridian's interactions with male characters in the novel? How does Walker show sex, or the desire for sex, as reproducing the social and political imbalance of power between men and women in the 1960s and 1970s?

   This topic could focus on the myriad ways that sex is used as a commodity whose value Meridian negotiates with various men. Whether it is Mr. Raymond who gropes Meridian as his price for a few items of food or the doctor's request for sex in return for sterilization, Meridian's subordinate position in her dealings with men is constantly reinforced sexually. This topic could be extended to include analysis of other characters who have been exploited sexually. Another way to write about this subject could be to critique the double standards applied to female sexuality. For example, Truman acknowledges that he would have never married Meridian because she had given birth, whereas he expected his wife to be a virgin. However, even before he knew about her child, he constantly pressured her to have sex with him. The politics of race can add another dimension to this topic. White men have branded black women as more sexually available than white women. This is exemplified through Mrs. Hill's harrowing memories of her employers' young sons begging her for sex.

3. **Interracial relationships:** How has the historical sexual exploitation of black women altered Meridian's perception of interracial relationships? How do the layers of meaning attached to white femininity affect relationships between Lynne and Truman, Lynne and Tommy Odds, and Lynne and Meridian?

In the context of racially segregated communities, interracial relationships become imbued with political overtones and they attract hostility from both sides of the racial divide. The person involved with someone from the other race is judged as traitorous, ignorant, or misguided. An essay could look at the three key interracial relationships (Lynne/Truman, Lynne/Tommy Odds, and Lynne/Meridian) and consider how each couple's interaction is shaped by history, by stereotypes, by hatred, and by forgiveness.

## Form and Genre

*Meridian* describes its protagonist's coming of age and thus can be considered an example of a bildungsroman, a term denoting a "novel of formation," a "novel of education," or a "novel of personal development." This genre of novel follows the protagonist's journey from childhood through a range of experiences and often through a spiritual crisis into adulthood. Usually, unhappiness propels the protagonist away from her/his home environment. The passage to maturity is full of conflicts with society and its values. The nature of those conflicts could be categorized as conflicts prompted by the individual's sense of self being at odds with society and the ensuant struggle between individuality and conformity. By the end of the novel, bildungsroman protagonists reevaluate their role in society, often coming to terms with the niche they have carved out for themselves within it. However, the form of *Meridian* is not consistent with the conventional bildungsroman, because it does not unfold chronologically and linearly. The novel interweaves the past and the present, through anecdotes, digressions, flashbacks, allusions, song, and poetry. Walker explained in an interview, in *Black Women Writers at Work*, that she was aiming to simulate the design of a "crazy quilt." A crazy quilt is a creative art form that uses irregular pieces of material to create asymmetrical designs that appear haphazard; however, the designer usually has some overall plan, which is realized by the piecing together of different types of fabric. Walker observed, "A crazy quilt story is one that can jump back and forth in time, work on many different levels, and one that can include myth. It is generally much more evocative of metaphor and symbolism than a novel that is chronological in structure" (Tate 176).

## Sample Topics:

1. **Meridian as a bildungsroman:** Why does Meridian have difficulties defining herself as an adult? How does Meridian develop and resolve her quest for identity at the end of the novel?

Many of Meridian's problems stem from her uncertainty about how to define herself as an adult woman because she cannot embrace the models of femininity that society presents. Her individuality strives to assert itself against the conformist, racist, and sexist attitudes of her environment. An essay on Meridian's coming of age could trace the development of this character to determine how she finds a place for herself in society. Does she ever compromise herself as a woman or as an African American? Alternatively, a paper could identify the various elements of a bildungsroman and determine which aspects of Meridian's journey correspond with those elements. Some of these elements are the conflicts of generations, an ordeal by love, and the search for a working philosophy. For a fuller list of elements, see "The Self in Bloom: Walker's *Meridian*" by Deborah E. McDowell. Are there any ways in which *Meridian* does not conform to the requirements of a conventional bildungsroman?

2. **The crazy quilt structure of *Meridian*:** How does Walker create an effect of a crazy quilt through the structure of *Meridian*? How does the quilt structure enhance some of the primary meanings and goals of the novel? What is the effect of the quilt structure on the reader?

Many readers find that *Meridian*'s nonchronological structure initially inhibits access to its meaning. As critic Maria Lauret proposes, constructing the meaning of the novel involves reader engagement with all the different pieces of fabric that make up the novel as each patch of the quilt serves a function within the overall text. An essay could examine the different types of text that are sewn together to create the novel, determining what Walker was trying to achieve through each "patch" of the quilt. An essay could also analyze how the crazy quilt structure helps Walker promote some of the novel's themes and messages, such as the interconnectedness of the past and the present or silence and self-expression.

## Language, Symbols, and Imagery

One way to find coherence in *Meridian*'s "crazy quilt" structure is through analysis of the novel's symbols and motifs. The recurrence of references to specific objects or events creates links between disparate characters, places, and time periods. The novel's epigraph is taken from *Black Elk Speaks*, from the chapter "The End of the Dream," and it laments Native Americans' loss of hope in the future after a massacre of women and children by white soldiers. Black Elk metaphorically describes this loss as "the sacred tree is dead." In Native American legends, the sacred tree offers its people protection so long as they stay under its sheltering branches. If the tree is destroyed, great sorrow will fall on the people and they will lose their power. As long as the tree lives, the people live. At college, Meridian is drawn to The Sojourner, an extraordinarily large magnolia tree. Myths and legends of strong black women fighting for equality are embedded in the tree's history. The tree is cut down by the students in a misguided protest against the maltreatment of a homeless girl by the college administration. The college authorities do not want the Wild Child to receive a funeral service in the college's chapel. In *Meridian*, the Wild Child is just one of many children who are killed or who die because their society did not provide adequate care for them. It is a damning indictment of a society when that society is judged as failing to protect its most vulnerable members. In the chapter "Camara," Meridian enters a church where a funeral is under way. The father of the murdered young man is overwhelmed by grief, but, as the service progresses, Meridian finally recognizes the value of the church in black life. As a child, she had only appreciated the aesthetics of the churchgoing experience—the music and the stained-glass windows. Now she becomes aware of the church's ability to uplift, sustain, and unite people; she grasps the relevance of church in everyday life. This chapter of the novel (whose title alludes to another murdered child) brings together the symbolism of trees, dead children, and church. Meridian is at a church funeral of a murdered son. As she leaves the service, she recognizes her unity with the people around her and her obligation to fight to make their world a place that does not murder its children. This epiphany occurs as she sits under a large tree by the side of the road. Her awakening brings to mind the story of the Buddha, who similarly found enlightenment under a tree. The interwoven structure of the chapter reinforces Meridian's realization that through a shared history, she shares "One Life" with the people around her.

A motif that Walker incorporates that underscores polarity, rather than unity, is that of hair. Meridian starts to lose her thick hair after the callous attitude of the college administration towards the Wild Child and after she becomes more involved in Civil Rights work. The regrowth of her hair does not occur until the end of the novel when she has found her purpose in life. There are many references to the differences between black women and white women's hair. Hair represents a distinctive but paradoxically unstable difference between black and white women. Meridian wonders whether, possibly, the only enviable feature of white women is their hair. Lynne seems aware of this possibility and takes every opportunity to flaunt her long hair when she suspects black women's resentment of her sexual activities with black men. Truman has an insight into the symbolic meaning of hair when he sees black children combing Lynne's hair in a way that accentuates their difference from her. Tommy Odds pulls Lynne's hair violently when he rapes her. However, white women's hair assumes more ambivalence in the first chapter of the novel when the mummified woman's skin keeps darkening, so her husband proclaims that her red hair is the proof of her original whiteness. Her hair is the only part of her that distinguishes her from a black woman, yet that hair is, pertinently, artificial (since the entire "mummy" is a deception) and has been placed on the mummy's head by a white male with a mercenary agenda.

## Sample Topics:

1. **The motif of trees:** How does Black Elk's reference to the "sacred tree" link to The Sojourner? What is the symbolic significance of The Sojourner? What is the importance of Meridian's epiphany under a tree?

Trees have symbolic importance in many world cultures. The Native American myth of the Sacred Tree sheds light on *Meridian*'s overall meaning. The relevance of the myth to Meridian's journey of self-awareness or its connection to The Sojourner could become the basis for an essay. A study of The Sojourner on its own is also viable as a paper. What does it mean that The Sojourner is reported to have started growing again at the end of the novel? Additionally, an essay could explore how all the trees described in the novel work together to enhance the novel's idea of interconnectedness.

2. **Dead, abused, and neglected children:** How do the various children's deaths affect Meridian? What is the significance of the fact that many of the dead children have been abused or neglected prior to their death?

Walker's descriptions of dead children are sometimes quite graphic. For example, Meridian carries a bloated and decomposing corpse to the mayor's office to force the authorities to acknowledge their responsibility for the child's death. The last dead child that Meridian hears about is the murdered child of a 13-year-old girl. What is the significance of including this example of a child killing a child toward the end of the novel? An essay could examine the different instances of dead children that appear in the novel and evaluate society's and/or Meridian's response to each corpse. Why is Meridian so driven to help children while being unwilling to raise or give birth to her own?

3. **Church:** What is the role of the church and Christianity in Mrs. Hill's life? Why does Meridian change her opinion about the relevance of church to black life?

An essay could investigate Mrs. Hill's reliance on the church and its teachings and show how faith allows her to manage her life. This approach would need to consider the historical context and social conditions for black women of Mrs. Hill's era.

Another approach could examine how *Meridian* portrays the benefits of churchgoing, for example, through the enjoyment of music and song that are shared in church. What is the symbolic significance of the B.B. King stained-glass window that Meridian notices in the chapter "Camara"? Why does Meridian wonder what the songs sung in church would be like if the singers committed murder? Throughout the novel, Meridian visits several different churches and chapels. How does Meridian come to understand the church's leadership role in black communities, and how does she define that role?

4. **The motif of hair:** How does the state of Meridian's hair parallel her psychological state? How does Walker use hair to symbolize both differences and similarities between *Meridian*'s black women and white women characters?

To write on this topic, the numerous references to hair need to be identified. The first important mention is in connection with the "Devoted Wife and Adoring Mother Gone Wrong." Marilene O'Shay's white husband claims her long red hair differentiates her from black women and, thus, from Meridian. How is white women's hair used to encapsulate their whiteness and thus their difference from black women throughout the novel? Another essay could look at the significance of hair to Meridian, in terms of her own hair and in terms of observations she makes about other people's hair or baldness. An analysis of Meridian's hair could be tied to an examination of her physical and psychological health at different moments in the narrative.

## Compare and Contrast Essays

Walker establishes a surprising connection between Meridian and Marilene O'Shay, the mummified woman in the side show. The parallels between a dead white woman and a living black woman comment on the role of women in society. Furthermore, some of the epithets that are used to promote Marilene O'Shay ironically mirror periods of Meridian's life. Marilene shows how an "Obedient Daughter," "Devoted Wife," and "Adoring Mother" "Gone Wrong" can end up: exploited by the man who murdered her. Marilene's death is sanctioned by society because of her failure to perform the role of perfect wife that was expected of her. Although Meridian has many similarities with Marilene, there are also significant contrasts. The most obvious of these differences is the two women's agency in their respective societies. Meridian is a leader in the communities she resides in, and people respect her because she stands up for equal rights. People only want to see Marilene as a spectacle. She serves as a warning to other women, such as Meridian, who transgress the roles and behavior that are deemed acceptable for a woman. After Meridian is carried back to her house in a catatonic state, she engages in a conversation with Truman as she starts to regain consciousness. The conversation triggers a flashback to her father and mother, whose essential differences are underscored by their reactions to church, singing, and the past. A comparison between Mr. and Mrs. Hill becomes a possible topic, especially given Walker's focus on the interconnectedness of past and present. Since parents are often the people instrumental in passing on value systems, traditions, and beliefs, Mr. and Mrs. Hill become key characters due to the spiritual and personal legacies passed on to Meridian.

## Sample Topics:

1. **Meridian and Marilene O'Shay:** What physical traits and behavioral patterns link the mummified woman and Meridian? How, and with what purpose does Walker contrast the two women in terms of their physical traits and behavior?

   An article that will prove helpful for this comparison is Michael Cooke's "Walker: The Centering Self," which lists similarities and differences between the two women. Creating such a list is a useful starting point for generating content and an organizational plan for this comparative essay. The essay could then evaluate what Walker achieves through her parallels and distinctions between the two women.

2. **Mr. Hill and Mrs. Hill:** What is Mr. Hill's attitude to the past and the present? What is Mrs. Hill's attitude to the past and the

present? How has each parent helped shape Meridian into the woman she is?

This essay topic could either compare the two parents in terms of their attitudes, beliefs, and actions or compare each parent's legacy on Meridian. The first approach could compare their attitudes to Christianity, spirituality, and Native American history or contrast the way they approach their life and relationships with Meridian. The second approach would look at which elements of their attitudes and personalities have helped form Meridian's distinctive character, be it positively or negatively.

## Bibliography and Online Sources

*Anniina's Alice Walker Page.* December 30, 2007. <http://www.luminarium.org/contemporary/alicew.htm>

Barnett, Pamela E. "'The Recurring Dream': Utopian Politics and Sexual Violence in Alice Walker's *Meridian*." *Dangerous Desire: Literature of Sexual Freedom and Sexual Violence Since the Sixties.* New York: Routledge, 2004. 61–89.

Callahan, John C. "The Hoop of Language: Politics and the Restoration of Voice in *Meridian*." *Modern Critical Views: Alice Walker.* Ed. Harold Bloom. New York: Chelsea House, 1989. 153–184.

Christian, Barbara. "An Angle of Seeing: Motherhood in Buchi Emecheta's *Joys of Motherhood* and Alice Walker's *Meridian*." *Black Feminist Criticism: Perspectives on Black Women Writers.* New York: Pergamon, 1985. 211–252.

———. "Novels for Everyday Use." *Alice Walker: Critical Perspectives Past and Present.* Eds. Henry Louis Gates, Jr. and K. A. Appiah. New York: Amistad, 1993. 50–104.

Cooke, Michael. "Walker: The Centering Self." *Alice Walker: Critical Perspectives Past and Present.* Eds. Henry Louis Gates, Jr. and K. A. Appiah. New York: Amistad, 1993. 140–154.

Hall, Christine. "Art, Action and the Ancestors: Alice Walker's *Meridian* in Its Context." *Black Women's Writing.* Ed. Gina Wesker. London: Macmillan, 1993. 96–110.

Lauret, Maria. "Meridian." *Modern Novelists: Alice Walker.* New York: St. Martin's, 2000. 60–89.

McDowell, Deborah E. "The Self in Bloom: Walker's *Meridian.*" *Alice Walker: Critical Perspectives Past and Present.* Eds. Henry Louis Gates, Jr. and K. A. Appiah. New York: Amistad, 1993. 168–178.

Nadel, Alan. "Reading the Body: *Meridian* and the Archaeology of Self." *Alice Walker: Critical Perspectives Past and Present.* Eds. Henry Louis Gates, Jr. and K. A. Appiah. New York: Amistad, 1993. 155–167.

Stein, Rachel. "Returning to the Sacred Tree: Black Women, Nature, and Political Resistance in Alice Walker's *Meridian.*" *Shifting the Ground: American Women Writers' Revisions of Nature, Gender, and Race.* Charlottesville: Virginia UP, 1997. 84–113.

Tate, Claudia, ed. "Alice Walker." *Black Women Writers at Work.* New York: Continuum, 1983. 175–187.

Walker, Alice. "The Civil Rights Movement: What Good Was It?" (1967). *In Search of Our Mothers' Gardens: Womanist Prose.* London: Women's Press, 1983. 119–129.

Winchell, Donna Haisty. *Alice Walker.* New York: Twayne, 1992.

# *THE COLOR PURPLE*

### READING TO WRITE

Dear God,

I spend my wedding day running from the oldest boy. He twelve. His mama died in his arms and he don't want to hear nothing bout no new one. He pick up a rock and laid my head open. The blood run all down tween my breasts. His daddy say Don't *do* that! But that's all he say. He got four children, instead of three, two boys and two girls. The girls hair ain't been comb since their mammy died. I tell him I'll just have to shave it off. Start fresh. He say bad luck to cut a woman hair. So after I bandage my head best I can and cook dinner—they have a spring, not a well, and a wood stove look like a truck—I start trying to untangle hair. They only six and eight and they cry. They scream. They cuse me of murder. By ten o'clock I'm done. They cry theirselves to sleep. But I don't cry. I lay there thinking bout Nettie while he on top of me, wonder if she safe. And then I think bout Shug Avery. I know what he doing to me he done to Shug Avery and maybe she like it. I put my arm around him.

An unwanted marriage, violence, parenting someone else's four young children, and sexual exploitation: Celie endures all this because Mr. _____ cannot find anyone else to take care of his household. This poor, uneducated, country girl feels that only God might listen to the details of her daily suffering, so she writes letters to him in her idiosyncratic English. Since Celie imagines God as a distant old white man, she is not expecting much divine mercy or compassion for her plight because she has routinely been exploited and overlooked by men. Additionally, the endemic discrimination of blacks by whites in Georgia means that her white God is unlikely to bother himself with a black girl's problems. Celie asks God for signs to prove that he is listening, but she receives nothing. Taking all these factors into consideration, the opening words of the excerpt—"Dear God"—can be used as a starting point for a variety of approaches to writing on *The Color Purple*.

The form of the novel is distinct. An epistolary novel is one that is written in the form of a series of letters exchanged among characters. This use of letters permits the author to present the viewpoint of multiple characters, and the multiple first-person voices give an immediacy to the characters' experiences, which is diminished when a third-person omniscient narrator mediates a narrative. An essay could analyze how the epistolary form of this novel helps Walker convey themes and ideas or develop characterization. For example, an essay could relate the epistolary form of the novel to the themes of finding one's voice and speaking out. The first line of the novel is a warning to Celie from her stepfather, who has raped her and impregnated her, to *"never tell nobody but God."* How are Celie's letters a response to this command to be silent? Later in the novel, Celie addresses her letters to her sister, Nettie. How does this shift in addressee mirror the psychological and intellectual growth that Celie is undergoing? How does Celie's language differ in the later letters from the earlier ones? How has she changed, and what has prompted her transformation?

The excerpt touches on several ideas and themes whose analysis could form the basis of a paper. Since Celie's letters are addressed to God, the novel engages the idea of religious belief. Even though Celie is convinced that her remote, authoritative God is deaf to her prayers, she also admits that she finds it hard to dispense with God totally. Shug steers her toward seeing God in a pantheistic way whereby God is immanent in all creation and all creation is interconnected. How the characters' religious beliefs influence the way they live their lives could become an essay topic. The excerpt describes Harpo's violence to Celie on her wedding day. His own mother had been murdered, and he had held her in his arms as she died. Violence, particularly toward women and children, is commonplace in the novel's world. You could think about the different types of violence presented in the novel. What is Walker's didactic intent in including graphic details of rape, murder, and domestic abuse? How does the novel propose that the problem of violence could be managed?

The excerpt explains that, at this point in her life, Celie responds to Mr. _____'s sexual use of her by drifting away in her imagination. Her thoughts of Nettie are replaced by sexualized fantasies of Shug. Betrayed and exploited by men all her life, Celie turns to women for support and love. One of Walker's goals in the novel is to promote the importance of women's solidarity, and this notion readily presents itself as a potential essay topic. With the support of a strong network of friends and family, the women are able to find self-fulfillment and acquire a sense of worth. Celie and Shug take this bond a step further by becoming lovers. A paper could analyze Celie and other female characters as womanists. Walker defined the word *womanist* in her essay collection *In Search of Our Mothers' Gardens* as someone who "appreciates and prefers women's culture" and who "loves other women, sexually and/or non-sexually." How does Walker use the novel as a vehicle for her womanist ideals?

Although Celie's English is nonstandard, she is forthcoming in revealing her feelings and unguarded in retelling the events of her life. As a result of this style, the novel might appear to be an easy read at first glance, despite Celie's broken syntax and unconventional spelling. However, as the excerpt exemplifies, a lot can transpire in just a few lines of the narrative. Furthermore, there are aspects of her life that Celie does not mention, such as the world beyond her horizon or how much time elapses between each writing of a letter. When preparing to write on this novel, a careful read is needed to avoid missing critical details and to fill in the gaps in her story.

## TOPICS AND STRATEGIES

The ideas suggested in the remainder of this chapter will propose a variety of essay topics on *The Color Purple*. These suggestions should be used as a starting point to aid you in generating your own innovative approaches to each topic.

### Themes

*The Color Purple* depicts a cruel, violent world where women and children are routinely beaten and exploited. Walker illustrates violence's many faces through multiple accounts of rape, wife-beating, and murder. Yet within this violent milieu, characters still yearn for, and find, love. Love, too, has many different faces in this novel. Some men love their wives, some parents love their children, and some friends and family come to love each other. Love is a healing force within the psychologically damaged community that Walker presents. By coming together in love, Celie's extended family becomes stronger, providing a healthier environment in which to raise children. Through love, understanding, and forgiveness, Walker suggests that the cycles of violence, in which some families are trapped, can be broken. Breaking free from cycles of violence allows both women and men the chance to find self-fulfillment. Although *The Color Purple*'s black community cannot elude the racist aggression that they suffer at the hands of the white population, family support and love can help lessen its impact on each individual. At the end of the novel, Albert observes that the more he opens himself to loving other people, the more other people love him back. As a result of his revised perspective on human relationships, Albert and Celie are able to speak to each other with honesty. They are not the only characters to find their true voice. Celie is transformed when she finds the courage to speak out because she is finally able to defend herself against oppression and exploitation. Mary Agnes asserts herself, too, and makes her needs known after years of timidity. Only Shug and Sofia consistently refuse to be silent and downtrodden by the sexist, racist society in which they live. Love, cruelty, violence, oppression, exploitation, domestic abuse, child abuse, family, marriage, male-female relationships: These are just some of the many themes that *The Color Purple* takes a controversial look at and which could become the focus of an essay.

### Sample Topics:

1. **Violence and cruelty:** Why are characters violent and cruel in the novel? What are the physical and mental effects on characters of acts of violence and cruelty? How does the novel judge the violent and the cruel?

   This essay could focus on either the violent or the victims of violence or both. You might want to consider how Walker shows violence to be perpetuated within families or the link she makes between family violence and violence in society more generally (particularly in terms of violent acts carried out in the context of racism). A thesis could also be developed that takes into account the novel's suggested remedies for violence.

2. **Love:** What social and personal factors interfere in the expression of love between characters? How does Walker demonstrate the power of love in the novel?

A possible approach to the theme of love is to analyze the different types of love that the novel presents and show the power love has to transform lives. The novel includes examples of love between husband and wives, between sisters, and between women, and this love is a driving force in making characters behave the way they do. Walker also moves toward an idea of universal love at the end of the novel. How is Celie able to feel universal love, and what is the effect of that on her and on others?

3. **Family:** In what ways does *The Color Purple* portray a negative image of the family unit? Conversely, Walker shows that the family can become a source of support and comfort. How?

Such an essay would start by looking at the specific family relationships in the novel. Some relationships provide characters with a reason to endure life's pain. For example, Celie's and Nettie's love for each other sustains both characters at difficult times in their lives. Walker depicts other relationships, particularly between husbands and wives and between parents and children, as sources of absolute misery and suffering. An essay could evaluate Walker's purpose in portraying the family unit in a negative light. Alternatively, a paper could focus on a specific type of family connection, such as husband and wife or sisters. These papers would analyze Walker's representation of marriage and sibling relationships respectively.

4. **Finding one's voice:** Which characters in *The Color Purple* have been compelled to be silent or felt compelled to speak out? What personality traits and attitudes determine whether a character will be silent or speak his or her truth?

This topic could be approached by analyzing certain characters' movement from silence to speech. What social and personal forces govern whether a character will be silent or self-assertive? What role does gender play in whether a character finds the will to speak his or her true thoughts? An angle that could be pursued is how the themes of silence and speaking out (for both black women and black men) are affected by the historical and social context.

## Character

In Walker's essay "Writing *The Color Purple*" in *In Search of Our Mothers' Gardens,* the author describes her characters as living spirits who demanded a pleasing location and silence in order for them to tell her their stories. Reading this essay will give you a good sense of how Walker viewed her vibrant and divergent cast of characters; she describes herself as their medium rather than their creator.

Many of *The Color Purple*'s characters are sufficiently dynamic and three dimensional that they provide ample material for an essay analyzing their development. Celie starts the novel as a reticent and abused child who blossoms through Shug's love into a self-assertive, successful businesswoman. Shug's presence is felt in the novel before she officially makes an appearance when Celie finds a photograph of her, which she treasures. When Mr. _____ brings Shug to their house, Shug ultimately responds to Celie's kindness and devotion. Despite her wild past and her affair with a boy less than half her age, Shug eventually settles down in the country with Celie. Mr. _____ transforms himself into Albert. Initially, he is a man so brutal and uncaring that only his constant love for Shug might salvage him slightly from readers' utter contempt. Through life experience, Mr. _____ becomes self-aware. Instead of being portrayed as a generic angry, aggressive, lazy bully, the novel shows how he becomes a man who earns love from other characters apart from Shug. Sofia enters the novel brash and confident. She refuses to be browbeaten by her husband's need to control her. Crushed by a racist encounter that leads to her imprisonment and then years of enforced domestic labor, Sofia stands strong and resilient once again in the final pages of the novel. These four characters could be written about using different approaches, and they could also be compared with one another and with other secondary characters. See the "Compare and Contrast" section for suggestions on comparative topics.

## Sample Topics:

1. **Celie's growth:** How does Celie develop over the course of the novel? What and who helps her to assert herself?

   To create a thesis on the topic of Celie's growth in awareness and self-assertion, the essay writer must determine the exact nature of Celie's change and what prompts it. Evidence for this can be found by comparing and contrasting how Celie responds to other characters at the start of the novel when she is young with how she deals with the same characters later in her life. Although she has obviously aged and had many experiences that have helped educate her, how does the changing social and historical context facilitate Celie's development?

2. **From Mr. _____ to Albert:** What events in this character's life cause him to transform himself from a nameless bully into a sensitive man capable of love and empathy?

   Similar to an essay on Celie, this paper is likely to look at the events and other characters who help Albert develop in terms of his behavior and attitudes. There are marked differences between Mr. _____ and the Albert who appears at the end of the novel, sewing with Celie on the porch. Why is Celie able to reconnect with her former brutish husband as a friend? What has Albert learned about himself as a man?

3. **Everybody's sugar—Shug:** Which of Shug's characteristics cause Celie and Albert to find her very attractive? How does she serve as a stimulus for change in Celie's and Albert's lives?

Shug educates Celie in many ways, both sexually and intellectually. Albert spends his entire life loving Shug but does not have the strength of character necessary to keep her with him. An essay on Shug could look at her function in the novel as a catalyst for love and transformation. How does Walker achieve sympathy for Shug despite her wild and sometimes mean behavior? How does the social and historical context of the early parts of the novel contribute to our judgment of Shug? Another approach to an essay on Shug could evaluate her as a symbol of resistance to traditional gender roles.

4. **Strong Sofia:** How and why does Sofia stand up for what she believes is right? How does Sofia contribute to other characters' growth in awareness?

Sofia's outspokenness and her preparedness to fight back against injustice and oppression are admirable qualities, but they bring her a lot of concomitant grief and suffering. An essay on Sofia could analyze her dominant character traits and show how they lead to positive and negative consequences in her life. How does she differ from other female characters in the novel in her attitudes and the choices she makes? How do the other characters respond to her? What is the significance of her relationship with Eleanor Jane to some of the novel's themes? The meaning of the name Sofia is wisdom. How is Sofia a source of wisdom for other characters?

## History and Context

How does Walker portray Africa? The stamp on Nettie's letter has a picture of Queen Victoria, "peanuts, coconuts, rubber trees and say[s] Africa"? Why does the stamp not read "Nigeria" or "Senegal"? The West has always inclined toward a homogenization of Africa, rather than acknowledging the specificity of each country and each country's diverse populations. Why does Nettie say that she has lessons in the "Olinka dialect"? African languages are repeatedly referred to as dialects in the Western media, but a dialect is a variation of a standard version of a language. What is "Olinka" a dialect of? Popular western images of Africa assume that all Africans live in thatched huts in rural areas; bustling African cities with their skyscrapers, malls, and cars are conveniently overlooked. Although Walker refers to Africa's colonial history through the allusion to Queen Victoria, Nettie does not question Corrine and Samuel's right as missionaries to go to Africa and impose their Christian views on the populace. Does it make a difference that Corrine and Samuel are African American and not white? Nettie is surprised that the Senegalese are not concerned with "the uplift of black people everywhere." The market traders are only interested in making a sale, and if there is no sale, there is no common purpose between African and African American. African-American attitudes toward Africa vary and shift over time; nonetheless, the goal of refuting white people's widespread belief that people of African descent are inferior to people of European descent has been constant. As Nettie travels to Africa, passing through New York and England, how do the different people she encounters add to the picture of Africa as either an inferior continent or as a place horribly misrepresented by the West? Does Walker compound the West's distorted representation of Africa (perhaps despite positive intentions), or is her mission to correct the West's misperception successful? As with *Possessing the Secret of Joy*, there is textual evidence that can be advanced both to criticize and defend Walker's representation of Africa.

In much of her work, Walker assigns the American South both positive and negative values. As a southern writer, Walker is able to draw on her lived experience of being raised in a sharecropper family in rural Georgia. She has firsthand knowledge of the daily toil involved in working the land and of the constant, violent brushes with white southern racism. Her thoughts on her southern heritage are explained in the essay "The Black Writer and the Southern Experience," which can be found in the anthology *In Search of Our Mothers' Gardens*. Another helpful essay on the South from the same anthology is "Coretta King: Revisited." These two essays should give you an understanding of the ambivalence that vexes Walker when writing about the South.

Alice Walker advocated womanism in *In Search of Our Mothers' Garden* as a tool to communicate the interests of black women and women of color. Targets of racism and sexism, black women had concerns that white feminism and the Civil Rights movement neglected. As Mr. _____ revels in telling Celie, "You black, you pore, you ugly, you a woman.

Goddam, he say, you nothing at all." Celie is perceived as being at the bottom of the social hierarchy because of her color, her gender, and her class. In the definitions of womanism included in the opening pages of *In Search of Our Mothers' Gardens,* Walker writes that "Womanist is to feminist as purple is to lavender." Thus, black women's feminism is associated with the color purple. (See the "Language, Symbol, and Imagery" section for more information on the color purple's symbolism.) How does Celie come to claim the color purple, or a womanist position, for herself?

## Sample Topics:

1. **Visions of Africa:** How does Walker offer a positive presentation of Africa and Africans? What aspects of the novel's depiction of Africa could provide evidence to accuse Walker of misrepresenting Africa?

   An essay on this topic would be evaluative, aiming to determine whether Walker's fictional construction of Olinka is tainted by Western assumptions on Africa or whether it redresses the West's repeated distorted representations of the continent and its people. How does she depict the relationships between the African characters and African Americans? What is the novel's position on colonialism and white involvement in Africa? To what purpose does Walker include the story about the white missionary (who Nettie eventually meets)? Essay writers on this topic might adopt a variety of different stances on this topic after examining the textual evidence of Walker's representation of Africa.

2. **The South:** In what ways does Walker show rural life in the South to be extremely difficult for both black women and black men? What are the positive aspects of southern life for Walker's black characters? How does the novel offer hope for change in the South?

   Walker's southern landscape is racist, violent, and oppressive. By the end of the novel, the characters are fighting back and have formed a community that can help its members with their struggles. An essay analyzing Walker's representation of the South could reflect on its conflicting features. How can a place be perceived as a home that offers a supportive community, yet many of the characters feel compelled to move away? What aspects of black southern life does Walker validate in the novel? Why do Celie and Shug move back home? How do the secondary characters, particularly Eleanor Jane and her baby son, shed light on Walker's judgment of the white southern mentality?

3. *The Color Purple* **as a womanist novel:** How does Walker show the effects of sexism on the black female characters when they interact with both black and white males? How does Celie come to espouse womanist ideas, and how are they reproduced in her behavior and actions?

An essay drawing on Walker's womanist philosophy will need to have a grasp of black feminist theory. First, you should read the definitions of *womanism* that can be found at the start of the essay collection *In Search of Our Mothers' Gardens: Womanist Prose.* Second, you will find reading a book on black feminist theory helpful. You will likely find an appropriate text, such as *Black Feminist Thought: Knowledge, Consciousness, and the Politics of Empowerment* by Patricia Hill Collins or Barbara Christian's *Black Feminist Criticism: Perspectives on Black Women Writers,* in your library. With an understanding of the meaning and goals of womanism, you could identify and analyze womanist concerns that Walker touches on in *The Color Purple.* For example, an exploration of how Celie and other female characters recast their relationships with the male characters and claim their power as black women is viable.

## Philosophy and Ideas

Since Walker makes black women's interests a primary focus in much of her work, thinking about gender is a logical place to start when trying to devise an essay topic for *The Color Purple.* Most societies around the world have expectations about the way men and women should behave. Failure to conform to these expectations can lead to a person being judged as aberrant or deficient. Popular explications of gender define women as weak, dependent, and sexually passive, whereas men are strong, independent, and sexually driven. In this schema, a strong, assertive woman is an anomaly, as is a man ridden with doubt or a desire to engage in domestic activities. Many of the characters in *The Color Purple* challenge traditional views of gender; however, there can be repercussions for their lack of conformity. For example, Shug's decisions to fulfill her sexual needs cause her society to label her a "loose woman." There is an imagined correlation between a woman's sexual behavior and her overall value as a woman. A man who cannot control his wife, such as Harpo, is deemed to be lacking masculinity. Women who reject standard models of femininity and men who do not conform to society's standards for masculinity find themselves marginalized from their society. Although *The Color Purple* shows that there can be negative consequences for those who defy traditional gender roles, the novel argues that behaving contrary to one's true nature is also detrimental to individual happiness and fulfillment. Society, however, will insist on conformity and, in the case of women, solidarity is crucial in order for society's pressures to be withstood. By the end of the novel, all the main female characters have stopped undermining one another, realizing that antagonism and jealousy only allow men and society to have power over their lives. The way that female characters, such as Celie, interact with men and society is often linked to their perceptions of God and religion. At the start of the novel, Celie sees God as a distant, disinterested white man. Her later adjusted understanding of God aids in the overhaul of her interpersonal relationships and her manner of conducting herself in society. Another facet of Celie's growth is the education she receives from Shug and Nettie. They broaden her knowledge in areas such as sexuality, geography, history, and religion. Women in this time period were often uneducated. As Nettie explains in one of her letters to Celie, the Olinka do not want girls educated by the missionaries because no man wants a wife who knows as much he does. Undoubtedly, a formal or informal education can be a catalyst in helping women break free of the traditional gender roles that curtail their freedom and choices.

## Sample Topics:

1. **Gender roles:** How does *The Color Purple* challenge traditional definitions of femininity and masculinity? According to the novel, what are the consequences of both challenging, and not challenging, stifling gender roles?

   This topic could either focus on just the male characters, or just the female characters, or make a comparison of male and female characters. An essay could examine not only how some of the characters defy society's expectations for them as women or men, but also the consequences on those characters who choose not to conform. How does conformity to traditional gender roles limit Mr. _____, Harpo, Celie, or Squeak? How does disruption of socially imposed gender roles affect Sofia and Shug?

2. **Female solidarity:** Why and how does the novel show female friendship and support as essential to women's well-being? What situations and emotions undermine women's solidarity at the start of the novel?

   By supporting one another, the female characters find the strength to stand up to the men who try to control, exploit, and oppress them. An essay on this topic could analyze specific characters' growth in awareness about the benefits of women's cohesion. For example, how does Squeak put aside her jealousy of Sofia and start to support her? Alternatively, a paper could look at the moments where the women are united. During these moments, how do the men respond to the women's unity, and what are the women able to achieve through their unanimity? How important is the sisterly bond in the novel?

3. **Religion and God:** The way a character views God is reflected in the way they act in the world and in the way they view their own agency. How is Celie's interaction with Mr. _____ indicative of the way she perceives God at any given time? How does Shug's perception of God carry over into the way she conducts herself?

An essay on this topic might link certain characters' perception of the divine to their sense of identity and self-worth. Why does Celie initially address her letters to God? What life events cause her to reject God as the recipient of her letters? Another approach to this topic could look at the role of religion in wider society as shown in *The Color Purple*. How do religious beliefs, whether Christian or otherwise, affect the Olinkan people and their traditional way of life? What does Nettie suggest have been the effects of Christian (whether European or American) missionaries in Africa?

4. **Education and learning:** Toward the end of the novel, Sofia observes that, "Everybody learn something in life." What do the different characters learn, and from where or whom do they get their education?

A feasible approach to this topic could look at the Olinka and the rural community of Georgia and determine how access to education (or lack thereof) is used to reinforce social inequities and to control segments of the population. Another approach might consider what different characters end up learning despite a lack of formal education. What ways can characters acquire an education? What does Walker's novel suggest can happen on an individual and social level when people become educated (whether that education is formal or informal)?

## Form and Genre

In the essay, "Writing *The Color Purple*," Walker asserts that she "knew *The Color Purple* would be a historical novel." She then goes on to note the differences between what a man might imagine as a historical novel versus her woman's definition. A male historical novel deals with wars over land or the lives of "Great Men," whereas her woman's history starts with "one woman asking another for her underwear." However, if a historical novel is defined as one in which the action is set during a specific period (earlier than that of the time of writing of the novel) and where the behavior and mentality of that period are reproduced accurately, then *The Color Purple* can be seen as a historical novel. Furthermore, a historical novel will often dwell on the conflicts that arise at an individual level because of the historical and social events that are happening "offstage" that are shaping characters' lives. *The Color Purple* describes the American South during the first half of the 20th century at a time when the South was still segregated and women were extremely limited in the choices they could make for their lives. However, Walker barely mentions the events that mainstream society would consider of supreme importance for this period, such as war or colonial conquest. Although some social and world phenomena and events are alluded to if they touch on Celie's or Nettie's lives, they are not at the forefront of the narrative.

The novel's lack of traditional history is explainable because the story is told through private letters. How would an uneducated, isolated black woman gain access to knowledge and information about the wider world? Celie's world only starts to expand once she meets Shug and once she starts reading Nettie's letters. An epistolary novel is one written in the form of a series of letters exchanged among characters. If letters from more than one character are used, the epistolary form can be undermined if an author does not differentiate the style and tone of the different characters' letters. In *The Color Purple*, Walker solved this problem by having Celie's letters written in a dialect appropriate for an uneducated, rural, black southern girl, whereas Nettie's access to a greater level of education is reflected in her use of a standard English that can employ a more sophisticated vocabulary and syntax.

Walker's creation of Celie's unique voice resonated with readers, and the novel's popularity led to Steven Spielberg directing a film version of it in 1985. The film version starred Whoopi Goldberg as Celie, Danny Glover as Albert, and Oprah Winfrey as Sofia. In order to appeal to mainstream audiences, aspects of the novel were glossed over. For example, Celie and Shug's sexual relationship is barely hinted at, since portrayals of lesbianism were not the norm in film in the 1980s. As Spielberg is a white, Jewish male who had not lived in the South, some critics felt that he was an unsuitable choice for director. He was condemned for having re-created a rather romantic representation of the South and for having shied away from showing its harsh realities. However, despite the mixed reviews, the movie made money and is still considered successful. *The Color Purple*'s ongoing popularity is shown by the musical version of the story that was brought to Broadway in 2005.

*Sample Topics:*

1. **The Color Purple as a historical novel:** In what ways is the setting of the novel a crucial foundation for Walker's thematic goals? Why is it significant that Walker deliberately sidelines mainstream historical events in her novel?

   An essay on the use and function of setting in *The Color Purple* could start by identifying the different historical events that Walker mentions. Why does she incorporate these particular events? In addition, she uses the southern mentality of the early 20th century as a backdrop that sheds light on many events that happen in the lives of her rural black characters. How does Walker challenge traditional understandings of history in the novel and why does she do this?

2. **The Color Purple as an epistolary novel:** How does the letter form of the novel enhance Walker's themes? How does Walker use the changing recipients of the letters to show character development?

   The epistolary form is not a commonly used novel form; however, it served Walker's goals for her novel very effectively. An essay could evaluate how the form of the novel is used by Walker to reinforce certain themes, amplify character traits, and reveal character development. The epistolary form could also be analyzed in conjunction with the novel's use of history. Since the letters are not dated, the passing of time becomes quite hard to pinpoint. Nonetheless, around 40 years elapse from the start to the finish of the novel. How does the epistolary form support Walker's beliefs about history? How can an uneducated girl's letters provide an alternative source of history?

3. **The film compared to the novel:** What are the critical differences between the film version and the novel? How do these differences undermine the novel's thematic intent? Why do you think the movie version made these changes?

Since the film version of *The Color Purple* has been successful, it must have something that appeals to audiences even if
it discarded some of the original foci of the novel. An essay
could compare and contrast the film version with the novel.
Remember though that you must construct a thesis that provides a purpose for the comparison, rather than simply listing
all the differences between the two versions.

## Language, Symbols, and Imagery

According to the essay "Writing *The Color Purple*," Walker was working
on a quilt at the same time she was writing the novel. Consequently, it
comes as no surprise that characters such as Celie and Sofia spend time
together sewing a quilt. Sewing, in *The Color Purple*, can be a communal or an individual activity; however, even when done individually, a
character can sew while in the company of others. Individual or communal, sewing is deemed to be a woman's activity. Thus, when Albert
starts sewing with Celie on his porch, it signifies a radical shift in his
attitude toward women and himself. Celie discovers that she has talent
for sewing and starts making pants for herself and Shug. The pants' prac-
ticality and aesthetic designs soon attract other customers. Before long,
Celie has a thriving business sewing pants. Although sewing and quilting can have simply utilitarian functions, many women, such as Celie,
express their creative proclivities through their sewing. This creativity
has limited other outlets within such women's daily lives of child-rearing, housework, and working on the land.

Celie's ability to find a sense of self-worth, partly through sewing,
is symbolized by her attainment of the color purple. At the start of the
story, when Mr. _____'s sister takes Celie to buy a new dress, they fail to
find the color purple among the possible fabrics. When Shug instructs
Celie in her view of God, she asserts that God is annoyed when people
fail to notice the color purple in a field. In the house where she settles
down with Shug, Celie finally decorates her room in purple and red.
Albert even gives Celie a carved purple frog. Celie's attainment of the
color purple is tied to Walker's definition of black feminism (womanism),
when she writes in *In Search of Our Mothers' Gardens* that "Womanist
is to feminist as purple to lavender." The importance of the color purple
to Celie is comparable to the importance of roofleaf to the Olinka. The

Olinka villagers have a ceremony documenting the loss and reattainment of roofleaf. The Olinka associate roofleaf with balance and harmony within their own community and with their environment. Loss of that balance can be hazardous. However, the harmonious way of life has been destabilized by greedy people in the past and in the time when Nettie is living with them. Sewing, pants, the color purple, and roofleaf are four significant symbols whose analysis could become the foundation of various essays.

## Sample Topics:

1. **Sewing and quilting:** What are the functions of sewing and quilting in the rural Georgia community that Walker depicts? What does the making of a quilt symbolize? Why is it significant that Albert learns to enjoy sewing?

   A quilt is constructed out of different types of fabric, which sewn together creatively can produce something useful and beautiful. Often the fabric pieces are chosen for the memories and associations they evoke. Why does Sofia propose to Celie that they make a quilt together? Given that the two women, and sometimes Shug, spend much time together working on this quilt, what does the sewing of this quilt symbolize? An essay could consider how the symbolic significance of quilting enhances some of the main themes and ideas of the novel. This topic could be extended to analyze the importance of all types of sewing and why sewing is so symbolically important to women, women's community, and interpersonal relationships.

2. **Pants:** How does pant-making contribute to Celie's development and self-assertion?

   Although the sewing of pants could be incorporated into one of the essay topics suggested above, pants have a special importance to Celie that could make them the focus of an essay in their own right. Why is it thematically important that although pant-making starts out as Celie's hobby, it turns into a money-making venture? Why is it significant, given the time period, that Celie starts making pants for women?

3. **The color purple:** Why did Walker give her novel the title *The Color Purple*? Why is the color purple so important to Celie?

If you want to write on the color purple, you could start by thinking of the associations that mainstream society has traditionally given to the color purple. Purple is the color associated with royalty. Bruises might be described as purple. An essay exploring the multiple meanings of the color purple probably should not overlook Walker's claiming of the color purple as the color symbolizing black feminism.

4. **Roofleaf:** What does the presence or absence of roofleaf signify to the Olinka? Why do the Olinka accord divine status to roofleaf?

A paper on the symbolism of roofleaf could address it in the context of the novel's linking of nature to divinity. Another approach could discuss the symbolism of roofleaf in the broader context of an analysis of the symbolism of trees. Why does Celie think of herself as a tree? What other meanings does Walker assign to trees later in the novel? For example, think about all the flowering trees Shug and Celie notice when they return together to Celie's former home. The topic of trees could be extended even further to think about how other flowers and plants are given significance in the novel.

## Compare and Contrast Essays

An essay that compares and contrasts characters is a place you might begin if faced with the task of writing a comparative paper. *The Color Purple* has several characters who have obvious similarities. For example, how does Shug compare to Sofia? They are both strong and unconventional women who, however, challenge societal norms in completely different ways. The female characters in general could provide material for an essay, and they could be compared using a variety of aspects.

For example, their respective attitudes toward men or sexuality, their respective attempts to find their voice within their families and within society, and their respective behavior toward other women could all be ways that Shug, Sofia, Squeak, and Celie could be compared. Alternatively, specific types of relationships could be examined, such as mother-daughter relationships or the bond of sisters. The male characters could be approached in a similar way. How does Mr. _____ compare to Harpo? What message is Walker trying to convey through the character parallels she establishes between Albert and Harpo? With a comparative essay, it is essential to go beyond simply detailing the similarities and differences between two or more characters. You need to prove the significance of the comparisons you draw.

In *The Color Purple,* there are also elements of the plot that could be compared. After Celie finds Nettie's letters, the novel splits into two parallel plots. The main plot still follows Celie's life and transformation; the secondary plot provides details of Nettie's difficult times with the Olinka in Africa. When an author includes a subplot in this way, its purpose is usually to elucidate events in the main plot. An essay centered on Celie and Nettie could compare and contrast the twists and turns in their respective lives. A thesis comparing Celie's plot with Nettie's plot would want to determine what Walker's purpose was in making the two sisters' journeys have so many elements in common.

## Sample Topics:

1. **Comparing the female characters:** How does Shug compare to Sofia? How does Squeak compare to Celie? How does Sofia compare to Squeak? How does Celie compare to Sofia? How does Sofia compare to Eleanor Jane? How do different mother-daughter relationships in the novel compare?

   There are many possible permutations that an essay comparing female characters could choose from. Your choice of characters will depend on the purpose of your paper. For example, if you choose to compare attitudes toward sexuality, Shug and Celie would be possible choices. An essay comparing women's attitudes toward gender roles could focus on Shug and Celie or

Squeak and Sofia. The different types of relationships between women could be compared. How do the different women raise their children? Why does Walker include so many different mother-daughter pairs in the novel? This topic could be extended to include appraisal of other black womanist texts, such as *I Know Why the Caged Bird Sings* by Maya Angelou or *Beloved* by Toni Morrison. How does Celie's life compare and contrast with the female protagonists of these texts?

2. **Comparing the male characters:** How does Albert compare to Harpo? How do some of the secondary male characters compare to one another?

Walker has often been criticized for her portrayals of black men. Many of her black male characters are shown to be abusive sexual exploiters and bullies. *The Color Purple*'s male characters were condemned by critics who felt that Albert and Harpo contributed to the negative image of black men perpetuated in mainstream media. How could Walker's depiction of Harpo and Albert be defended from these charges? An essay could compare and contrast these two men's growth in awareness and their changing attitudes and behavior. Another way to approach the male characters would be to compare some of the secondary characters such as Grady, Samuel, or Jack with the purpose of illustrating Walker's condemnation or endorsement of certain types of masculinities.

3. **Celie's plot and Nettie's plot:** What are different areas of overlap between the two plots? What is the point of Nettie's subplot in the novel?

Both Celie and Nettie are forced away from home and find themselves in difficult situations to which they must adjust. Both sisters struggle to survive in a triangle of two women and one man, raising another woman's children. What other parallels are there between the two plots? An essay could examine the two plots' similarities and differences.

## Bibliography and Online Sources

Abbandonato, Linda. "Rewriting the Heroine's Story in *The Color Purple.*" *Alice Walker: Critical Perspectives Past and Present.* Eds. Henry Louis Gates, Jr. and K. A. Appiah. New York: Amistad, 1993. 296–308.

*Anniina's Alice Walker Page.* December 30, 2007. <http://www.luminarium.org/contemporary/alicew.htm>.

Berlant, Lauren. "Race, Gender, and Nation in *The Color Purple.*" *Alice Walker: Critical Perspectives Past and Present.* Eds. Henry Louis Gates, Jr. and K. A. Appiah. New York: Amistad, 1993. 211–238.

Christian, Barbara. "Alice Walker: The Black Woman Artist as Wayward." *Black Feminist Criticism: Perspectives on Black Women Writers.* Ed. Barbara Christian. New York: Pergamon, 1985. 80–101.

Collins, Patricia Hill. *Black Feminist Thought: Knowledge, Consciousness, and the Politics of Empowerment.* Boston: Unwin Hyman, 1990.

Dieke, Ikenna, ed. *Critical Essays on Alice Walker.* Westport, CT: Greenwood, 1999.

Henderson, Mae G. "*The Color Purple:* Revisions and Redefinitions." *Alice Walker: Modern Critical Views.* Ed. Harold Bloom. New York: Chelsea House, 1989. 67–80.

hooks, bell. "Reading and Resistance: *The Color Purple.*" *Alice Walker: Critical Perspectives Past and Present.* Eds. Henry Louis Gates, Jr. and K. A. Appiah. New York: Amistad, 1993. 284–295.

———. "Writing the Subject: Reading *The Color Purple.*" *Alice Walker: Modern Critical Views.* Ed. Harold Bloom. New York: Chelsea House, 1989. 215–228.

Katz, Tamar. "'show Me How to Do Like You': Didacticism and Epistolary Form in *The Color Purple.*" *Alice Walker: Modern Critical Views.* Ed. Harold Bloom. New York: Chelsea House, 1989. 185–194.

Lauret, Maria. "The Color Purple." *Modern Novelists: Alice Walker.* New York: St. Martin's, 2000. 90–120.

Simcikova, Karla. *To Live Fully, Here and Now: The Healing Vision in the Works of Alice Walker.* Lanham, MD: Lexington, 2007.

———. "Coretta King: Revisited." *In Search of Our Mother's Gardens: Womanist Prose.* London: Women's Press, 1983. 146–157.

———. "The Black Writer and the Southern Experience." *In Search of Our Mother's Gardens: Womanist Prose.* London: Women's Press, 1983. 15–21.

Walker, Alice. *The Same River Twice: Honoring the Difficult : A Meditation on Life, Spirit, Art, and the Making of the Film, The Color Purple, Ten Years Later.* New York: Scribner, 1996.

———. "Writing *The Color Purple.*" *In Search of Our Mothers' Gardens: Womanist Prose.* London: Women's Press, 1983. 355–360.

Wall, Cheryl A. *Worrying the Line: Black Women Writers, Lineage, and Literary Tradition.* Chapel Hill: U of North Carolina P, 2005.

Winchell, Donna Haisty. "Letters to God: *The Color Purple.*" *Alice Walker.* New York: Twayne, 1992. 85–99.

# THE TEMPLE OF
# MY FAMILIAR

## READING TO WRITE

A S ROCK star Arveyda starts to sing to Carlotta, the wife he has betrayed, he has a flash of insight into the role of the musician: to unite people through song. From this perspective, art can occasion redemption and atonement, transforming both artist and audience. Arveyda's song takes on a shamanic flavor as he strives to heal both Carlotta and himself. A shaman draws on unique knowledge of cosmic power and the spirit world to assist healing. Often, the shaman uses specific objects to help communicate wisdom from the spirit world. Before he starts to sing, Arveyda instructs Carlotta to bring three sacred stones that were entrusted to her safekeeping by her mother. Although she is ignorant of the stones' history, they provide a bridge to her ancestors in South America. Through the power of the stones and his song, Arveyda connects the past and the present, unites mother, father, and child, and blurs the boundaries of time and space:

> He sang of the red parrot feathers in their ears—for they had brought the parrot with them; it was their familiar, symbolic of their essence—and the long rough hair that made a pillow for their heads. He sang of the coming of the enslavers and the cruel fate of the enslaved. He sang of two people who loved for a moment and of one of them who died, horribly, with nothing to leave behind but his seed that became a child, and some red parrot-feather earrings and three insignificant stones. He sang of the confusion and the terror of the mother: the scars she could never reveal to the child because they still hurt her so.

Arveyda and Carlotta would make interesting characters for analysis. Other characters are drawn to Arveyda because of his spirituality; however, Arveyda needs to heal himself even though his music is a healing force for other people. His troubled childhood in Indiana has left him searching for a sense of identity and belonging. In the course of that search for meaning, he devastates Carlotta by leaving her for Zedé, her own mother. Carlotta strives to overcome this betrayal, and Arveyda's song is a first step to try and salve the pain that has overwhelmed her since the infidelity. A possible topic that emerges from this is to argue for the power of creative expression. Although Arveyda is a highly successful musician and his particular art form is song, the novel shows how creative expression in any of its forms (for example, writing, music, or painting) permits the artist to experience the joy of the act of creation.

Arveyda's song recounts Carlotta's personal history. For the first time, she learns of her father, Jesús, and how he risked his life to protect the sacred stones in the village. She also hears about her mother's brutal tale of captivity and her father's murder after the captors discover her mother's love for him. One feature of this story that is essential to Carlotta's healing is the reconnection to the past through memory. As the passage hints, the breach between mother and daughter has been exacerbated by Zedé's reluctance to talk about her past. However, trying to avoid distressing memories by not talking about them does not stop pain. Worse, the pain gets passed on to the next generation if the trauma is not addressed. *The Temple of My Familiar* explores the notion of memory and the role memories could have in aiding in the construction of both individual and collective histories. The novel proposes that memories could constitute one strand of an alternative history for all the people who have been dispossessed by mainstream versions of history. *The Temple of My Familiar* is concerned with rewriting history to include the voices of all formerly marginalized peoples. An essay could address the importance of memory or the different sources of knowledge about the past that could be used to produce an inclusive history.

*The Temple of My Familiar* is a novel of ideas. In a novel of ideas, characters debate the pros and cons of moral, ethical, or intellectual issues; characterization and plot are subordinated to the ideas under debate. Even though the characters come and go and even though it would be a challenge to summarize the plot of the novel, Walker weaves in unifying threads to substantiate the text's primary focus: the interconnectedness of all components of the universe. The passage, for example, mentions "red parrot-feather ear-rings." Throughout the novel, many of the characters demonstrate a bond with a particular animal, bird, or reptile. Red parrot feathers symbolize the mythological origins of Carlotta's father's ancestors from the continent of Zuma who brought the parrot to the village where Jesús was later born. An essay could inquire into the significance of specific animals or birds to individual characters. Similarly, many of the characters are distinguished by affinity with a certain color. An essay could look at the usage, function, and meanings of color throughout the novel. Apart from the parrot feathers, the color red is mentioned in other unusual contexts, such as Olivia's wedding. To facilitate writing about *The Temple of My Familiar*, you could find other unifying symbols, motifs, and images and see how Walker applies them throughout the novel.

Despite the novel's emphasis on ideas, the characters are still important because they function as windows onto those ideas. Analysis of each character's disposition, behavior, and relationships will be helpful in grasping the fundamental concerns of the novel. Each character can be handled as the mouthpiece of a key idea or concept, but he or she can also become the subject of a traditional character study. Since *The Temple of My Familiar* incorporates a broad range of characters, analyzing character will provide many possible essay topics.

## TOPICS AND STRATEGIES

The remainder of this chapter will focus on possible topics for essays on *The Temple of My Familiar* and different approaches that could be deployed in writing about those topics. Remember that the topics are suggestions and should be used as prompts to aid you in creating your own original papers.

### Themes

The novel deals with a multitude of themes that are concerned with the way humans relate to one another. Walker's depiction of human relationships shows egregious mistreatment, neglect, and exploitation as key factors that sabotage successful interaction. People do not take time with one another to find out what anyone thinks or feels. Everyone is searching to fulfill their own desires and needs, and emotions are often repressed or unacknowledged. In the case of Zedé and Carlotta, an enemy could not betray Carlotta more effectively than her mother does when she starts an affair with her son-in-law. Many of the characters are living with deception, but their responses vary. Fanny chooses not to confront Suwelo about his infidelities, whereas Arveyda visits Carlotta to try and atone for his betrayal of her. Trust is rare between two people and frequently cannot be achieved because of lack of authentic communication. If dishonesty prevails more often than not when people interact, *The Temple of My Familiar* illustrates that honesty and openness in relationships is a realizable goal. Lissie, Hal, and Rafe, for example, are eventually able to live in trust with one another. The warmth and openness of Celie and Shug in their old age attracts like-minded visitors who want to be part of the caring, openly demonstrative environment they have created. Fanny's memories of her childhood focus on Celie and Shug's household as a place that was full of love. Love, in this novel, is not limited to romantic love between a man and a woman. As the example of Celie and Shug proves, a loving relationship between two women can also provide a nurturing environment in which to raise children. The love that the novel ultimately promotes is a universal love, founded on forgiveness, empathy, compassion, and wholeness. This kind of love is an approach to life whereby a person recognizes the connection between self and other. Nine of the beatitudes in "The Gospel According to Shug," incorporate the word *love.* Shug's congregation is urged to love "the diversity of life" and the "entire cosmos." An all-embracing love for the universe will allow everyone to live an authentic life. An essential element of an authentic life is open and direct communication with other people. There are numerous forms of communication that occur in the novel. In each case, so long as the message is truly heard, a better understanding of the character's self takes place. Failure to communicate causes obstacles in the development of nurturing and supportive relationships.

## Sample Topics:

1. **Personal relationships:** How does Walker present family relationships? How is marriage portrayed in the novel? How do the characters respond to their relationship problems?

   To write an essay based on an investigation of personal relationships, begin with consideration of the different marriages and the different family relationships depicted in the novel and determine what Walker's attitude is toward them. The marriage between Fanny and Suwelo is one that is predominantly flawed. Lissie and Hal's marriage fails. A productive line of inquiry would be to examine what Walker insinuates are the causes of difficult personal relationships. What does Walker suggest is responsible for making a marriage unhappy? Fanny and Suwelo and Lissie and Hal ultimately manage to salvage their respective relationships. How do they resolve their problems? A paper could examine the way that particular characters respond to their problematical personal relationships. Although Walker's perspective on marriage could be the basis for a paper on its own, the topic can be broadened to consider personal relationships in general. Examine other family relationships in the story. How does Walker represent the parent/child relationship? Are there any similarities between her representation of the married relationship and, for example, the parent/child relationship? An essay on this topic could select one of the more important relationships and appraise how each character manages his or her emotional problems caused through interaction with family members.

2. **Love:** How is love between the characters shown? What social and personal factors obstruct the expression of love between characters?

Essays on the theme of love can be approached from one of various angles. One approach is to analyze the occurrences of love that the story describes and show the power they have to counteract life's adversity. Another essay could focus on the different manifestations of love to demonstrate how love takes different forms. Hal demonstrates a kind of brotherly love toward Lissie, even though they were passionate lovers at one time. The love between Rafe and Hal is nonsexual; nevertheless, the two men are extremely important to each other. The notion of universal love is broached. An essay could examine Walker's concept of universal love and show how it is illustrated through Lissie's multiple incarnations or through Suwelo's and Fanny's respective evolutions.

3. **Honesty and dishonesty:** Identify the different acts of deception and betrayal that Walker depicts in the novel. How do the deceived characters respond to their betrayal? How do the betrayers react to their own dishonest behavior? How and why are characters able to forgive the dishonesty of others?

The novel opposes honesty and openness with dishonesty and deception. However, dishonesty is slowly bested by honesty. A character such as Suwelo comes to understand that his own sense of wholeness is compromised by treating another person dishonestly. An essay on this topic could either focus on dishonesty, deception, and betrayal as independent themes, or it could negotiate the interplay between honesty and dishonesty. Another approach could look at the role of forgiveness as it relates to the dynamics of honesty and dishonesty. Why does each character find it necessary to forgive the harm done to them by others?

4. **Communication:** What different forms of communication, verbal and nonverbal, does Walker describe? How do different characters learn and grow through their willingness to communicate with others?

Storytelling, diaries, songs, audio cassettes, plays, paintings, conversations: These are just some of the forms of communication that *The Temple of My Familiar* presents. The differences in form notwithstanding, the purpose of communication in this novel is largely didactic. What are the older characters trying to teach Suwelo through their stories? What does Mary Jane hope to learn through reading her great-aunt's diary? Why are Nzingha and Fanny writing a play? What is the significance of the fact that the Olinka hum as a way to represent the ineffable? Essays on this topic could discuss the didactic purposes of the various types of communication. Additionally, the relationship between different communicators and communicatees could be analyzed to determine the effects of sharing knowledge and experiences.

## Character

Analysis of characters in *The Temple of My Familiar* is complicated by the lack of continuity in their various histories. The novel starts with Zedé's story, but this character loses her central position in the text after part one. Similarly, part three puts the spotlight on Mary Jane Briden, who is a peripheral character throughout the rest of the novel. One of the explanations for this nontraditional character development is that the characters function in the text as mouthpieces for various intellectual ideas.

Some of the characters do feature prominently in more than just one part of the text, and these characters could readily become the focus of an analysis. In *The Temple of My Familiar*, the name of a character is often indicative of her or his function in the novel. Beyond this specific function, however, each character has distinctive traits and is dynamic, offering the potential for analysis of their interaction with others and their growth throughout the novel. Fanny is the granddaughter of Celie, who was the protagonist of *The Color Purple*. She is the daughter of Olivia and Ola, a radical African playwright. Her middle name is Nzingha, derived from the Angolan Queen Nzingha of Ndongo (c.1582–1663), a formidable warrior, leader, and diplomat in a time when black women had to contend with rampant racism from white colonialists and sexism from all men. Suwelo was born Louis, Jr., but changed his name to Suwelo; Suwelo (Sowelu) is the rune for wholeness, life forces, and the sun's energy. The rune represents a journey toward complete knowledge of one's physical, mental, spiritual, emotional, and psychological self. The meaning of the name Carlotta is womanly, feminine, and petite; it is also the female equivalent of the name Charles, which means manly. Carlotta's name, thus, insinuates that this character will be implicated in gender issues. Betrayed by her husband and her mother, Carlotta retreats into an exaggerated simulation of femininity, wearing extremely high heels and paying excessive attention to her physical appearance. Carlotta refers to herself during this phase as a "female impersonator." The goal of her ultra-feminine appearance is to generate male desire. Toward the end of the novel, Carlotta cuts off all her hair and wears sports clothes, seeking a more androgynous look. Lissie informs Suwelo that the name Lissie means "the one who remembers everything." Her detailed memories of past lives span the entire history of humankind. Lissie remembers being male, female, black, white, master, slave, and a lion. She recounts her stories to people who are ready to listen and learn from her past.

## Sample Topics:

1. **Fanny's development:** What steps does Fanny take to deal with the anger that the racism and sexism of her environment provokes in her? Since Fanny finds value in "The Gospel According to Shug," what changes does she make in her life to live according to the beatitudes?

   Fanny consciously evolves throughout the novel and makes choices that will allow her to behave and live differently. An essay could examine the decisions that Fanny makes, looking at how she addresses the racism and sexism that she knows limit her. Why does she visit Africa and her father? What does she learn from her half sister, Nzingha? How does she renegotiate her relationship with Suwelo? The novel's last glimpse of Fanny is an account of a sexual episode with Arveyda. What does this incident tell the reader about Fanny's spiritual growth?

2. **Suwelo's journey:** What event from his past has traumatized Suwelo and affects him as an adult? What does Suwelo learn from Lissie and Mr. Hal? How does Suwelo achieve wholeness in his life?

   As an American history college teacher, Suwelo starts out largely uncritical of his job, even though he essentially articulates a white perspective of history. Similarly, he believes that his enjoyment of pornography and other women has no bearing on his marriage. What causes Suwelo to begin the process of reevaluating himself and his behavior? An essay could analyze this character's evolution as he searches for more meaningful interaction with his world and with others. Different characters provide him with different sources of information that slowly allow him to reshape himself.

3. **Carlotta's rebirth:** How does the failure of her marriage cause Carlotta to behave? How does knowledge of the past help Carlotta re-create herself?

When Suwelo meets Carlotta after a long hiatus, he is unable to recognize her because she has changed so drastically from the ultra-feminine woman with whom he had an affair. How and why has Carlotta changed? An essay on this character could examine her transformation, taking into consideration the role of the past on her development. Not only must Carlotta overcome her own past, she also has to contend with her mother's and father's pasts and the history of her South American ancestors.

4. **The many lives of Lissie:** What philosophical ideas does Lissie articulate through her storytelling? What effect does Lissie have on the men to whom she tells her stories?

Lissie's symbolic function in the novel would make a viable topic for a paper. What does she want to convey to Suwelo through her storytelling? Mr. Hal claims that, "Lissie is a lot of women." How do the various Lissies compare with each other? Another essay could look at the relationship between Mr. Hal and Lissie. Why does the novel end with Mr. Hal trying to see and make sense of one of Lissie's paintings? What is the significance of the reddish spot? Alternatively, Lissie can be viewed as an unconventional woman for her time and place, whether she is a young woman on her island birthplace or an old woman sharing a house with two men in Baltimore. What characteristics allow her to defy society's code of conduct for black women?

## History and Context

*The Temple of My Familiar* was published in 1989; however, Alice Walker spent eight years working on the manuscript. In other words, the novel was written throughout the 1980s. Not surprisingly, the novel can be seen as redolent with issues and beliefs that gained ground in the 1980s but that may be less in style today. New age beliefs acquired considerable popularity throughout the 1980s, particularly in California, where Walker was living while writing this novel. The spiritual practices of new age followers are eclectic but are derived from multiple world religions such as Hinduism, Shamanism, and Buddhism. Each new age believer devises his or her own spiritual path. As we see in the novel, some adherents explore reincarnation, astrology, Tarot, the occult, and the power of crystals. Holistic healing is advocated by means of massage and other nontraditional therapeutic practices. Beliefs, similar to practices, vary considerably throughout the new age movement. However, some beliefs predominate, such as the idea that all living beings, the natural world, and the entire universe are interconnected or that love is the paramount principle of human existence. Love, in this sense, is love for the whole of creation, not simply romantic or sexual love. Although the new age movement still resonates in society, the 1980s hope for social transformation has more generally been replaced with the aim of individual spiritual growth. Since Walker uses many new age beliefs and practices as revolutionary, counterculture forces in *The Temple of My Familiar,* the novel could be analyzed as epitomizing various new age ideals of the 1980s.

The mission to rewrite history from an inclusive standpoint also gathered momentum in the 1980s. Arguments by feminists in the 1970s posited that history had been written from the perspective of the conquerors; thus, history as it was taught in schools and colleges was the history of white men. The Herstory movement's undertaking was to rewrite the annals of history to include the contributions of people hitherto excluded from mainstream accounts. In this way, previously ignored archives were researched to add the contributions of women to the tale of humanity. *The Temple of My Familiar* both introduces female historical and contemporary personages previously consigned to virtual oblivion and retells the story of the formation of civilization as one of oppression and loss as males sought to dominate women and to appropriate the professions, such as the priesthood, formerly occupied by women.

The proposition that the world was once a happier, egalitarian, and freer place is not a theory originating from the 1980s. Treatises on utopias and golden ages have been produced by writers since the times of the ancient Greeks. In many of these utopian blueprints, the role of women has been debated. For males who were themselves hostile to the direction that civilization had taken, the notion that there was a time when feminine values (but not necessarily women) had predominated allowed the possibility of an alternative way of living for mankind. Under such systems of thinking, the feminine principle is perceived as holistic, simultaneous, and communal, whereas the masculine is associated with the linear, the sequential, and the individualist. Civilization becomes defined as an ongoing process of degeneration that overtook the natural, free people of the golden age of the matriarchies and imposed on them aberrant institutions such as the church, the state, and patriarchy. The exclusion of women from the building of civilization is one explanation for their association with nature. Proponents of the golden age of matriarchies use the widespread existence of powerful goddesses in ancient civilizations as historical proof of the golden age's actuality. While golden age ideas have long been propounded, some feminists recontextualized them in the 1970s and 1980s as part of the process of redefining the role of women in history and of challenging mainstream (white male) anti-ecological and unegalitarian theories of progress.

## Sample Topics:

1. **1980s new ageism:** What new age practices and beliefs does Walker incorporate into *The Temple of My Familiar* and to what aim? What is Lissie's role in promoting new age beliefs?

An essay investigating the influence of new age beliefs and practices on the content of *The Temple of My Familiar* could start by identifying and analyzing all the different examples of new ageism that Walker's text endorses. Alternatively, an inquiry into Lissie's function in the text as a mouthpiece for many new age ideas could form the basis of a paper. What is her role in Suwelo's spiritual journey? How does the ending of the novel depict new age ideals?

2. **The Herstory movement:** Which nonfictional female personages does Walker allude to in the novel, and what is her goal in using these allusions? How does *The Temple of My Familiar* rewrite history from a woman's perspective?

This topic could examine the multiple ways that Walker fulfils the mandate of the Herstory movement by putting women back in the historical process. For example, what is the significance of Fanny's discovery of writer Bessie Head? How does Nzingha restate the story of Medusa? Walker's female characters are drawn from a wide spectrum of ethnic and racial backgrounds. Which female perspectives does Walker include? What does each character contribute to a revamped account of history?

3. **The golden age of matriarchies:** How does Walker validate the theory of the golden age of matriarchies? How are powerful women shown to be leaders in the novel? Why does Walker locate her golden age in Africa?

This topic overlaps with the rewriting of history discussed above, but it also offers enough material as a separate area of focus. The golden age of matriarchies theory of prehistory has negative and positive connotations for women. The positive side of the theory presents women as powerful. Their leadership was not destructive to the environment, nor was it oppressive or unegalitarian. A paper could look at the way Walker presents women's leadership, in spiritual, political, or cultural terms. The negative side effect of the golden age theory has been to align women with nature. This has become a thorny issue because its essentialism runs the risk of reducing women to being only mothers and nurturers and ill-suited to contributing to the intellectual advancement of civilization. A paper could consider how the novel address the issue of women's bond with nature and the notion that women are essentially nurturing and caring. What different attitudes toward motherhood does Walker present? How does it show women as contributing to the advancement of civilization? Another approach would be to consider why Walker situates her golden age in Africa. How does this contribute to Walker's political goals in the novel?

## Philosophy and Ideas

Many of the ideas in *The Temple of My Familiar* that you could write about are linked to a well-established tenet of new ageism, namely universal connectedness. The force that everything in the universe shares and that causes this unity is energy. Energy is a life force that creates a bond between humans and animals, humans and nature, and humans and the spirit world. With this way of thinking, god is no longer explained as a distant creator who controls and directs. God is immanent. These pantheistic ideas date back hundreds of years and have been incorporated into Western and Eastern religions. Awareness of this shared energy and spirit permits psychic bonding between people who recognize a kindred spirit in one another. Such is the case with Fanny and Arveyda when they share their personal stories of their foremothers. Similarly, two different women who have a child by Ola name their offspring Nzingha. Universal connectedness or consciousness means that everything that happens, or is said or thought, is connected to everything else. Shug's Gospel refers to this as the "unbroken web of life." With this in mind, Walker depicts the oneness of the universe through the structure and content of the novel. Her all-encompassing and entwined spectrum of characters, of settings, and of historical periods artistically reproduces this sense of oneness. Each character in *The Temple of My Familiar*, however, is not born with awareness of interconnectedness. Whether female or male, each character must undertake her or his own spiritual journey to find an authentic self. The spiritual journey to wholeness is underscored in the novel by many physical journeys. Fanny travels to Africa to unearth her African inheritance. Zedé returns to her origins in South America. A meeting with a parent is crucial to both women's spiritual journey to find self-understanding. Information and wisdom from the past is an invaluable source of direction. Suwelo seeks out the wisdom of elders through his conversations with Lissie and Hal. In the case of Lissie, her stories do more than supply wisdom accrued through age. Her memories of her many pasts serve as lessons from spirits and ancestors. Her memories lead Suwelo to a new vision of dynamics between man and woman and between humankind and the world. Understanding the lessons of the past is essential if a character is to appreciate the oneness of all experience. In the same vein, the pursuit of creative art forms connects the artist to the unity of the universe. Again, The Gospel According to Shug clarifies this notion: "HELPED are those who create anything at all, for they shall relive the thrill of their own conception, and realize a spiritual partnership in the creation of the Universe that keeps them responsible and cheerful." By the end of *The Temple of My Familiar*, the four main characters are all experimenting with different forms of artistic creation. However, they are quick to point out that the quality of the end product is not the point of art; the artistic process is what makes them "cheerful."

## Sample Topics:

1. **Universal connectedness:** How does the structure and content of the novel enhance Walker's message of universal connectedness?

   An essay on this topic could explore the numerous ways that Walker depicts the interconnectedness among the characters. In some places, readers are aware, but the characters are unaware, of their complementarity. Another approach to this topic could look at how Walker uses the plot structure of the novel to promote the idea of oneness. The novel eschews linearity, jumping from one setting to another with digressions whose relevance sometimes has to be determined by the reader.

2. **The journey to the authentic self:** How do the main characters overcome the limitations of their particular situations and create a life that allows true expression of self? How does Walker employ the motif of traveling to support the idea of spiritual journeying?

Both female and male characters strive to find a way of living that will not force them to be subject to the racist, sexist dictates of society. The spiritual journey to find this authentic way of being is not easy. An essay could select Suwelo, Fanny, Carlotta, or Arveyda, or several of the secondary characters, and analyze where they look for answers to find spiritual, mental, and physical satisfaction. Another approach to this topic could look at Walker's use of the motif of traveling to see how she involves traveling in each character's spiritual journey.

3. **The importance of the past:** What does Suwelo learn from Lissie's and Hal's memories/stories of the past? What does Mary Jane learn from her research into her aunt's and great-aunt's past? What is the significance of the story of M'sukta living in the Museum of Natural History?

Mary Ann Haverstock's boat is named *Recuerdo* (memory). How does the boat's name link to Mary Ann's rescue of Carlotta and Zedé, to her name change, and to her abandonment of her former life? Memory and the past play a critical role in all of the main characters' lives. A paper could investigate the legacy of the past and repressed memories on Mary Ann/Jane, Suwelo, Fanny, or Carlotta. Using M'Sukta's or Lissie's stories as evidence, what seems to be Walker's position on the importance of memory in the rewriting of history? How does Walker's presentation of memory and the wisdom of elders compare to her attitudes toward museums and colleges as sources of knowledge? An essay could address either of these questions.

4. **Creative art forms:** What different creative art forms do the various characters pursue? Based on the novel's presentation of art, what is Walker's position on the political, spiritual, and cultural values of artistic production?

Writing novels (Bessie Head) and plays (Ola, Nzingha, and Fanny), painting (Lissie and Hal), music (Arveyda), and photography (of Lissie) are some of the more traditional art forms that are validated in *The Temple of My Familiar.* An essay could examine the importance of any of these art forms as shown in the novel. Alternatively, a paper could comment on the less traditional art forms presented throughout the novel, such as Zedé's feathered items, Carlotta's bell music, or Arveyda's bread baking. Each artist produces something of beauty. Awareness of beauty allows characters to embrace the positive elements of life. An essay could show how the nontraditional art forms improve characters' lives.

## Form and Genre

A novel is an extended, fictional prose narrative, which is traditionally expected to have characters that interact with one another within the framework of some form of recognizable plot. Of the numerous varieties within the novel genre, the novel of ideas prioritizes polemics on intellectual issues over characterization or plot. The characters often become mouthpieces for particular viewpoints. Further, the characters sometimes personify the idea that they represent through their personality and actions. With this definition in mind, *The Temple of My Familiar* can be analyzed as a novel of ideas. Another unconventional aspect of *The Temple of My Familiar*'s form is its reliance on storytelling. Many of its chapters comprise stories that one character tells another character. The characters' stories can transport their listeners into the past or to different places in the present. Lissie's stories, for example, communicate ideas across cultures and inspire Suwelo's imagination to envision possibilities in his own life. In *The Temple of My Familiar,* the purpose of the stories is to share knowledge of the world. The novel's preponderance of storytelling recreates the idea of an oral narrative, insofar as a written narrative can do this. The novel argues for the importance of the spoken word as a source of knowledge. Human society has been shaped by stories, from early creation myths to modern legends that are acted out in movies. Many societies, particularly Native-American and African, have orality entrenched in their culture and traditions. For such societies, storytelling is more than a conduit to transmit knowledge; it is also an art form. For Walker, the ancient wisdom of myth and memory ties into the Jungian concept of the collective unconscious. In this theory, archetypal symbols (e.g. the snake), themes (e.g. the loss of innocence), characters (e.g. the great goddess), or patterns of circumstances (e.g. a journey where the hero is forced to face many trials before he can return home) are noted to have recurred throughout literature, myths, folklore, and rituals around the world. The collective unconscious is a part of the unconscious mind and is shared by a society or all humankind, because it is the product of our common ancestral experience. Therefore, analysis of myths and other oral traditions can allow us to access ancient scientific, religious, or moral knowledge. These alternative sources of wisdom, discredited by mainstream Western thinking as superstition or groundless, counterpose the rational, scientific, Western worldview.

## Sample Topics:

1. *The Temple of My Familiar* **as a novel of ideas:** How does Walker use her characters to propound key ideas and theories? How does the structure of the plot and the use of characters within that plot support some of Walker's intellectual theories?

   This topic can take one of a number of different approaches. First, analysis of any combination of the characters can have as its goal the elucidation of the ideas that each character embodies. Second, an overview of the novel's plot and structure and the untraditional use of character can be explored for its intention of bolstering some of the philosophical and political ideas that Walker upholds. Finally, an essay could argue that Walker does not completely sacrifice character and plot to ideas or that the novel works on two levels—as a novel of ideas and a novel that realistically portrays the growth and development of its main characters.

2. **The oral tradition:** How do stories and storytelling affect the characters in *The Temple of My Familiar*? What is Walker's political goal in asserting the value of oral traditions?

   Stories and storytelling have always played a significant role in the education and acculturation of young and old people. How important are stories and storytelling in *The Temple of My Familiar*? An essay on this topic could consider the effect of stories on characters such as Suwelo or Carlotta. How does the form of the novel reinforce the value of orality? An essay addressing this question could also take into consideration Walker's use of archetypal symbols, motifs, and themes that are common to many oral narratives around the world and are perhaps indicative of humankind's psychic connectedness.

## Language, Symbols, and Imagery

A familiar is a spirit whose job is to help a witch or wizard and who often assumes the form of an animal. Black cats, for example, are readily associated with magic and superstition because of their reputation for being in the service of witches. Familiars usually have some magical abilities themselves, but the degree of independence they have from their mistress or master varies from story to story. In Lissie's dream about her familiar, the creature is part bird, part fish, and part reptile and is resident in Lissie's temple. In order to conduct a conversation with a white man, Lissie repeatedly imprisons the familiar to prevent it from disrupting the conversation. Each time, however, the familiar breaks free from whatever receptacle Lissie uses to trap it. Ultimately, Lissie realizes that her behavior has destroyed the bond between the familiar and herself. When the familiar escapes for the final time, it looks at Lissie "with pity" as it flies off. Lissie is left watching its departure with a group of white people. The temple also vanishes, replaced by a white stone building. Before the familiar leaves for good, it is notable for being the color of a rainbow. After its departure, the setting where Lissie is left standing is remarkable for its absence of color. Although the temple of Lissie's familiar is described only once in the novel, its symbolic significance plays out in the rest of the novel. In contrast, references to color and animals recur throughout the novel. Many of the characters are associated with a particular color. Olivia describes Celie as "very much influenced by color." Celie's electric blue clothing was felt to give off energy and power. Mary Jane dyes her hair a startling shade of blue. Similarly, the color red functions as a motif in the novel. For example, at the end of the novel, Hal can make out a reddish spot in Lissie's painting. Red parrot feather earrings are important to Carlotta as an item that connects to her past. The familiar and the red parrot feather earrings involve another motif: the recurrence of references to animals and other creatures from the natural world. Fanny and Suwelo's house is bird-shaped; this permits cohabitation with freedom. In one incarnation, Lissie describes herself as a lion living in a harmonious relationship with humans. The Edenic dream unravels when "Adam" is expelled from paradise because of his pale skin that does not love the sun. The bitter man forms a bond with a dog for companionship. According to Lissie, when men asserted themselves over women, they trained dogs to chase women. Man's controlling relationship with dogs symbolizes the loss of harmonious living that women and all the other animals shared before men's drive to power.

## Sample Topics:

1. **The temple of Lissie's familiar:** What does the familiar's escape and disappearance symbolize? What does the alteration of the temple symbolize?

   The story of Lissie's temple and her familiar could be analyzed for their symbolic meaning in terms of Lissie's interpretations of the history of humankind. Each specific detail of the dream about the familiar can shed light on Lissie's worldview and her status as goddess. The importance of this symbol is signaled by Walker's choice of title for this novel. How do the temple and the familiar incident help elucidate the wider meanings of the novel? An essay could also analyze Walker's use of familiars throughout the novel.

2. **Colors:** Why does the novel end with Hal discerning a reddish spot, which "marks the return of [his] lost vision"? To what ends are specific colors associated with specific characters?

   Different cultures around the world have different symbolic meanings associated with specific colors. Caution is needed, therefore, when analyzing color symbolism. Red is the color of blood, so can be a symbol of life. In China, brides wear red—as does Olivia's entire wedding party. However, American brides traditionally wear white as a symbol of purity. In *The Temple of My Familiar*, the color white is often laden with negative connotations, such as when Lissie (as an "Adam" figure) is forced to leave the paradise of Africa because the sun is not kind to his pale skin. Analysis of color symbolism could become the basis of a viable paper, but such an essay would need to be alert to when and why Walker deviates from usual American interpretations of certain colors.

3. **Creatures from the natural world:** What does Lissie's story about lions illustrate? Why are dogs hostile creatures in Lissie's worldview?

An essay on this topic could focus on an analysis of the importance of birds and feathers for many of the novel's characters. Alternatively, a paper could examine the importance of references to four-legged animals to the novel's overall meaning. Why is it significant that Hal is uncomfortable with cats? What does the story of Husa reveal about the relationships between humans and animals? What is the message that Lissie wants to transmit to Suwelo through her memory of her "animal cousins"?

## Compare and Contrast Essays

As people grow up and start to wonder who they are and what they want from life, they often reflect back on their childhood, identifying formative events and influences. Relationships with parents are reconsidered with the wisdom of maturity. Sometimes, traumatic events are chewed over to clarify their effect on our personality. Suwelo, Arveyda, and Carlotta all reflect on how the deaths of parents affect their adult behavior and attitudes. The truths of their parents' stories, moreover, have to be faced in order to facilitate reconciliation with the past. Carlotta and Fanny also have living parents whose pasts are hidden from their children. Finding out the truth allows the children to better understand choices that their parents have made. Whether parents are alive or dead, the parent-child dynamic is one that leaves its lingering imprint on a person's sense of self. Lissie tells Suwelo that "if our parents are not present in us, consciously present, there is much, very much about ourselves we can never know." Parental attitudes can influence a child's behavior in the arena of sexuality as parents often unconsciously model what they believe are appropriate means of expressing sexuality and appropriate forms of interaction with sexual partners. Alternatively, problems with a parent can manifest themselves later in life in analogous problems with a sexual partner. In the patriarchal society that Walker critiques in her novel, male sexuality can be exploitative (Suwelo's use of pornography) and denigratory (Suwelo's assumption that Carlotta lacks substance). Aware of this, female characters such as Fanny and Lissie have problems responding to men sexually or finding men who will not be constrained by their expectations of femininity and women. One possible solution to this dilemma is for women to turn to other women where sexuality is free from sexual politics. Celie and Shug live and love together in a warm and harmonious environment. In *The Temple of My Familiar,* the male characters' attitudes toward sexuality are molded by their societies. It becomes the women's task to try and show them alternative modes of interaction that will be as emancipatory for the men as for the women.

## Sample Topics:

1. **The characters' attitudes toward sexuality:** What is the difference between male and female sexuality in the novel? Which male and which female characters have problems relating to the opposite sex and why? How do these characters overcome their problems?

   This topic can be approached in one of several ways. A comparison between male and female attitudes toward sexuality is one possibility. Such an essay could also consider Walker's proposed solutions for bridging sexual differences between men and women. Another approach would be to compare and contrast different male, or different female, attitudes to sex, looking at sexuality's political overtones and how political outlook shapes sexual behavior.

2. **The characters' relationships with their parents:** How does parental legacy affect each character's behavior as an adult? How does each character achieve understanding of his or her parents?

If each generation can gain full knowledge of its parents, Lissie asserts that this facilitates reconnection with the ancient past and "the preancient current of life itself." An essay could discuss the correlation between knowing the truth about one's parents and self-truth. How do Suwelo, Arveyda, Carlotta, and Fanny make the journey into the past to learn their parents' stories? What effect does knowledge of parents have on each character? Conversely, how does ignorance of one's parents affect a child?

## Bibliography and Online Sources

*Anniina's Alice Walker Page*. December 30, 2007. <http://www.luminarium.org/contemporary/alicew.htm>.

Dieke, Ikenna. "Walker's *The Temple of My Familiar:* Womanist as Monistic Ideal." *Critical Essays on Alice Walker.* Ed. Ikenna Dieke. Westport, CT: Greenwood, 1999. 127–139.

Gates, Jr., Henry Louis, and K. A. Appiah, eds. *Alice Walker: Critical Perspectives Past and Present.* New York: Amistad, 1993.

King, Jeannette. "Recovering the Power of the Goddess: Alice Walker—*The Temple of My Familiar.*" *Women and the Word: Contemporary Women Novelists and the Bible.* New York: St. Martin's P, 2000. 171–186.

Lauret, Maria. "The Temple of My Familiar." *Modern Novelists: Alice Walker.* New York: St. Martin's, 2000. 121–158.

Simcikova, Karla. *To Live Fully, Here and Now: The Healing Vision in the Works of Alice Walker.* Lanham, MD: Lexington, 2007.

Winchell, Donna Haisty. "Harmony of Heart and Hearth: *The Temple of My Familiar.*" *Alice Walker.* New York: Twayne, 1992. 115–131.

# POSSESSING THE SECRET OF JOY

## READING TO WRITE

SUPPORTERS OF traditions often suppose that the custom or belief has been handed down unaltered from generation to generation. The longevity of a tradition is assumed to increase its authenticity and its value to the community since it establishes continuity between the past and the present, communicating ancestral wisdom. However, people rarely know the true origins of the traditions they follow, or are aware of how traditions mutate over time. When Tashi returns to Africa to murder the old woman who carried out her traditional circumcision, she manipulates the value attached to tradition to gain access to M'Lissa:

> It was I who shooed Mbati from her post; I who told M'Lissa: Mama Lissa, give the girl a break. Your other daughter has come from America just to look after you! Since this coming back to care for the elderly was such a strong characteristic of the ancient traditions, how could she refuse?
>
> Oh, M'Lissa had said, it is too much happiness. Too much! To see the daughter of Nafa, here, right beside my bed. Oh, surely I shall die of it!
>
> I thought it an odd thing to say.
>
> How did the defendant appear to you? the prosecuting attorney asks.
>
> There is a long pause. Motherly, Mbati replies.
>
> The young man is surprised. What, his look implies, this demon, *motherly*!

Yes, Mbati continues in a definite voice. I lost my own mother when I was an infant, and yet never believed she died. When Mrs. Johnson showed up at the door—

Childhood memories are quite irrelevant to this court, says the attorney, cutting her off. Though surely the humane response would have been to let her finish; even if one felt quite unable to ask the question: How did your mother die? It is a taboo question, in Olinka. One never asked for fear of the answer.

Mbati subsides into silence, but looks me in the face and holds my gaze. I see she has not condemned me.

Few people in either African or American communities would challenge the value of the tradition of the young caring for the elderly. Many people in America, however, would denounce the practice of female genital cutting and lament its status as tradition in some African societies. Most American women would view female genital cutting as cruel physical mutilation and a violation of individual human rights. Some African women feel that circumcision is necessary in order to make a daughter marriageable. Following traditions or not frequently results in conflict between the individual and the community. How are traditions used to define a community? How can traditions be used by those in power to control the behavior of a certain group of people? How and why does a community enforce adherence to traditions? What happens to an individual if she or he refuses to conform to traditional practices? Thinking about these questions could become the starting point for various essays on *Possessing the Secret of Joy*.

One reason that traditions can survive unchallenged for generations is that it is made taboo to even talk about them. In the excerpt, the attorney prevents Mbati from giving details of her mother's death because the Olinka have made such discussions taboo. Similarly, *Possessing the Secret of Joy* explains that talking about the female initiation ceremony is taboo in Olinkan society. As a girl becomes a woman, the ideal situation would be a mother instructing her daughter in everything that will happen to her as she matures. However, in this novel the mother-daughter relationship is complicated by a sense of betrayal. Mothers are complicit in giving their daughters pain since they take their children to be circumcised and sometimes participate in the procedure. The mother-daughter relationship is explored in depth in this novel and could readily be analyzed in an essay. As the excerpt illustrates, the feeling of a mother-daughter bond can arise between two unrelated women who feel empathy for each other. For example, Mbati found Tashi "motherly" when she arrives at the house to kill M'Lissa. Mbati does not condemn Tashi, perhaps out of a sense of female solidarity and perhaps because she has finally encountered a woman who is making sure the story of her life and death will not be consigned to silence. How is the attorney's denial of the relevance of childhood memories pitted against the women's growing feelings of resistance? Lisette observes to her son in part eight of the novel that "men refuse to remember things that don't happen to them." What is Walker's stance on men's attitudes toward women's suffering and pain? Women's suffering, women's solidarity, resistance, memory, taboos, and male attitudes to women's pain: These themes could all become the focus of a paper.

Mbati's unexpected description of Tashi as motherly is made even stranger by the fact that Tashi, although Olinkan by birth, has spent a large part of her life in the United States and has always been on the margins of her African community. Even as she faces the death penalty for murder, there is speculation that her American citizenship might help her be spared. During psychoanalysis, she is encouraged to come to terms with both her American (Evelyn) and African (Tashi) sides. An examination of Tashi/Evelyn's conflicting dual identity would make an interesting essay. The tie between black Americans and Africa is another topic that Walker addresses in the novel. In the passage, this tie is imaged as a familial relationship between two women (even though Tashi is African by birth). However, it is not awareness of shared ancestral origins that draw the women together emotionally, so much as a sense of the need for solidarity in speaking out for women's rights. In the excerpt, Tashi's goal of murdering M'Lissa is to eradicate, at least symbolically, an Olinkan tradition that cripples women. However, Tashi could be accused of imposing American values on an African society. Walker's portrayal of Africans and Africa has been judged as problematic by several critics, and an essay exploring her representation of Africa would certainly have merit. Does Walker's political agenda (to make the world aware of the insidious practice of female genital mutilation) make her lose sight of the variations and specificity of the different populations in Africa? Could she be accused of cultural imperialism in her account of the imaginary Olinka?

# TOPICS AND STRATEGIES

Suggested topics for essays on *Possessing the Secret of Joy* will be the focus of the remainder of this chapter. Additionally, the chapter will propose general approaches that could be used to develop those topics. These proposals will ideally help you to generate your own creative approaches to the topics.

## Themes

Walker took the title of this novel from Mirella Ricciardi's narrative *African Saga* (1982) in which Ricciardi proclaims, "Black people are natural, they possess the secret of joy, which is why they can survive the suffering and humiliation inflicted upon them." What is the secret of joy? Several possible answers (women's sexual organs, love, understanding, friendship, solidarity) to this question are insinuated throughout the novel, but in the final chapter, Walker baldly states that "RESISTANCE IS THE SECRET OF JOY!" *Possessing the Secret of Joy* thereby identifies itself as a novel with a political purpose: to encourage women to fight against the practice of female genital cutting. The novel's final chapter describes a group of African women flaunting their girl babies' naked genitals as a signal that they, at least, will fight to keep their daughters' sexuality intact. This symbolic gesture with their children is done in defiance of the threats of male soldiers who are trying to maintain civil order with phallic machine guns.

Tashi is the character who is at the forefront of this female rebellion. Her misguided choice to be circumcised as a young adult isolates her from everyone, rather than drawing her into her African community in the way she had hoped it would. As a result of her decision, sex, childbirth, and urination are so painful that she descends into a form of madness at the realization of what she has lost in her life. However, she is fortunate to have the emotional support of her husband, Adam, her friend Olivia, and various other characters (Mzee, Raye, Mbati, Pierre, and Benny). Some of these characters are related to Tashi through family ties; others bond to her in a familial way. For example, Mzee writes to his daughter to explain that the process of psychoanalyzing Tashi has awakened in him a sense of affinity with her suffering that links him back to his "ancient self." He acknowledges the prehistoric unity of all humankind through their shared African origins.

Tashi fights back from the brink of insanity by returning to Africa to confront the woman whom she feels is responsible for murdering her sister, Dura, and for spoiling Tashi's own life. This woman, M'Lissa, was the principal circumciser of Olinkan girls. Tashi's plan is to revenge herself on the old *tsunga*. M'Lissa's murder will pay her back for the painful deaths she has inflicted on many young girls and will symbolize the death of the archaic and oppressive tradition. Is this murder an example of vengeance or retribution?

## Sample Topics:

1. **Resistance:** What different forms of resistance does the novel depict? Why does Walker claim that resistance is the "secret of joy"?

   An essay on this important theme would need to examine the political purpose of *Possessing the Secret of Joy*. How does Walker propose that resistance should be enacted? Tashi uses violence as a means to bring about social transformation. Tashi, however, murders an old woman, who arguably is a victim of the patriarchal Olinkan system herself. What does Tashi achieve through this murder? Does the novel show any other methods that could be used to resist oppression? For example, what is the significance of the sign that Tashi writes on the paper having the same colors as the Olinkan flag?

2. **Retribution and revenge:** Is Tashi's murder of M'Lissa an example of revenge or of retribution?

   Whereas revenge could be considered as simply getting even with someone who has wronged another person, retribution implies that the punishment is justly deserved for the wrong committed. Thus, retribution has connotations of greater legitimacy than revenge. An essay on this topic needs to decide whether Tashi is vengeful or whether she is trying to correct some wrong. Alternatively, could she be acting with both an individual and a communal purpose in mind? What other examples of revenge and retribution does Walker include in the novel? Examine, for example, the Dogon creation myth. How does this myth tie in with Tashi's decision to commit murder?

3. **Family relationships:** How does Walker portray male and female interaction in the story? How does she present sibling and parent/child relationships?

There are various possible approaches to writing an essay based on an examination of Walker's representation of family relationships. One type of relationship explored through different pairs of characters is the mother/daughter relationship. An essay could examine how Walker presents this important relationship, analyzing both negative and positive aspects. Note that the mother/daughter bond can be claimed by characters who are not biologically related. Although Walker's perspective on this specific relationship could be the basis for a thesis, the topic can be broadened to consider family relationships more generally. Look at other family relationships in the story, such as mother/son, brother/sister, or sister/sister. How does Walker represent them? A paper could examine the way that supportive family relationships affect a particular character. Similar to the mother/daughter topic, other family relationships do not necessarily have to be biologically based; they could be relationships that achieve the status of family through the intensity of the bond that is established between two characters.

## Character

*Possessing the Secret of Joy* is structured so that the voices of several different characters are heard from a first-person perspective. This allows the reader direct access to each character's thoughts; however, the majority of their thoughts that the narrative presents pertain to Tashi's story rather than their own lives. The novel is essentially about Tashi's journey toward spiritual and psychological wholeness, and writing about her journey could make an interesting paper. Her shifts in development are signaled by Walker through the changing title headings. A conflict is created between her African and her American identities, and this split is indicated by the different names—Tashi and Evelyn— that she uses. However, she is not always just African or just American. As the chapter headings imply, the interplay between the two strands of her personality alters depending on her frame of mind. Thus, the headings Tashi-Evelyn or Evelyn-Tashi indicate which influence predominates at given moments in her life. Additionally, there is another facet of her complex character that is evident in her identification as "Mrs. Johnson," Adam's wife.

The secondary characters will be more difficult to write about than Tashi because there is less information provided about them. Nevertheless, their analysis could still lead to a range of possible character studies. For example, the character Adam could be approached through an investigation into his relationships with women. A lot of information about M'Lissa is garnered from other characters' memories of her, although she does claim the narrative voice at the time when Tashi comes to kill her. M'Lissa could be approached through analysis of her symbolic role within Olinkan society. Pierre's role in the novel is multifaceted. Despite Tashi's initial rejection of him, he becomes an important person in her life since he educates her on the origins of genital cutting. Beyond his interaction with Tashi, the text shows Pierre as having complex traits in terms of his sexuality and in terms of his relationships with his mother and his father's family. Furthermore, his physical appearance is used by Walker to add to the uniqueness of his character.

### Sample Topics:

1. **Tashi's journey:** How does Walker use variations in the chapter headings to signal Tashi's conflicts and development? How does Tashi eventually find wholeness?

Analysis of Walker's use of changing chapter titles when referring to Tashi would provide sufficient material for a viable essay. Their analysis would be linked to discussion of Tashi's spiritual journey as she searches for respite from the physical and psychological pain that has been her lot in life since her genital cutting. How and why does Tashi refuse the position of victim? Tashi's mental journey is acted out through another type of journey—the return home. Why is the return home an essential component of Tashi's psychological journey? Another approach to this character could look at her relationship with her place of birth. Why does she have an unusual position in her society? How does this position lead to her choice to become circumcised as an adult?

2. **M'Lissa:** M'Lissa is revered as an Olinkan mother figure. How does she betray her position as "mother" to the girls in her trust? What does M'Lissa symbolize to Olinkan society? What does her murder symbolize?

When Tashi comes to murder M'Lissa, M'Lissa sees her intent in her eyes. M'Lissa has seen a lot of blood and death in her life, and she has become immune to other people's pain and suffering. An essay could examine M'Lissa's function in her society. Why do women become the enforcers of brutal traditions on other women? What might they gain from this position of power? Does Walker vindicate M'Lissa's behavior and actions in any way? Alternatively, an essay could analyze M'Lissa's significance to Tashi. Why does murdering M'Lissa allow Tashi to start the process of healing?

3. **Adam's loss of joy:** How does Tashi's pain affect Adam physically and psychologically? What is the significance of the fact that it is American Adam who rescues Tashi from the rebel camp where she has been circumcised? Why does Adam maintain a relationship with Lisette?

Adam is committed to loving and helping Tashi from the time they are young together in Africa throughout their adult lives.

An essay could investigate why Adam makes this commitment to Tashi and how this commitment affects his own life. Another way to approach analysis of Adam could be through his relationships with other characters. Why does he form a bond with Lisette? How does he treat their child? How does he respond to Benny? Adam could also be analyzed for his symbolic function in the novel, which is alluded to when a character jokes about Adam being married to Eve(lyn). In the novel, how does Eve's eating from the tree of knowledge cause Adam to be expelled from paradise?

4. **The stone—Pierre:** How does Pierre embody multiplicity and multivalency? How does he help and support the other characters? How has his own life been affected by Tashi's situation?

In French, *pierre* means stone, but it is a word whose gender is feminine (*une pierre*). In Jungian symbolism, a stone represents wholeness and successful individuation. Pierre is part European, part American, and in a sense, part African. When he discusses his sexuality with Adam, it is implied that he is bisexual (even though he finds that term limiting). An essay could explore the function of Pierre's multiplicity in the novel. How does his defiance of categories allow him to assist other characters?

## History and Context

The Western media has had a tendency to represent Africa as a homogeneous country, as opposed to an extremely diverse continent. People in Europe and Asia, in contrast, are nearly always differentiated according to their specific country of origin. Media images of Africa usually focus on the negative: famine, poverty, AIDS, and war. Common stereotypes attached to Africa and Africans have been taken as fact by many Westerners as a result of these repeated negative portrayals. Additionally, anthropological representations of various African "tribes" have established an image in many Western minds of a primitive world where all Africans still live in huts and wild animals roam around freely. Africa is often imagined as needing the help of the West, because of its representation as lagging behind the West in terms of social, intellectual, and moral development; the West's role in creating and perpetuating Africa's problems is rarely addressed. The African-American position on Africa is multifaceted and has changed over time, but one common thread has been to disprove white America's notion that people of African descent are inferior to people of European descent. Some African Americans feel affinity to Africa as their ancestral homeland. Alice Walker refers to this idea in the address to the reader at the end of *Possessing the Secret of Joy*. Walker avers that since she is ignorant of the specifics of her origins, she will claim the entire continent of Africa as her motherland. Olinka is her fictional construction of this lost Africa. After its publication in 1992, critics attacked Walker for her overarching picture of "Africa." The fictional construction of Olinka was seen as another example of the American denial of Africa's regional cultural specificity. Uninformed readers of *Possessing the Secret of Joy* might conclude that the practice of genital cutting, as described in the novel, is the traditional norm throughout Africa. Other contentious issues found in the novel were the portrayals of African helplessness in dealing with AIDS and corruption. This helplessness implied that Americans needed to save Africa from itself. Walker was accused of cultural imperialism because of the implication in the novel that Africa would be better served if it adopted American standards of behavior. However, defenders of Walker's project pointed out that Tashi was an African character and her choice to be circumcised as an adult was atypical for African women. Furthermore, within her Olinkan community, Tashi was an outsider because of her close relationship with the American missionary family. Overall, there are arguments that can be proposed both to critique and defend Walker's representation of Africa.

## Sample Topics:

1. **The American vision of Africa:** In what ways does Walker positively validate Africa and Africans? What aspects of the novel's portrayal of Africa could provide evidence to accuse Walker of cultural imperialism?

An essay on this topic could examine the different components of Walker's fictional construction of Olinka and her African characters. How does she depict the relationships between Africa and African Americans and between Africa and people of European descent (whether in Europe or America)? In some instances, Walker shows Africa as helpless and uninformed; on the other hand, aspects of African life and its people are validated. Additionally, Walker seems to have taken steps in the novel to pre-empt expected critique of her American intervention in an African issue. A thesis on this topic could argue different propositions depending on the conclusions you draw after assessing the textual evidence of Walker's representation of Africa.

## Philosophy and Ideas

Female circumcision, female genital cutting, or female genital mutilation: These are all terms for the same practice. The difference in the terms lies in their connotations. Circumcision downplays the painful physical reality of the practice and puts emphasis on the cultural value attached to it. The term *genital cutting* attempts to find neutral ground where the actuality of the physical aspect of the practice is recognized without resorting to heavily emotive words. Female genital mutilation ignores the cultural meanings of the tradition and stresses the misery and torture inflicted on women. By using the phrase *female genital mutilation* throughout the novel, Walker makes her political position on the practice clear. The novel's intent is to expose the insidious nature of the procedure and to encourage women to speak out against it. The novel's final chapter urges women to join together in a mission to eradicate this brutal mutilation. Female solidarity takes several forms throughout the novel and is an effective force in overcoming men's exploitation of women. When writing about the subject of genital cutting, it is important not to make generalizations about the practice as there are different types of genital cutting carried out in specific parts of Africa and the Middle East. Walker describes the most extreme type of genital cutting: infibulation. Sociologists are uncertain how the practice originated. Pierre offers up the Dogon (who live in

Mali) explanation that excision of both sexes is necessary to differentiate male and female. According to this myth, female circumcision rids the woman of her masculinity.

One reason why an African mother may decide that her daughter should be circumcised is so that the girl is not socially disadvantaged later in her life. Circumcision is a rite of passage that ensures that the girl will be viewed as marriageable. Tashi recalls how the girls of her village taunted her for not being circumcised. Her intact genitals were a symbol of her outsider status within Olinkan society. Her decision to be circumcised is partly motivated by a desire to achieve a sense of belonging. Her final argument with Olivia shows that she equates her circumcision with resistance to cultural assimilation by non-Africans. Similarly, her desire for tribal scarring on her cheeks is intended to define herself overtly as an Olinkan. She accuses Olivia, as American missionary, of working on behalf of white people to undermine African cultural authenticity and Africanness in general. From her African perspective, American cultural imperialism is an anomaly because the behavioral standards that Americans want to enforce on Africans are not even authentically American. Similarly, M'Lissa taunts Tashi with the question, "What does an American look like?" Tashi offers multiple answers to this conundrum, but ultimately concludes that America is formed of a multiracial community of people who are seeking refuge from suffering. America, Tashi wants to believe, can allow individual difference and creation of an identity that can withstand the pressures of social conformity.

Psychoanalysis is a tool that an American may use to help overcome traumas from the past, and it is a healing process that has European origins. Tashi is analyzed by a character who evokes Carl Jung. Walker acknowledges Jung at the end of the novel as having been "so real in [her] own therapy that [she] could imagine him as alive and active in Tashi's treatment." A discussion of the Jungian concepts that Walker uses as part of Tashi's cure in Switzerland would make a feasible paper.

## Sample Topics:

1. **Female genital cutting:** What is Walker's aim in writing *Possessing the Secret of Joy* vis-à-vis genital cutting? How does

Walker depict the practice of genital cutting through the characters of Dura and Tashi?

Before starting to write on this topic, you might find it helpful to watch Walker's documentary film, *Warrior Marks: Female Genital Mutilation and the Sexual Blinding of Women*, which was made with the collaboration of Pratibha Parmar. A corresponding nonfiction book was published with the same title, and this text would provide a wealth of information on Walker's attitude toward the tradition. An essay could examine Walker's perspective on genital cutting as revealed in the novel and elsewhere and possibly critique her position for any oversights or generalizations.

2. **Female solidarity:** How does the novel depict the importance of women's unity when fighting the political, social, and cultural status quo? How does the novel illustrate the value of women's support of one another in everyday life?

   M'Lissa is the novel's example of a woman who allows her individual desire for power and money to supersede the welfare of other women. She is a tool used by the dominant males of her society to keep other women in subjection. An essay could analyze the novel's perspective on the benefits to women of female solidarity and expose the threats to women's interests that can arise if women are divided. Another approach to this topic could look at how different female friendships and enmities aid or harm women's well-being on a personal or on a political level.

3. **The individual and the community:** How does Walker compare and contrast Olinkan and American societies? In each continent, according to the novel, how is the individual able to meet her or his individual needs without compromising the needs of the community?

   Although this topic might overlap with the idea of female solidarity discussed above, it could also take a more comprehensive approach by looking at both men and women in Africa and America. In Olinka, how is a sense of community forged? Consider, for example, Tashi's memory of a conversation among Olinkan elders. Is a sense of community shown to be possible in America? What happens in both continents, according to the novel, to the individual who is thought to have transgressed the norms of the community? How can community be created for people who are marginalized from mainstream society?

4. **Psychoanalysis:** Which features of Jungian psychoanalysis does Walker show to be helpful in Tashi's therapy? How does Walker use Mzee's interaction with Tashi to validate some Jungian hypotheses?

An essay on this topic would need to do some research on Carl Jung and his ideas. A possible place to start is with Jung himself. Jung's *Man and His Symbols* explains his theories of dream symbolism in language suitable for nonprofessional readers. This text will help you to start writing an essay on Walker's use of Jungian theories in the novel. How does Walker illustrate the therapeutic benefits of art? How does Tashi strive for wholeness in the Jungian sense? An extension to this topic would be to examine the character of Mzee (Jung). How does Walker characterize Mzee?

# Form and Genre

*Possessing the Secret of Joy* uses multiple first-person narrative voices. This structure lets the reader feel the immediacy of the character articulating her or his thoughts since there is no mediation by an external narrator. Walker does not use multiple voices to retell the same incidents from different perspectives. Each voice furthers the story according to that character's contribution to Tashi's situation. Within the framework of these characters' interaction with Tashi, additional insights and thoughts of a more personal nature are presented. There are advantages and disadvantages to using this type of narrative point of view. As mentioned, multiple first-person points of view offer access to a diverse range of voices with the intensity and openness denied third-person narration. The author can speak through male and female characters from different classes and cultures. On the other hand, many authors find it challenging to create truly distinct voices for their characters. If the characters all sound the same, then the benefits of this choice of point of view are negated. Furthermore, dialogues that are reproduced within this type of narrative sometimes sound forced, as if the character needs to learn a piece of information and this is the only way they could feasibly gain access to it.

### Sample Topics:

1. **The use of multiple first-person narrative points of view:** What are the advantages of using multiple first-person narrators in *Possessing the Secret of Joy*? How does Walker use this point of view to promote the novel's theme of the necessity of speaking out about pain and suffering?

   An author's choice of narrative point of view is critical as it must not undercut the goals of the narrative. An essay on the narrative point of view of *Possessing the Secret of Joy* could assess how the form relates to Walker's thematic and intellectual goals. The advantages and disadvantages of using multiple first-person voices could be considered in connection with how they promote or inhibit those goals.

## Language, Symbols, and Imagery

The multiple first-person narrative point of view contributes to the minimal number of well-developed symbols in *Possessing the Secret of Joy*. After all, people rarely speak using complex figurative language. The symbols that are present in the text are, thus, alluded to by one character usually no more than once or twice. An important theme in the novel is resistance, and there are several symbolic items that help to underscore that theme; an essay on symbols of resistance becomes possible by analysis of a selection of these objects. Similarly, Walker uses symbolism to highlight the psychological and physical damage caused by female genital cutting. These symbols can be analyzed to show how Walker aims to prove the hurt done to society by the practice of genital cutting that extends far beyond the pain of any individual woman.

## Sample Topics:

1. **Symbols of resistance:** Why does Tashi write her protest sign on paper having the colors of the Olinkan flag? Why do African potters start to produce sculptures of women enjoying their sexuality?

A flag is a symbolic representation of a country. Walker mocks the idea of a flag when she describes how the Olinkan colors were chosen and then the flag was mass-produced in Germany. Protest signs are a Western way to express opposition. Why does Tashi use this form of protest, and why does she deliberately aim to dishonor the Olinkan flag? When the women potters visit Tashi in prison, they explain that the statuettes of women fingering their genitals with pleasure were originally symbols of the Goddess or the Life Force itself. They represent a time when it is supposed that women were not subjugated by men. What is the significance of the fact that Tashi bequeaths her statuette of Nyanda to Mbati before her execution? An essay could examine how Walker uses symbols as markers of women's resistance.

2. **Symbols of pain:** How does Tashi's tower dream link to termite hills? How is the character of Benny used to show how a woman's circumcision pain affects others?

An essay on symbols of pain could analyze the textual elements that are used by Walker to add weight to the idea that the psychological and physical suffering a woman undergoes as a result of genital cutting affects more people than just the individual woman herself. How do Benny's slowness and his mother's treatment of him exemplify how the legacy of genital cutting affects men as well as women? What is the significance of termite hills in the origins of the genital cutting tradition? In her imagined role as termite queen, what provokes Tashi's horror?

## Compare and Contrast Essays

Tashi and Carlotta in *The Temple of My Familiar* are two women in search of wholeness. Their sense of fragmentation and dislocation from their respective societies is aggravated by their society's sexist attitudes and practices. For both women, a confrontation with the past is critical in steering them toward the Jungian-inspired individuation they seek, even though the journey into the past is completely different for the two women in terms of goals and outcome. Both women have a dual identity (African and American in the case of Tashi and American and South American for Carlotta), which raises questions and causes conflicts for them. Relationships with other women are vital for the support they offer each woman. Although the mother/daughter relationship is critical to both of them, coming to terms with negative memories and knowledge of their mothers is an important component of each of their journeys. Both women are married to men who are unfaithful to them, although the circumstances of the betrayals vary significantly. These two characters have many similarities, and comparing them could provide a promising foundation for an essay.

### Sample Topics:

1. **Tashi and Carlotta:** How does each woman respond to the values of her society pertaining to female appearance and behavior? How does each woman eventually heal and find wholeness?

   These two characters could be compared on the basis of their response to society's expectations for female behavior, their intimate relationships with other characters, and the contrasting ways that they achieve wholeness. Another approach for a paper would be to use Jungian theories and ideas to compare and contrast each woman's journey to individuation. For example, how does each woman use art, dreams, or the duality of the anima/animus to reintegrate the lost parts of themselves?

## Bibliography and Online Sources

*Anniina's Alice Walker Page.* December 30, 2007. <http://www.luminarium.org/contemporary/alicew.htm>.

Gates, Jr., Henry Louis, and K. A. Appiah, eds. *Alice Walker: Critical Perspectives Past and Present.* New York: Amistad, 1993.

Lauret, Maria. "Possessing the Secret of Joy." *Modern Novelists: Alice Walker.* New York: St. Martin's, 2000. 159–192.

Simcikova, Karla. *To Live Fully, Here and Now: The Healing Vision in the Works of Alice Walker.* Lanham, MD: Lexington, 2007.

# BY THE LIGHT OF
# MY FATHER'S SMILE

## READING TO WRITE

$B$ Y THE *Light of My Father's Smile* campaigns for the healing power of truth and reconciliation. In the excerpt below, Mr. Robinson hovers in a space between life and death, charged with the mission of fulfilling two tasks. His first task is to "guide back to the path someone [he] left behind who is lost," and his second mandate is "to host a ceremony so that [he] and others [he has] hurt may face eternity reconciled and complete." Mr. Robinson is aware that his two tasks are linked to his daughters, Susannah and Magdalena respectively, whom he hurt when he was alive because of his hypocritical attitudes toward sexuality:

... What we do know is that each of us will have a little bit of time, a window of opportunity, so to speak, in which to make amends, to say goodbye, to bring love back to a love-forsaken heart. And then we are gone, and no one even thinks of us anymore.

As Manuelito spoke, I was thinking of my literal haunting of my younger daughter, Susannah. To her surprise, she was dreaming about me constantly. She was "feeling" a presence lounging and lurking about her house. She was wearing black more and more, as if in imitation of my bogus priestly frock. She was wearing onyx on her finger, jet about her throat. When she slipped into her black car on her way down the mountain, it was as though she were entering me, her dark father, of whom she had once been so proud. So trusting, and so unafraid.

And I, my nose pressed now against the window of her love life, and especially her sex life. Trying to have a place in an area I had nearly destroyed. Was this natural? I asked Manuelito.

One of the most important foci in the novel is an examination of the father/daughter relationship. As Manuelito has made clear, Mr. Robinson's task is to make amends with Susannah, his youngest daughter, who turned against her father after she witnessed him beating her older sister, Magdalena. Magdalena's crime was having had sexual relationships with a local Mexican boy, Manuelito. Now, many years have passed, but Susannah is still searching for peace of mind and wholeness, and her primary method of striving for a better state of being is sexual experimentation. Her father, in a benign ghostly form, repeatedly spies on his daughter when she is in the throes of sexual passion. In the passage, the idea of any kind of participation in his daughter's sexuality seems "unnatural" to him. The Christian American society, in which he has been reared, has indoctrinated him into believing that he should isolate himself from, deny, and even subvert his daughters' sexuality. If a daughter is to be "Daddy's little girl," then both father and daughter must pretend that she has no sexual desire. The hypocrisy of this type of father/daughter interaction is reinforced by Mr. Robinson's savage beating of Magdalena, who, just as she is finding a sense of self through her own unique sexual identity, has shame and punishment inflicted on her for something natural. Mr. Robinson enjoys an active sex life with his wife and so would have been, ironically, one person who could have instructed his daughter in anything she might have needed to know about sexuality and pregnancy. Instead, he violently crushes her burgeoning sexuality and emerging self. The themes of father/daughter relationships, sexuality, the double standards of sexuality for men and women, hypocrisy, lies, and dishonesty are all possible topics for an essay.

The reason why Manuelito is able to explain to Mr. Robinson the post-death tasks he must perform is because Manuelito is Mundo. The Mundo are a part-Indian, part-black tribe who live in relative isolation in Mexico. Their beliefs, which include a celebration of sexuality and promotion of the father's role of support and encouragement in a daughter's reaching of sexual maturity, are in stark contrast to Mr. Robinson's Christian attitudes in which fathers absent themselves from all aspects of their daughter's sexual maturation. Throughout the novel, Walker juxtaposes the spiritual beliefs of the Mundo with those of Mr. Robinson, showing how assumptions of Western intellectual superiority have undermined indigenous beliefs to the detriment of all. An essay could compare the Mundo beliefs with those of Christian America (personified by the behavior and beliefs of Mr. Robinson), showing how the Mundo ideas are presented as liberating and natural, while Western beliefs are restrictive and unnatural. When characters start to lose their natural, instinctive celebration of the body and sex and begin to live by hypocritical, Christian, patriarchal proscriptions, the novel describes this as being "sucked into the black cloth." Susannah is depicted in the passage as being in a critical state because her spirit is being drained off into the color black. Her car, her jewelry, and her black clothing all symbolically indicate her precarious state of mind. Mr. Robinson knows that he must intervene before she is erased completely. Susannah's journey toward wholeness could be the focus of an essay. How responsible is Mr. Robinson for his daughter's happiness and choices?

Even though the Mundo and Americans are a world apart, Walker stresses that there are shared beliefs that span the globe. For example, nearly every culture has created the notion of angels, often giving a role to the dead in the lives of the living. In the excerpt, Mr. Robinson is conscious of his "haunting" of his youngest daughter; however, he is also haunted by her and is unable to move on to eternity (according to the Mundo belief system) until he has corrected the wrongs he has done to her. An analysis of Walker's blurred boundary between life and death could make a compelling paper. In some Western thinking, life and death are often conceived of as mutually exclusive. One of Walker's epigraphs asserts that love and friendship are about the "interpenetration of one another's soul by way of the body." Thus, Walker brings together another pair of concepts that are usually conceived of as binary opposites by fusing the body and the soul, rather than making them distinct entities. In her schema, sexual relationships allow characters to heal and to connect with the spiritual. This challenge to Western dualistic thinking could be the focus of a paper, examining Walker's merging of life and death or body and soul, or any other polarities that the novel dismantles.

*By the Light of My Father's Smile* raises many questions, suggests answers, and presents scenarios that go against the grain of mainstream Western thinking and accepted norms. In order to write about this novel, an essay writer must have an open mind. The controversial spiritual and sexual ideas advanced in the novel could become the focus of papers whose goal is to interrogate, debate, and evaluate.

# TOPICS AND STRATEGIES

The remainder of this chapter will focus on potential topics for essays on *By the Light of My Father's Smile* and different approaches that could be deployed in writing about those topics. Remember that the topics suggestions are simply a place to start from and should be used to inspire your own original papers.

## Themes

*By the Light of My Father's Smile* incorporates consideration of a number of themes; however, some of them overlap and writing on one theme may lead to the essay's touching on a different but related theme. Alice Walker has often been condemned by critics for her representation of African-American male characters. Some of her work, such as *The Color Purple* or *The Third Life of Grange Copeland,* has included graphic examples of spousal and child abuse, with men as the perpetrators of this sort of violence. However, other critics have pointed out that the goal of these works has not been to degrade black men or perpetuate negative portrayals of them, but to depict how they have the capacity for redemption and how their changed perspective and behavior would promote healing within the family. Furthermore, her work always shows black men's violence as evolving out of the racist environment that restricts their fulfillment as men. In *By the Light of My Father's Smile,* Walker explores the possibility of black men's redemptive potential, by showing the importance of the father/daughter relationship. To focus on this message, she locates the father beyond the immediate influence of any racist society (he is dead), so that his only purpose in the afterlife is to make amends with his two daughters for a single act of violence which has left both girls feeling betrayed and broken. His beating of Magdalena, out of hypocritical fear of her sexuality, causes both sisters to reject their father for his inappropriate rage. Mr. Robinson's mission is to reconcile with Magdalena and to facilitate both girls' healing. An important component of this mission is that both girls need to break free from the past to find their path in life. Many other characters also struggle to overcome difficult legacies from their parents and the past. Strong characters, such as Irene or Pauline, do not let the past crush them or erase their desires, even though, arguably, their pasts are far more traumatic than Magdalena's or Susannah's. Thus, the novel asks: How much responsibility must we bear for the choices that we make in our lives? At what point does blaming our parents become an excuse for our own weaknesses?

## Sample Topics:

1. **Father/daughter relationships:** How does the novel argue for a revolution in the way fathers interact with their daughters? How does the novel show the ways that a failed father/daughter relationship affects the rest of the family?

   Media representations of the father/daughter relationship still regularly advance the "Daddy's little girl" scenario as being an acceptable way for fathers to relate to their daughters. An essay could show how Walker reveals the hypocrisy of this type of father/daughter relationship because it tries to deny the daughter's sexual being and instead works to maintain the illusion of a girl's perpetual innocence and fidelity to Daddy. How does Walker suggest the father/daughter relationship could be reconfigured? How does she use Mundo beliefs to challenge Judeo-Christian beliefs of the role of the father in the family? An essay could focus on Mr. Robinson's relationship either with Magdalena or with Susannah, or it could compare and contrast his interaction with both girls.

2. **Rejection:** How do the novel's characters respond to their experiences of interpersonal rejection? How does Magdalena's rejection by, and of, her father lead to her self-imposed social rejection?

People frequently respond to rejection with depression or aggression. Why does Magdalena believe that her father loved Susannah, but not her? How does she respond to this perceived rejection? How do the themes of jealousy, power, and love tie into the theme of rejection? An essay could address any one of these themes in an analysis, perhaps looking at Magdalena's belief of having been rejected by her father, Susannah's awareness of her "rejecting power," Irene's rejection by her family, and the various other romantic and interpersonal rejections that the novel describes. What personality traits determine whether a character reacts to rejection with self-doubt or with self-determination?

3. **Reconciliation, forgiveness, and healing:** According to the Mundo, what are the missions of the recently dead? How does the novel show Mr. Robinson reconciling with Magdalena? How do different characters heal themselves from the pain of their childhoods?

   The novel demonstrates the necessity for reconciliation. Overcoming the wrongs of the past allows characters to find wholeness and heal. A key method to overcoming the negative legacy of the past is through forgiveness. The themes of forgiveness, healing, and reconciliation overlap in this novel, but any one of these themes could be used as the basis for a thematic analysis. Several character relationships are used to illustrate these themes, such as the relationships between Mr. Robinson and his two daughters, the fraught relationship between the two sisters, Susannah's relationships with Pauline and Irene, and the relationships between Mr. Robinson and his wife. Your essay could select any number of these relationships for examination. Another approach to this topic could examine the novel's depiction of the role of sexuality in healing.

4. **Breaking free from the past:** Which characters successfully break free from the past, and which characters stay trapped

in the past? Why does the past haunt some characters more than others?

Although this theme could easily be linked to the themes of forgiveness and healing, the novel provides sufficient textual support for this theme to be treated independently. The focus of such as essay could evaluate why some characters are destroyed by the past, while others move beyond the terrible things that were done to them as children. In the novel, which strategies for overcoming the past seem to be more successful than others? Why do some characters lack the ability to cope with the past? Could any characters be accused of contributing to the hold their past has on them? Do any characters believe they have broken free of the past, but this turns out to be a delusion?

# Character

Similarly to *The Temple of My Familiar,* Walker uses the names of her characters in *By the Light of My Father's Smile* to hint at the function of the character within the novel. In the Bible, Susannah is spied on by two lecherous elders as she bathes nude in her garden. They attempt to blackmail her by saying that they will accuse her of meeting a young lover in the garden unless she agrees to make love with the two of them. Susannah is rescued by Daniel, who questions the two elders and their discrepancies in their stories expose their lies. Daniel tells the two elders that an angel is waiting to cut them in two—indeed, they are put to death. The name Susannah is derived from the Hebrew word for *lily.* The novel indicates the relevance of the Stephen Collins Foster (1826–64) song "O Susanna!" to the character as well. The final line of this 19th-century song is, "And when I'm dead and buried/Susannah don't you cry!" Ironically, the song was written by a white songwriter as part of the racist "blackface" minstrel tradition, which was so popular throughout the 19th century. The etymology of Lily Paul's name is explained in the novel by Irene. A lily (which links her to Susannah) is the "flower of Lilith, the first mother" and is an "ancient symbol for the yoni." *Yoni* is a Sanskrit word that describes all the female reproductive organs. The name Paul can be traced back to St. Paul the apostle, whom Irene implicates in the Christian Church's repression of women. Magdalena's name originates from another biblical figure, Mary Magdalene, the repentant sinner and prostitute who was a disciple of Jesus. Finally, the name Irene has its roots in the Greek goddess, Eirene, who was the goddess of peace. Thus, thinking of the symbolic connotations of each character's name will help steer you toward valid approaches for character studies that link character to some of the foremost themes of the novel.

## Sample Topics:

1. **"O Susannah!":** How do Susannah's life choices as an adult arise out of her response to her father's beating of her sister? How does the ending of the novel, when Susannah dies and all her books are burned by her friends, reinforce Walker's message about legacy and remembrance?

    Susannah could be analyzed as a dynamic character who combats her past through sexuality and connection with others. Another approach to this character is to consider her symbolic functions within the novel. How do the different implications of her name point toward her symbolic meaning in the novel? Susannah is the only character that lives into old age and dies a natural death in her bed. How does Walker use Susannah's death and funeral to impart her vision of ideal interaction between humankind and the natural world, between different generations of humankind, and between friends and lovers?

2. **Lily Paul—the woman-man:** How does Lily Paul overcome a childhood in which she was repeatedly exploited? What is Lily Paul's (Pauline's) symbolic function in the novel?

    An essay on this assertive and aggressive character could analyze her development from exploited young wife to successful, sexually-assertive restaurateur. An alternative approach is to look at her importance in the novel for showcasing the power of women's sexuality. How does Pauline destabilize traditional views of female sexuality? Another essay could examine this character's role in Susannah's journey to wholeness. What are the parallels between Lily Paul and Magdalena? What does Pauline teach Susannah? What is the significance of Pauline's appearance at Susannah's funeral at the end of the novel?

3. **The "repentant sinner"—Magdalena:** Why is Magdalena's spirit broken by her father's beating of her? How do Magdalena's choices as an adult embody her attitude to her past and reveal her dominant personality traits?

An essay on this troubled character could consider how her family experiences as a child have shaped who she becomes as a woman. How do her unconventional appearance and her lifestyle reflect her inability to reconcile with the negative judgment she felt she received as a girl from her father? Another essay could explore Magdalena's function in the novel in bringing out the themes of love and sexuality. An analysis of the symbolism of her different names could also be the basis of a paper. Why does Magdalena change her name to June? Juno was the queen of the gods and the goddess of marriage and women's well-being. Why is this choice of name for herself significant, and why does her father always refer to her by it? What other traits are associated with Juno (or Hera in Greek)? Why do the Mundo call Magdalena Mad Dog? Why does her father modify this name to MacDoc?

4. **Irene—the goddess of peace:** How does Irene manage to triumph over her inauspicious beginnings in life? How does Irene function as Susannah's spiritual adviser?

An essay based on this character could analyze her function in contributing to the themes of breaking free from the past, the treatment of women in Western civilization, or the role of the church in restricting women's freedoms. Another approach to writing about Irene could be to contemplate her role as Susannah's adviser and educator. What does she teach Susannah? How does her advice and friendship with Susannah influence the main character's choices and decisions? Finally, a paper could appraise her symbolic purpose as an emblem of peace. How does she elucidate the theme of peace in the novel?

## Philosophy and Ideas

As with other Alice Walker novels, an articulation of philosophical ideas is emphasized in the narrative, with some characters becoming primarily mouthpieces for those ideas. Consideration of these ideas can readily generate possible essay topics. In the "Afterword," Walker writes, "I thank the spirit of Eros for its presence in my life and for the lessons it has taught me." Father Matthew Fox's quotation, which is used for one of the epigraphs, asserts that "Human sexuality is a mystical moment in the Universe. All the angels and all the other beings come out to wonder at this." Thus, the novel is framed by declarations extolling the importance of sexuality. Furthermore, the epigraph connects sexuality to death through its reference to angels. According to Freudian psychology, all humans have an instinct for life and survival (Eros) and a compulsion toward death and nonexistence (Thanatos). The desire for love and passion falls into the realm of Eros, whereas risk-taking or self-destructive behaviors are manifestations of Thanatos. However, even though the two drives are usually talked about as a pair of opposites—Eros versus Thanatos—these two principles are thought to stage an ongoing battle within our psyches. As a result, the pursuit of Eros can easily turn into self-destruction or aggression, as Walker illustrates in the way Magdalena behaves after her father beats her for being sexual. Similarly, Walker shows the instability of other dualities in the novel, such as life and death and body and soul. In *By the Light of My Father's Smile,* none of these interconnected pairs are as distinct from each other as might normally be imagined. The living and the dead are haunted by each other and involved in each other's existence through memory or ghostly observation. The Mundo claim that spirituality resides in the sexual organs, and this means that the soul can be penetrated through the body. One duality in the novel that is not dismantled is that of truth and lies. The Mundo believe that it "takes only one lie to unravel the world." Several of the characters have to deal with the realization that a lack of truth has contributed to the derailment of their lives. The Mundo speculate whether some Christian tenets have led to the chaos of the Western world. For example, they cannot accept the notion that God gave Man dominion over all earth. Man's assumption of control of the earth has resulted in wide-scale destruction and exploitation of the planet and its resources. Walker's novel emphasizes the dangers of the assumption that the earth belongs to man. Throughout history, people from more developed nations have traveled to other lands in search of resources that could be exploited for profit. The consequence of such travel was the corruption of indigenous populations, whose frequently more peaceful attitudes and harmonious way of life came under attack. The novel exposes this corruption through the history of Kalimasa's changing response to the tourists that throng to their country year after year.

## Sample Topics:

1. **Eros and Thanatos:** Which characters pursue love and passion and to what end? Which characters demonstrate self-destructive or aggressive behavior and to what end?

   To write such an essay, you will probably want to read Sigmund's Freud's *Beyond the Pleasure Principle* (1920), where you can find an explanation of his theory of Thanatos in conjunction with his earlier concept of Eros. With an understanding of these two drives, an essay could examine how Walker shows the conflicting impulses of Eros and Thanatos in characters such as Magdalena or Manuelito. Does the novel resolve the conflict between the two drives?

2. **Life and death:** How does the novel blur the expected boundaries between the living and the dead?

   An essay on the topic of life and death could consider the different techniques that Walker deploys to undermine the usual clear demarcation between the two states. For example, many of the narrators are dead, whereas some of the living characters are trapped in a deathlike existence. According to the novel, why have so many cultures created the notion of angels? In *By the Light of My Father's Smile*, what is the function of an angel?

This topic could be extended to include analysis of the dualism of body and soul. What does the novel propose is the function of sexuality in accessing the human spirit? Why are angels, according to the epigraphs, envious of human sexuality? How can the pursuit of sexuality lead to connection with one's spirit or to the spirit's destruction?

3. **Truth and lies:** Why do the Mundo not lie? How have lies damaged the lives of some of the characters?

This essay could identify some of the lies that different characters and/or cultures have perpetuated and analyze the effects of the lies on others. Analysis of truth and lies might also touch on the themes of hypocrisy and deception. For example, Mr. and Mrs. Robinson pretend to be Christian missionaries when they go to study the Mundo. This deception has terrible consequences for the entire Robinson family.

4. **Traveling and tourism:** Many of the characters make journeys to other continents and places. What are the effects of traveling on the traveler? What are the effects of tourism and traveling on the countries and populations being visited?

You could start this essay by looking at the various types of journeys that different characters make. Susannah, Irene, and the Robinson family are all described making trips to foreign countries. How does the novel depict the negative and positive sides of travel? Overall, does the novel condone or critique traveling and tourism? This topic could also consider traveling as the passage from life to death, which is presented as a journey with tour guides.

## Form and Genre

*By The Light of My Father's Smile* mostly uses multiple first-person narrative voices to tell its story, although some chapters slide into third-person omniscience, often where the primary focus is dialogue between Susannah and Irene. Some of the narrators are dead (Mr. Robinson and Magdalena), and some are alive (Susannah and Pauline).

Each voice articulates its experience of sexuality's role in forming and severing bonds between people. This choice of narrative point of view allows Walker to include the perspectives of male and female characters from different backgrounds. A limitation of this narrative point of view is that extended dialogues between characters sometimes sound as if the author wants to expound particular ideas, and a rather unnatural-sounding conversation is the only way that such ideas can be incorporated. An essay could evaluate how successfully the chosen narrative point of view backs up, or undermines, the novel's themes and ideas.

### Sample Topics:

1. **The use of multiple first-person points of view:** What are the advantages and disadvantages of using multiple first-person narrators in *By the Light of My Father's Smile*? How does Walker use this point of view to engage the novel's exploration of truth and lies, life and death, Eros and Thanatos, and cultural variances in attitudes toward women and their sexuality?

   When an author selects a narrative point of view, we can assume that she or he feels that the choice will successfully facilitate the goals of the narrative. An essay on the narrative point of view of *By the Light of My Father's Smile* could evaluate how the first-person/third-person blend supports the novel's intellectual objectives. The advantages and limitations of using multiple first-person voices could also be assessed. What are the advantages of using third-person narration for some chapters? How successfully does Walker differentiate the various voices of the narrators?

## Language, Symbols, and Imagery

The Mundo initiation song is repeated at intervals throughout the novel. Manuelito acts as the teacher of this song, coaching Magdalena while he is alive and Mr. Robinson after their deaths. As a boy, Manuelito rides a horse named Vado, which the novel explains means "a place in the river where it is easy to cross." The initiation song, entitled "Vado," is geared toward helping the living cross over to death. If someone dies singing, then she or he will continue to sing and live on the other side until they have completed their two tasks of healing the living. The song also serves as the Mundo's guide to correct living. Some stanzas address the idea of destiny, others assert the equality of woman and man; some verses express the necessity for love of children, while others extol the primacy of sexuality in life. As Mr. Robinson struggles to learn the song, he repeatedly confuses one line. Instead of saying, "by the light of my father's smile," he chants "by the light of my father's eyes." Manuelito sees this as a revealing slip and explains in detail the significance of a "father's smile" in the Mundo belief system. The father's smile is a symbolic interpretation of a phase of the moon when the Mundo believe that women are sexually receptive but less likely to conceive. The Mundo father celebrates his daughter's sexuality, rather than judging it critically or repressing it. This initiation song is critical in conveying some of the novel's central messages; therefore study of the song's different stanzas would lead to an essay engaging several themes and ideas.

When a daughter's sexuality is not allowed to express itself because of patriarchal restraints, laws of the church, and a society that wants to maintain the illusion of female innocence, the results (according to the novel) can be catastrophic. Magdalena turns to food and chronic overeating to assuage her pain and sense of loss. Ultimately, she dies from her gluttony. Her death occurs while she has a piece of cake in one hand and a can of beer in the other. However, the novel also provides many examples where eating food is a sensuous experience. When Susannah goes to Greece with Petros, the natural and wholesome food seems to act as a precursor to lovemaking. Susannah meets Pauline for the first time at her successful restaurant. The link between these two episodes is signaled in the novel by the recurrence of a cabbage rose oilcloth that adorns the restaurant's tables and, coincidentally, the table at Petros's parents' home. The oilcloth indicates the presence of good food, which is linked to the power of sexuality.

## Sample Topics:

1. **The Mundo initiation song:** How does the song express some of the central messages of the novel? Why is it essential for Mr. Robinson to learn the song after his death?

An essay on the initiation song could examine it for its importance in putting forth ideas that Walker uses to refute many mainstream Western beliefs. What beliefs does Walker want to question by promoting the perspectives of the song? Another approach could look at the way that knowledge and understanding of the song affects different characters. Why does Walker make Manuelito Mr. Robinson's spiritual teacher? Why are the phases of the moon important to the song and to Mundo men and women?

2. **Food and eating:** Why does Magdalena eat herself to death? In the world of the novel, how is food linked to sexuality?

Eating natural and organic foods can be a sexually charged experience for the novel's characters. To write on this topic, you will need to find all the meals that are described in detail in the text and consider the imagery that Walker uses in connection with the food items. What is the effect of this imagery? What is the significance of the oilcloth that appears on different tables? Another approach to the topic of food could consider its symbolic function in Magdalena's adult life. Why does she resist dieting or pursuing a healthy life? What does her resistance suggest about the relationship between food and sexuality?

## Compare and Contrast Essays

Siblings rarely respond in the same way to their shared upbringing. In the case of Susannah and Magdalena, tensions exist even before their father beats Magdalena. The two girls differ in terms of their behavior and outlook on life. Magdalena feels as if their parents love Susannah more than her, so jealousy and resentment are two emotions that undermine any possible sisterly relationship. Their reactions to Mr. Robinson's beating of Magdalena could not be more divergent. "Bad girl" Magdalena becomes self-destructive and repressed, whereas "good girl" Susannah adopts a bold lifestyle of crossing boundaries, literally and figuratively. A comparison of the two sisters' choices and their behavior is possible since Walker places the two characters in contrast to each other.

Susannah's adult sexual life is part of her path of trying to find emotional wholeness. Walker provides many details of her two most significant sexual relationships with Petros and Pauline. She travels with each lover, and in each case traveling away from the United States brings to light psychological and emotional gulfs between Susannah and the lover. Ultimately, each relationship founders even though they have a sexual connection. What is Susannah looking for that Petros and Pauline are unable to provide?

## *Sample Topics:*

1. **Magdalena and Susannah:** How do the two girls differ as children? How do the two women differ as adults? How does their shared upbringing unite them? How do their respective deaths affect their sisterly relationship?

   An essay on these two sisters could compare and contrast their respective experiences growing up in the Robinson family during their time in Mexico. How does Mexico shape who they become as adults? Why do the two girls respond so differently to the emotional damage caused by their father's brutal beating of Magdalena? When the two sisters meet as adults, what is the nature of their relationship? How does each sister have an emotional hold over the other one?

2. **Susannah's marriage to Petros and her relationship with Pauline:** What parallels does the novel establish between Susannah's two lovers? What does each lover teach Susannah? Why do both relationships ultimately fail?

   Like many of Walker's characters, such as Fanny (*The Temple of My Familiar*) and Celie (*The Color Purple*), Susannah is on a journey to find emotional, sexual, and spiritual wholeness. Relationships with men and with other women are key in propelling the character forward on this journey. An essay could compare and contrast Susannah's two most important relationships. What does she learn from each lover? Why must her journey eventually continue without them? Another approach would be to compare Susannah with female protagonists from other Walker novels. For example, how does Susannah compare to Celie in terms of their journeys to wholeness? For Susannah and Celie, how do critical relationships with a woman help show each woman a different vision of how life can be lived?

## Bibliography and Online Sources

*Anniina's Alice Walker Page.* December 30, 2007. <http://www.luminarium.org/contemporary/alicew.htm>.

Lauret, Maria. "Postscript: *By the Light of My Father's Smile.*" *Modern Novelists: Alice Walker.* New York: St. Martin's, 2000. 206–212.

Simcikova, Karla. *To Live Fully, Here and Now: The Healing Vision in the Works of Alice Walker.* Lanham, MD: Lexington, 2007.

# *NOW IS THE TIME TO OPEN YOUR HEART*

## READING TO WRITE

**A**LICE WALKER'S novel *Now Is the Time to Open Your Heart* has received mixed reviews. Some critics have praised the novel as profound, declaring that its easy-to-read style makes the novel's mystical ideas accessible. Other critics have accused the novel of being clichéd, arguing that its loose plot and structure work together to create a story that is difficult to relate to and hard to follow. In an interview with Rose Marie Berger in 2007, Walker asserted:

> In my writing, my focus is often on heightening awareness of spiritual teachings that might not be so easily understood. One of the problems with a mystic is that you're often out there by yourself. People will read a book like my last novel [*Now Is the Time to Open Your Heart*] and have no idea what you're talking about. [. . .] The aim of the Buddhist or the Christian person's meditation is to open the heart. That's what *Now Is the Time* is basically about.

What does Walker mean by the idea of opening the heart? The novel suggests that with an open heart, humans will be able to recognize and acknowledge one another's full humanity. Protagonist Kate Talkingtree wonders how murder could ever be committed if one person truly sees another. A closed heart leads to a violent world due to human fear and distrust of one another. The novel proposes methods that people can use to look inward and promote spiritual healing, resulting in an open heart. These methods include going on spiritual retreats, adhering to indigenous beliefs and customs, communicating with ancestors, and immersing one's self in nature. All of these methods come into play when Kate's search for an authentic life takes her to the Amazon to take part in a shamanistic retreat where consumption of a plant derivative impels participants to connect to their true self through dreamlike visions. Kate's journey and the different routes toward wholeness that she experiments with could become the focus of an essay. How does each method advance her spiritual healing?

The process of opening the heart is not necessarily an easy one. Each character has erected mental walls that initially obstruct them from achieving their enlightenment:

> How many shamans, perhaps even more gifted than Armando, had the Spanish slain? How many had they taken captive, pressed into slavery? How many had died in the gold and silver mines?
>
> And yet, here they were, tending the sick descendents of the people who'd almost destroyed them. Even their bodies, for hundreds of years, had not belonged to them. Armando and Cosmi carried the Indian spirit of their ancestors, but their bodies showed traces of the long Spanish domination, as did their last names.
>
> A sick person has no history and no nationality, said Armando when they were discussing the past.
>
> If you cannot feel that way there is no possibility of becoming a *curandero*.
>
> Kate pondered this. She was still plagued by those ancestors of hers who'd lived and died miserably. They wanted her to rectify their wrongs, she felt. There were weeks when they seemed to visit her every night.

The passage shows that, at this point in her life, Kate is blocked from being healed by her feelings about past wrongs done to people of color by white people. The anger provoked by knowledge of endemic, racist violence torments her with the conviction that she should pursue retribution. Specifically, she is visited in her dreams by a mutilated slave ancestor whom Kate suspects wants her to avenge his brutal murder by white racists. However, Remus teaches Kate that healing cannot be achieved "by settling a score." In the excerpt, Kate discerns the difference between herself and the two Indian shamans. Armando, similar to Remus, argues that a healer must not be concerned with race or past wrongs; otherwise, healing will not take place. An essay could examine the role of ancestors or dreams in the characters' lives. In this novel, ancestors are not only foremothers and forefathers from a character's direct lineage, but they can be an inspirational person, such as Saartjie Bartmann, whose spirit affects the living. Likewise, dreams are crucial in influencing characters' choices and attitudes in their lives.

The excerpt also brings out a recurrent topic in Walker's work: how white people's history of conquering and destruction has resulted in the loss of indigenous wisdom around the world. This loss has greatly affected not only the lives of people who were once the original inhabitants of a land, but also the lives of all other populations. In the passage, Kate reflects on how much shamanistic knowledge must have vanished because of the murder of so many Indians at the hands of the Spanish. The novel depicts a similar legacy of loss and injury in the aboriginal Australian and Hawaiian communities. A paper could explore what Walker thinks these communities and mainstream American society have lost as a consequence of the attempts to assimilate indigenous populations to dominant Western ideologies and behavior. How does the novel argue that the Hawaiian and Australian indigenous populations could try to regain their own traditional way of being?

It is likely that any essay on this novel will engage some features of Walker's spiritual beliefs. Character studies, analyses of symbols, or comparative essays will probably touch on consideration of the author's proposals for how to establish better relationships between individuals, between communities, and between humanity and the environment. Essay writers should be willing to open their hearts to these ideas and give them the consideration that Walker expresses hope for in her interview with Berger. An alternative method of approaching the novel would be to write a constructive critique of the ideas presented in the novel, analyzing possible oversights, contradictions, or ironies.

## TOPICS AND STRATEGIES

The balance of this chapter will suggest topics related to *Now Is the Time to Open Your Heart* and a variety of approaches that could be used to write essays on those topics. The suggested ideas should be used to help develop your own original approaches to these topics.

## Themes

The word *devotion* has a variety of different meanings: It can refer to intense love between people; it can be used to describe commitment to a specific purpose; or it can signify the following of religious observances. All three of these meanings are touched on in the novel. At the beginning, Kate dismantles her altar, which had been consecrated to a mixture of people and religious and secular beliefs. In the final chapter, Kate reconstructs her altar with Yolo's help as they prepare for a celebration of their love for, and life with, each other. In the middle of the novel, a secondary character, Hugh, narrates a story of an old Indian man's devotion to his ancestors. Every year, the man collects water from a spring that emanates from an ancient burial site to sprinkle it on a more recent graveyard. Hearing this story makes Kate ponder on the meaning of devotion in her own life. She speculates that one facet of devotion in any of its forms is the pleasure and the sense of purpose that it gives the devotee. Walker's exploration of the meanings and manifestations of devotion is a theme that offers the potential for an analytical essay. When Kate initially takes down her altar, it is because she feels as if her life is shifting. She is 57 years old, and her body is beginning to show signs of aging: Her knees have started creaking. She resolves to take a journey down the Colorado River as part of the process of healing herself spiritually. On the river trip, she meets other older women and they talk about the problems of aging in a youth-oriented society. The novel consistently argues for the reinstatement of the value and power of older women, questioning society's fear of old age. Another negative societal characteristic that Walker condemns is pervasive violence. Many of her novels have remonstrated with the problem of men's violence against women and white people's violence against nonwhite peoples. *Now Is the Time to Open Your Heart* also engages these themes but, in addition, it condemns the way that politicians simulate a pretense of working toward world peace. According to the novel, unless humans acknowledge their own fear of being annihilated and empathize with that fear in others, true peace will never genuinely be sought. Any of these forms of violence could be discussed in an essay.

## Sample Topics:

1. **Violence and peace:** What different forms of violence does Walker comment on in the novel? What are the physical and mental effects on characters of acts of violence?

   An essay could analyze the legacy of violence on the victims of male brutality against women or on the victims of racist aggression or both. How does the novel judge the violent? A paper could also be developed that investigates the novel's suggested therapies for overcoming violence on an individual level and on a community level. What steps does Grandmother explain are necessary for humans to achieve peace? What is the role of the individual in creating a state of peace?

2. **Male/female relationships:** How is marriage depicted in the novel? What are the causes of antagonism between men and women?

   If you write on the topic of male/female relationships, you could start by examining the main couple in the novel: Kate and Yolo. What does each character initially find appealing in the other? What makes them feel that their relationship is over as they set off on their respective journeys? A paper could analyze the nature of this relationship and how it changes over time. Why does the couple ultimately stay together and celebrate their union publicly? Another approach to this topic could look at men and women who are not in romantic relationships with each other. What are some of the ways that the novel shows men interacting with women? How do socially constructed gender roles affect the interaction between men and women?

3. **Devotion:** What different types of devotion does the novel illustrate? How and why does the novel extol acts of devotion?

   An essay on this topic could consider the different examples of devotion in the novel and show how they interconnect.

Alternatively, a thematic analysis could select just one of the types of devotion and make it the focus of a paper. For example, a thesis could be created that discusses devotion as an expression of love or that analyzes devotion in the sense of religious or spiritual observance. Regardless of the type of devotion, what are the human qualities that are needed in order to be a genuine devotee?

4. **Aging:** How does the process of aging affect the different characters? How does the novel depict the dangers to individuals and society by trying to conceal aging?

Kate, Yolo, and some of their friends are in their fifties. Many of these characters have been faced with the issue of whether to try and make themselves look younger or not. How does the novel judge the youth-oriented ethos of the United States? An essay could look at the issues surrounding aging as presented through the various characters and through Grandmother. Aging characters mention the idea that they become invisible as they age. Kate feels that eradicating a part of her "hard-won existence," for example by dying her gray hair, would result in her missing a part of her life. An essay could also look at the theme of invisibility, not only in terms of aging, but also in the way the novel describes white men as invisible. What causes invisibility?

## Character

Many of the characters in this novel serve as mouthpieces for philosophical ideas and appear only in specific sections of the novel; therefore, they do not make particularly effective subjects for conventional character studies. For example, Hugh might be discussed in conjunction with the theme of devotion or an examination of the value of indigenous beliefs. Lalika's story could be used to illustrate the process of spiritual healing or how men abuse and violate women. The two main characters, however, are dynamic and present opportunities to write about the transformations they make in their lives. Kate and Yolo both change as a result of the journeys they make. Kate boats down the Colorado and then voyages into the Amazon to take part in an unusual kind of spiritual retreat. Yolo travels to Hawaii with the intention of enjoying a standard beach vacation. However, his life changes forever when a local man asks him to stand guard over a young man's dead body. After this, Yolo is drawn into the lives of Hawaiians and can no longer ignore their harsh realities, such as the fact that many Hawaiians are addicted to toxic substances, which are killing them and undermining their traditional, community values.

## Sample Topics:

1. **Kate's journey:** Why does Kate decide to boat down the Colorado and what does she learn as a result of this trip? Why does Kate travel to the Amazon and what does she learn through the experience of this spiritual retreat?

   At 57, Kate feels that her life is coming to an end, but resists the thought of giving up on her life. She makes two significant journeys that help her reevaluate what and who is important to her. An essay on Kate could start by considering her psychological condition at the beginning of the novel. Why is she so dissatisfied? Why is she thinking of ending her relationship with Yolo? How do the two spiritual trips help her reassess her life path? What truths about herself must she confront? What adjustments does she make to her way of thinking and behaving? Why does she decide to stay with Yolo at the end of the novel?

2. **Yolo's journey:** Why does he call himself Yolo? Which characters influence Yolo on his journey? How do they do this? What does Yolo come to realize about his own life and the way he has been living it?

   A simple beach vacation takes a dramatic turn when Yolo is made aware of the Hawaiians' degradation at the hands of white America and the incredible strength and wisdom Hawaiians have within their traditional community. This knowledge forces him to realize that his life has not been one of reflection and awareness. Various characters provide him with different sources of wisdom and knowledge that oblige him to re-create himself. An essay on Yolo could chart his journey from unquestioning artist to a man who chooses to be Kate's spiritual and sexual partner in life.

# History and Context

A reconsideration of indigenous beliefs is an important goal of this novel. When Kate goes to the Amazonian rain forest, her purpose is to join in a shamanistic ritual where participants drink a sacred drink (the grandmother medicine or yagé), which allows them to look deep into their souls and find balance and a clearer sense of self. Armando, the shaman, draws on unique knowledge of cosmic power and nature to assist the visitors' healing. He also uses the grandmother medicine to help communicate wisdom from the spirit world. The use of this drink dates back thousands of years, and knowledge of its powers is passed from generation to generation of shamans. Kate realizes that such types of indigenous knowledge have been endangered by the destructive behavior and cultural superiority that accompanied European conquering of foreign lands. Yolo discovers wisdom and alternative worldviews in Hawaii when he is invited to join in a Polynesian circle, where discussion of local problems is headed by a Mahu (men who live as women). Two Australian aborigines also talk about the problems faced by their population as they struggle with the knowledge of what has been lost as a result of the imposition of white culture and values. *Now Is the Time to Open Your Heart* incorporates characters from different indigenous populations with the aim of showing how valuable knowledge is in danger of being lost because of the ascendancy of white beliefs and way of life. The novel shows that indigenous beliefs have value to nonindigenous populations, but also that they have intrinsic value for the indigenous people themselves and so should not be judged only for their potential contribution to a wider community.

## Sample Topics:

1. **The value of indigenous beliefs and way of life:** Which indigenous beliefs, customs, and traditions does the novel validate? How do indigenous beliefs, customs, and traditions offer a

viable alternative to mainstream white beliefs, behavior, and attitudes?

The novel contends that if indigenous populations are going to save themselves from destruction caused by their interaction with colonizers, they need to reconnect with their old ways and renounce negative white influences. An essay evaluating the value of indigenous beliefs and their benefits to both indigenous and other population groups could examine the information that Walker provides on native North Americans, South Americans, Hawaiians, and Australians. What does Walker find so insidious about some mainstream American attitudes and interpersonal interaction? How can utilizing indigenous customs help people open their hearts to one another?

## Philosophy and Ideas

Many of the ideas expounded in *Now Is the Time to Open Your Heart* are linked to the broad notion of healing the body and mind. Once the problems of the body and mind are addressed and rectified, then the heart can open itself in love. Although healing could be the focus of an essay in a more general way, some of the connected ideas could also form the basis of a paper in their own right. The novel proposes different techniques that people can use to help in their healing. For example, the power of nature is shown to be restorative. Kate first starts to experience a personal connection with nature during her trip down the Colorado. After retching and vomiting for some time, Kate picks up a wild plant and spontaneously eats it; immediately, she feels a lessening of her symptoms. Nature does not only have the power to purify the body, it can also aid in the attainment of spiritual goals. Canyon or rain forest, the novel presents nature as a cathedral where harmonious living with natural elements facilitates communion with a higher power that emanates from within the individual. Another method to connect with one's authentic self is through analysis of dreams. At the start of the novel, Kate's dreams of dry rivers propel her to make her journey on the Colorado. After her departure, Yolo begins to dream for the first time. A dream can affect a character significantly if she or he heeds its message. Kate has a life-changing dream about Remus, one of her slave ancestors, who was tortured by his white master. Kate initially feels that she must avenge the wrongs done to him. In her dream, Remus explains to her the function of ancestors: to remind the living of how not to live their lives. In her dream, Kate is able to restore the wholeness of Remus's body which, in turn, helps her to resolve her own conflict with her ancestors and the past.

## Sample Topics:

1. **Healing:** How do the characters come to realize that they are in need of healing? What techniques does the novel show can help in healing? How do retreats facilitate the characters' healing? Why must the characters open their hearts if they are to heal?

   An essay on this topic could look at the different procedures that the characters use to assist their physical, mental, and spiritual healing. Such an essay could draw on the stories of the secondary characters that Kate and Yolo meet on their journeys to exemplify the process of healing, or it could focus just on the two main characters. Another approach to this topic could show why the phrase "open your heart" is so important to the healing process. Take a look, for example, at the chapter where Grandmother explains to Kate how opening the heart is necessary to receive the full benefits of her plant medicine.

2. **The power of nature:** How are different plants used throughout the novel to cleanse and purify various characters? Why are water and trees important to Kate and Yolo? How can nature inspire spiritual regeneration?

   For this type of essay, you could select one or a few natural elements, such as water, trees, or plants, and show their significance to the characters and to the idea of nature having healing and spiritual properties. Why does Grandmother say that her medicine should be consumed only in the jungle? According to the novel, how are humans destroying nature, and what is the impact of this destruction on humanity?

3. **Dreams:** How do dreams influence decisions that characters make? How do the dreamlike visions induced by drinking yagé promote characters' healing?

Some characters' dreams are recounted in the novel, and there are overlaps between their dream and their life. The dream might reveal a truth to the character, or it might compel a character to make changes in his or her life. Why does Walker establish this confused boundary between dream and the state of being awake? One approach to this topic could examine the symbolic significance of the characters' dreams. Alternatively, an essay could discuss Walker's blurring of the distinction between dream and reality.

4. **Ancestors:** How do memories, dreams, or stories of ancestors affect the way various characters view their life? What do characters learn from communication with ancestors while under the influence of yagé?

If writing on the topic of ancestors, you could consider the ways that Walker shows how communication with spirits can lead to the gaining of wisdom and strength. How can knowledge of past wrongs done to ancestors empower the living? Alternatively, how can knowledge of past wrongs done to ancestors cause someone to close his or her heart? What role have the Mahus been given by their ancestors? What do the Hawaiians and the Australians feel has been lost by moving away from the traditional ways of their ancestors?

## Language, Symbols, and Imagery

The most important symbols and images in the novel support Walker's exploration of spiritual and physical healing. The novel introduces the concept of Grandmother each time Kate drinks yagé. The spirit of Grandmother is loving and allows communicants to reach a higher level of knowing when they are in her presence. The shaman Anunu informs Kate that the absence of Grandmother in the lives of people is what causes a constant feeling of fear. However, although the Grandmother that is accessed through drinking the plant medicine is not a tangible person, there are some women characters who are presented as embodying the Grandmother spirit. One such woman is Saartjie Bartmann, the so-called Hottentot Venus. Her story of abuse and exploitation helps Lalika and Gloria find the strength to withstand their repeated rape and mistreatment. By connecting with Saartjie's spirit through prayer, the two women feel that they are in the presence of pure love, and they are able to remove themselves mentally from the violence being done to them. When Lalika tells Kate her horrific story of abuse, the two women are sitting out in the rain near a waterfall and a river. Kate's initial decision to start seeking a new path in her life is precipitated by dreams of dry rivers. Water, in all its forms, is a very important natural element to the characters in search of higher knowledge of self and surroundings. Similarly, there are many instances where the characters observe or discuss animals, fish, insects, and reptiles. During a meal with Armando, the participants in the retreat discuss which creature has visited them in their jungle house. Armando offers an explanation of the possible meaning of each specific creature, whether it be a moth, bat, or gecko. A character's companion animal spirit sheds light on the behavior and attitudes of a particular character. An essay on the novel's depiction of Grandmother, or water, or animals would likely engage with philosophical ideas linked to the healing forces of nature and humanity's need for transformed interaction with the natural world.

## Sample Topics:

1. **Grandmother:** What do characters learn by drinking the grandmother medicine? Which female characters embody the spirit of Grandmother?

   An essay on the concept of Grandmother could examine the various female characters who are embodiments of the Grandmother spirit. Look, for example, at the story of Saartjie Bartmann or the account of Anunu. How do these older women guide and love the younger women with whom they are connected? What qualities do these older women have that are inspirational? Another approach to this topic could consider the ways that communication with Grandmother liberates characters from their pasts. How does Grandmother make freedom possible?

2. **Water:** How are rivers, waterfalls, rain, and the ocean important to different characters? What does Yolo's tattoo of waves symbolize?

The importance of water to Kate would make a valid essay topic because many of her most significant experiences take place near water. What does Kate's dream of dry rivers symbolize? Another approach to the topic of water would be to analyze the different meanings of water to a selection of characters such as Yolo or the old Indian who visits Hugh.

3. **Animals, reptiles, fish, and insects:** According to the novel, how are nonhuman creatures important to humans? To what purpose does Walker incorporate so many descriptions of natural creatures?

Writing on this topic could take one of two main approaches. A paper could discuss the relationships between characters and specific creatures. Walker depicts many characters as being associated with a particular species of creature. How does the specific creature shed light on the nature of the character? Another approach could look at Walker's use of animals, reptiles, fish, birds, and insects in general. Why does the second chapter of the novel recount a fable about a snake? How does this fable tie into the rest of the novel's plot?

## Compare and Contrast Essays

The main plot of Kate's journey is paralleled by the separate voyage of discovery that Yolo makes. The novel switches back and forth between the two plots, although the story starts and finishes with Kate and Yolo together. At the beginning of the novel, the two main characters feel that their relationship has run its course, and they are resolved to part.

However, after the events and epiphanies of their respective journeys, they end up publicly celebrating their love and shared life. Although the two plots are set in separate locations and although the main characters meet a completely different range of secondary characters, what the characters experience ultimately brings them together. How does Walker create parallels in Kate's and Yolo's journeys?

## *Sample Topics:*

1. **Kate's journey and Yolo's journey:** What do the two characters learn from their journeys? How do the two separate journeys culminate in the two characters healing their relationship?

   An essay comparing and contrasting Kate's and Yolo's journeys could assess a variety of elements that are common to both journeys. For example, what does each character realize about himself or herself during the journey? Whom do they meet on their trips and how do these encounters affect all involved? How does the past affect the present in the lives of the characters in both plots? How do the characters in both plots try to heal their individual and community problems?

### Bibliography and Online Sources

*Anniina's Alice Walker Page.* December 30, 2007. <http://www.luminarium.org/contemporary/alicew.htm>.

Bates, Gerri. *Alice Walker: a Critical Companion.* Westport, CT: Greenwood, 2005.

Simcikova, Karla. *To Live Fully, Here and Now: The Healing Vision in the Works of Alice Walker.* Lanham, MD: Lexington, 2007.

# "IN SEARCH OF OUR MOTHERS' GARDENS"

## READING TO WRITE

"IN SEARCH of Our Mothers' Gardens" is an essay. Essays discuss specific subjects or pursue lines of argument, usually of a short length. Analysis of essays follows along comparable lines to short story and novel explication; however, in the case of an argumentative essay, it is essential to have a clear understanding of the author's thesis. The most common type of essay written in high school and college is the five paragraph deductive essay. This style of organizing an essay places its thesis in the introduction, and then proves its assertion through three supporting paragraphs, before concluding with a paragraph that summarizes the main points made throughout the essay. "In Search of Our Mothers' Gardens," however, is an essay that uses inductive reasoning as its organizational strategy. In other words, it does not state its thesis and then prove it; it stacks layer upon layer of points as it builds toward its thesis at the end of the essay. Being aware of the type of organizational pattern that an essay uses will be helpful in figuring out the author's thesis.

The excerpt below is taken from the beginning of Walker's essay and is part of her plan to set the scene by explaining why black women were unable to express their creativity for so many years and the effect this had on their spirits:

In the still heat of the post-Reconstruction South, this is how they seemed to Jean Toomer: exquisite butterflies trapped in an evil honey, toiling away their lives in an era, a century, that did not acknowledge them, except as "the *mule* of the world." They dreamed dreams that no one knew—not even themselves, in any coherent fashion—and saw visions no one could understand. They wandered or sat about the countryside crooning lullabies to ghosts, and drawing the mother of Christ in charcoal on courthouse walls.

They forced their minds to desert their bodies and their striving spirits sought to rise, like frail whirlwinds from the hard red clay. And when those frail whirlwinds fell, in scattered particles, upon the ground, no one mourned. Instead, men lit candles to celebrate the emptiness that remained, as people do who enter a beautiful but vacant space to resurrect a God.

Our mothers and grandmothers, some of them: moving to music not yet written. And they waited.

The historical context is critical in understanding the societal restrictions that Walker presents as limiting the opportunities for black women's creative expression. The post-Reconstruction era covers the period of American history from the end of the 19th to the early decades of the 20th century. Race relations in the South at this time were characterized by violence against African Americans and a denial of their civil and human rights. In addition to discrimination on the basis of their race, black women were suffering the effects of widespread sexism. As the excerpt describes, their lives were constant toil; they were obliged to perform the labor that no one else wanted to do. An essay could examine the effect of the historical context on opportunities for black women to express themselves through art. Tied to this analysis could be an exploration of Walker's use of allusion. The excerpt alludes to Jean Toomer (1894–1967), an important writer of the 1920s Harlem Renaissance. His most highly regarded work, *Cane* (1923), explores black women's search for self-realization in the South during the post-Reconstruction era.

The passage contrasts black women's potential with their reality. According to Walker, Toomer metaphorically portrays these spiritually starved women as "exquisite butterflies." However, a butterfly must emerge from its cocoon in order for the world to see its beautiful display. The actual experience of these women was to be treated as the "*mule* of the world." A mixture of a donkey and a horse, a mule is known for its patience, endurance, and strength. A paper could consider how and why these qualities have been attributed to black women. How does Walker illustrate the strength of her black female ancestors? How did women's patience and endurance manifest itself? One explanation the passage mentions is that the women separate their spirits from their bodies in order to survive their situation. The contrast between the women's spirits and their bodies is also reinforced through Walker's use of religious imagery. Reminiscent of the biblical parable of the sower and the seed, the women's spirits are described as falling like wasted seed on hard ground where they cannot take root. The use and effects of nature or religious imagery could be explored in an essay.

Although the women are condemned to a life of spiritual emptiness, ironically their spirituality, although displaced, is passionate and intense. Their separation of mind and body forces their spirituality and creativity to seep out in the extremely limited ways that are socially acceptable. The women see visions, converse with ghosts, and draw the image of the Virgin Mary on courthouse walls. Religious fervor and mystical behavior are areas of their lives where the women are allowed to express themselves. Their vacancy goes unnoticed by men who are content to label them saints and are not concerned to understand their pain. Since they are perceived to be on the lowest rung of the social hierarchy, black women's concerns are invisible to others. However, their creative spirit was latent and was passed to their children through the arts that were open to them: cooking, sewing, quilting, storytelling, or gardening.

Thus, even though these women were denied the opportunity to find self-fulfillment, they did sow the seeds for future generations. As the whirlwind tossed their spirits on the hard ground, some seeds did fall on fertile ground. This is implied by Walker's phrase that asserts that some of "our mothers and grandmothers" were "moving to music not yet written." The desire to compose that music was within them, and they bequeathed that desire to their daughters. They taught their daughters the *"notion of song,"* if not the song itself. The thesis of Walker's essay is connected to the idea of black women's creativity and the importance of heritage and artistic legacies. What assertions does she make about these topics? Essays could consider Walker's position on forms of creative expression and on the connection between the past and the present.

# TOPICS AND STRATEGIES

The ideas suggested in the remainder of this chapter will propose a variety of possible topics on "In Search of Our Mothers' Gardens." These suggestions should be used as a starting point to aid you in generating your own innovative approaches to each topic.

## Themes

Although an argumentative essay will primarily be focused on persuading the reader of particular ideas, the author may still touch on certain themes within that framework. As Walker traces the history of black women's possibilities for creative expression throughout past centuries, a theme that is reiterated is the strength of these women who had to endure so much. Contemporary critics may scoff at Phillis Wheatley's verse, but if her personal history is taken into account, it is extraordinary that she wrote poetry at all. (For more information on Wheatley, see the "History and Context" section.) Even in more recent times, Walker's mother, who was raising eight children and laboring in the fields, made the time to nurture a beautiful garden and fulfill the creative needs of her soul, when other people might have just collapsed with exhaustion. According to Walker, such women as Phillis Wheatley and her own mother are owed respect for bequeathing "possibilities" and exemplifying "the will to grasp them." For black women of Walker's generation who do not have so many restrictions in place to obstruct their pursuit of art, there is almost a feeling of obligation not to betray the memory of those women who endured so much suffering just to leave a legacy of the possibility of being an artist.

### Sample Topics:

1. **Strength:** According to Walker's essay, in what different ways have black women demonstrated their mental, physical, and spiritual strength?

   The strength of a mule and the strength of a saint: These are two popular metaphors that Walker draws on in her essay to comment on the widely acknowledged strength of black women. An essay could examine the various ways that Walker shows how black women have proved their strength over the centuries. An extension of this topic could consider the negative legacy on black women of being labeled "strong." For example, Walker mentions that black women have been called "Mean and Evil Bitches" and "Superwomen." How does this assumption of extreme strength impede black women from finding fulfillment in their relationships and in their daily lives?

2. **Respect:** What is the legacy of respect that Walker's mother leaves to her daughter? How does Walker use her poem to demonstrate her respect for women of her mother's generation?

Referring to her mother, Walker writes: "Her face, as she prepares the Art that is her gift, is a legacy of respect she leaves to me, for all that illuminates and cherishes life." What exactly does she mean by this? An essay could consider the different reasons Walker presents as to why her generation should respect their female ancestors. This essay would likely encompass analysis of the theme of strength, but it would include discussion of other aspects in addition.

## History and Context

The argument of "In Search of Our Mothers' Gardens" spans hundreds of years of history, but focuses on two eras in particular: the late 1700s and the 1920s. By focusing on these periods of history, Walker establishes continuity between black women's experiences as artists in the past with black female artists' experiences today. Thus, writing on the historical context is a viable topic because Walker's argument stresses the relevance of historical context to black female artistic production. To write on this topic, you may need to do some secondary reading. Phillis Wheatley was sold into slavery at age seven, yet is the first published black poet in America. Her *Poems on Various Subjects: Religious and Moral* (1773) would make important reading for an understanding of Walker's position on Wheatley's achievements as a poet. Jean Toomer's *Cane* (1923) could prove constructive in gaining a broader perspective on the post-Reconstruction era, the era of Walker's mother. This period of American history is sometimes referred to as the nadir of American race relations because of a marked rise in white supremacist activities and escalating violence against blacks.

## Sample Topics:

1. **The position of black women in the late 18th century and the early 20th century:** How does the historical context of these two eras affect opportunities for black women in general and as artists? How does Walker establish continuity in terms of black female experience between the different historical periods?

Such an essay could analyze the effects of historical context on black women's artistic production. Additionally, it could include a look at how changing stereotypes of black women play into how they are judged as women and as artists. How have African-American women passed on a legacy in the arts despite the restrictions of their social and historical context? How do their foremothers' experiences as artists affect black women living in present times?

## Philosophy and Ideas

The main thrust of "In Search of Our Mothers' Gardens" shows how black women have felt compelled to express themselves creatively, even when social forces have conspired to silence them and block any possibility of artistic production. Walker goes back to the 18th century to tell the inspirational story of Phillis Wheatley, who despite being a slave, black, and female, had a volume of poetry published which received some critical acclaim. Walker asserts that Wheatley's poetry is riddled with "contrary instincts," which become understandable in light of her biography. The quality of the poetry from a contemporary perspective becomes irrelevant in face of Wheatley's achievement of getting her work published. Although Wheatley was successful in pursuing the more traditional art form of poetry, Walker argues that black women often expressed themselves through nontraditional media, using the materials that were available to them. Consequently, sewing, quilting, cooking, storytelling, and gardening are places where black women can find examples of their foremothers' creative vision and love of beauty. Although the topics of black women's creative expression and heritage overlap to a degree, they could each be the focus of an essay.

## Sample Topics:

1. **Black women's creative expression:** How have black women expressed themselves creatively during times when social realities prevented them from pursuing traditional art forms? What does Walker mean by the "contrary instincts" that can be discerned in the work of black women? What does Walker claim is the role of spirituality in artistic inspiration?

   One approach to this topic would be to consider the various nontraditional art forms that Walker claims became the foci of black women's creative spirit. Walker's redefinition of art provides a broader spectrum of artifacts that demonstrate black women's artistic impulses and love of beauty. The nontraditional art forms that can be considered are gardening, cooking, quilting, and storytelling. These activities are not marred by the contrary instincts that Walker finds in traditional art forms, such as the poetry or novels produced by black women in earlier times. Another approach to this topic would be to look at Wheatley's *Poems on Various Subjects: Religious and Moral* (1773), Nella Larsen's *Quicksand* (1929) or *Passing* (1928), and Zora Neale Hurston's novel *Their Eyes Were Watching God* (1937) or her autobiography *Dust Tracks on a Road* (1942) to find evidence of these contrary instincts. Although these three writers died in poverty or obscurity, how did they achieve literary success at a time when black women were given little encouragement or support to pursue the arts? Is there any evidence of Walker's work being affected by "contrary instincts" or breaking with traditional literary forms and conventions?

2. **Heritage:** According to Walker, what are the qualities that black women's foremothers have bequeathed to subsequent generations? How should black women of today respond to the artistic efforts of their ancestors?

In Walker's essay, although the focus is on establishing an artistic legacy derived from black women, she also demonstrates the importance of artistic heritage in general. She uses quotations from the work of Virginia Woolf and Okot p'Bitek to represent a female and a black legacy respectively. An essay could examine how Walker uses literary heritage in her essay. How does she build on ideas from the past to make them relevant for the present? How does she prove the contribution and value of black women to her artistic heritage?

## Form and Genre

Although "In Search of Our Mothers' Gardens" is an essay, it uses elements of other genres in its composition. Notably, it includes a poem by Walker, which is entitled "Women" when it is anthologized independently of the essay. A paraphrased stanza from p'Bitek's poem "Song of Lawino" is also incorporated into the essay. Additionally, Walker uses personal anecdotes and autobiographical memories of her family to flesh out her argument. "In Search of Our Mothers' Gardens" could be analyzed for its blend of genres, exploring the function and effect of this mixture of features. Why does Walker use a nontraditional form of essay writing?

### Sample Topics:

1. **A mix of genres:** Why does Walker write her tribute to her foremothers as a poem? Why does Walker mix the genres of the autobiography, the essay, and the poem in "In Search of Our Mothers' Gardens"?

   Such an essay could analyze the elements from the different genres that the text incorporates. How does the use of aspects from different genres enhance the text's philosophical and thematic goals? For example, what is the main message of the poem "Women," and why does Walker articulate this particular message through poetry (as opposed to prose)? As a black female writer, Walker embraces her nontraditional artistic heritage and recognizes the value of using whatever materials come to hand to express oneself creatively. Does the mix of genres reflect her heritage in any way?

## Language, Symbols, and Imagery

Essays employ language and rhetorical devices to bolster their arguments, and "In Search of Our Mothers' Gardens" is no exception. Its title hints at an area of figurative language that Walker uses throughout the essay, namely imagery related to the natural world. The most significant symbol is Walker's mother's garden. In the essay, she considers its divinely inspired beauty, its originality, and its attractiveness to others. Additionally, she observes that when her mother works in her garden, her face is transformed with radiance as she fulfills the dictates of her soul. When someone is skilled as a gardener, a popular expression describes such a person as having "green fingers." This saying implies that their skill in growing plants and flowers is a creative gift from God, not something that can be learned. Walker also deploys other images relating to the natural world in the essay. For instance, Walker repeats Toomer's description of post-Reconstruction era women as "vacant and fallow fields." Why are women so often described in the context of nature and the natural world? Linked to her usage of nature imagery and symbols, Walker also exploits religious images to convey the spirituality of black women in the past. In this way, the black women Toomer wrote about in the 1920s are invoked as "Saints." Their emptiness is comparable to an unoccupied church. Walker describes her foremothers as creators without the opportunity for creation. Along with both the nature and religious imagery, "In Search of Our Mothers' Gardens" incorporates many historical and literary allusions. Analysis of the function and effect of these multiple allusions could form the basis of an essay, showing how the allusions support Walker's arguments.

### Sample Topics:

1. **Imagery linked to the natural world:** What does Walker's mother's garden symbolize? In what circumstances are black women shown to be connected to, or working with, nature?

Such an essay could select any of the nature images and symbols that Walker uses and analyze how they add to the arguments she is making about women's lives and opportunities in earlier eras. How does the use of natural imagery create a link between women from different generations? Folklore referred to a black woman as the "mule of the world." Thus, imagery from the natural world can be used to denigrate black women as well as validate them. How does Walker validate black women's association with nature?

2. **Religious imagery:** Why were early 20th-century black women perceived as saints? How does Walker use biblical language and religious images to critique the treatment and perception of black women in the post-Reconstruction era?

Walker establishes art as the missing link between the popular perception of black women in the post-Reconstruction era and their seemingly insane behavior. Why does Walker describe their frustrated artistic impulses using religious imagery? For example, take a look at the paragraph where Walker alludes to the biblical parable of the sower and the seed or the section where black women are compared to temples. An essay could analyze why these post-Reconstruction women are described using religious terms. What is the connection between spirituality and art according to Walker?

3. **The use of allusion:** Which historical, literary, and religious allusions does Walker use and to what effect?

An essay could explore how Walker's allusions illuminate the arguments that she is making throughout the essay. How does Walker use allusions to Virginia Woolf and *A Room of One's Own*? Why is it significant that the literary quotations that support Walker's arguments are taken from the work of white women, black women, and black men? How and why does Walker alter other authors' work? How does Walker's use of allusions to black female writers differ from her use of allusion to Woolf, p'Bitek, or Toomer?

## Bibliography and Online Sources

*Anniina's Alice Walker Page.* December 30, 2007. <http://www.luminarium.org/contemporary/alicew.htm>.

Lauret, Maria. "Alice Walker's Life and Work: The Essays." *Modern Novelists: Alice Walker.* New York: St. Martin's, 2000. 1–29.

Wall, Cheryl A. *Worrying the Line: Black Women Writers, Lineage, and Literary Tradition.* Chapel Hill: U of North Carolina P, 2005.

Winchell, Donna Haisty. *Alice Walker.* New York: Twayne, 1992.

# "BEAUTY: WHEN THE OTHER DANCER IS THE SELF"

## READING TO WRITE

MANY YOUNGER siblings know what it is like to be hurt physically by an older brother or sister and then pressured to lie to parents about what happened. In Alice Walker's case, her brother shoots her in the eye with a BB pellet, which blinds her and leaves an unsightly scar on the eye's surface:

> "Yes, I will say that is what happened." If I do not say this is what happened, I know my brothers will find ways to make me wish I had. But now I will say anything that gets me to my mother.
>
> Confronted by our parents we stick to the lie agreed upon. They place me on a bench on the porch and I close my left eye while they examine the right. There is a tree growing from underneath the porch that climbs past the railing to the roof. It is the last thing my right eye sees. I watch as its trunk, its branches, and then its leaves are blotted out by the rising blood.
>
> I am in shock. First there is intense fever, which my father tries to break using lily leaves bound around my head. Then there are chills: my mother tries to get me to eat soup. Eventually, I do not know how, my parents learn what has happened. A week after the "accident" they take me to see a doctor. "Why did you wait so long to come?" he asks, looking into my eye and shaking his head. "Eyes are sympathetic," he says. "If one is blind, the other will likely become blind too."

As the excerpt explains, Walker's parents are unable to get their child to a doctor until a week after the "accident." Prior to this visit, the parents' medical therapies—lily leaves and soup—show their lack of awareness as to the severity of the injury. In fact, their assessment of their daughter's injury is limited only to the physical; they fail to notice how Alice's self-esteem has been damaged. The idea of blindness, both literal and figurative, is explored throughout this essay, and its analysis could become the focus of a paper. Walker's parents are blind to the psychological pain that their child is suffering. The doctor's cruelty in the passage ironically supports his idea that blindness can be contagious. He brutally tells the child that her other eye may lose its vision. His blindness is demonstrated by his insensitivity to the feelings of a child in pain. His words resonate with Walker, and she spends part of her adult years rushing around the world trying to see everything she can before her vision totally fails.

Walker's literal blindness is rendered through the image of the disappearing tree, which is the last thing her ruined eye observes. As her eye fills with blood, the tree vanishes from her field of vision, starting with its trunk and moving upward to its leaves. In other words, Walker is robbed of the ability to look upward. Raising the head and looking down are actions that are used symbolically by Walker in this essay as each action reflects respectively whether she feels beautiful and chosen or rejected and different. Acceptance and difference are themes that the essay explores through elements such as symbolism and repetition. The image of the vanishing tree provides an example of Walker's use of nature throughout the essay. When Walker is an adult, the sight of the desert overwhelms her because of its beauty. In the poem "On Sight," which can be found also in the poetry collection *Horses Make a Landscape Look More Beautiful,* she writes how trees in the desert always have their branches pointing upward toward the heavens. The desert is a source of intense poetic inspiration for Walker, who comes to realize that, with her one good eye, she is able to appreciate the beauty of the natural world and, for this, she should be grateful. Thus, the tree that slowly disappears from her vision, in the excerpt, rematerializes in a more powerful form in the desert, compelling her to look upward once more.

Another theme that emerges from the dynamics among Walker, her parents, and her brothers is that of family relationships. Sibling rivalry is commonplace within families, and it is not rare for children to believe that a brother or sister has deliberately harmed them. Walker indicates her skepticism toward her brother's claim that his shooting of her was an "accident" through her use of quotation marks around the word. Furthermore, her outrage that her brothers are more concerned about getting into trouble with their parents than her immediate pain intensifies her sense of injury at their hands. Walker's parents are struggling to raise eight children with inadequate resources in a racist society. Is it possible that they do not see their daughter's pain because she conceals it or because they are stretched to their limits in trying to take care of every member of their family? An examination of family relationships presents itself as a possible essay topic. Walker does not shy away from criticism of her family members—including herself—in this candid and emotive essay that incorporates personal memories.

## TOPICS AND STRATEGIES

The remainder of this chapter will propose various topics for essays on "Beauty: When the Other Dancer Is the Self" and different approaches that could be deployed in writing about those topics. Remember that the ideas are simply suggestions; you should use them as starting points to aid in creating your own topics.

### Themes

This essay engages with themes such as family relationships, perception, difference, and acceptance, any of which could provide the basis for a thematic analysis. Since "Beauty: When the Other Dancer Is the Self" can be considered partly a memoir, Walker's depiction of the interaction between the different people becomes an exploration of the dynamics of real-life family relationships. Walker addresses the nature of interaction among siblings, particularly focusing on the roles of power and empathy in such relationships. An important feature of Walker's sometimes critical look at family relationships is that there are often massive gulfs of understanding between family members. Only one of her brothers seems to have any awareness that the young Alice is traumatized by the altered appearance of her eye and battles with a loss of self-esteem as a consequence. The other family members' perception is off-kilter from

Walker's perspective. She is shocked that they fail to perceive modifications in her behavior and demeanor as a result of her disfigurement. In fact, the young Alice feels that her eye injury becomes the cause of her different status within the family. Some weeks after the incident, Walker starts performing poorly at school for the first time ever and gets sent to live with her grandparents. From her child's perspective, Walker concludes that she is "the one sent away from home," whereas her brothers get to keep their BB guns and stay with the rest of the family. The injured Alice makes a connection between the unsightliness of her eye, her own lack of beauty, her difference from others, and the degree of acceptance from other people. Walker interprets her return to her grandparents as a form of rejection.

## Sample Topics:

1. **Family relationships:** How does Walker portray sibling relationships in the essay? How does she present parent-child relationships?

   To write an essay based on an examination of familial relationships, determine what Walker's attitude is toward them by looking at the different examples depicted in the essay. The marriage between Walker's parents is shown as one that is caring, but that is marred by the pressures placed on them to provide for, and take care of, their large family. How do these economic pressures affect the relationship between the parents and their children? Look at the sibling relationships in the essay. How does Walker show them to be both constructive and destructive? A paper could examine the way that positive and negative relationships affect Walker throughout her life. Another line of inquiry would be to examine what Walker suggests are the causes of difficult personal relationships. For example, why does Walker insinuate that it may be possible to interpret her brother's shooting of her as deliberate?

2. **Perception:** In what ways do the people Walker writes about have gaps of understanding when they judge one another? What is the significance of the varying assessments the people in the

essay have of the same events? How does Walker perceive her eye injury in contrast to other people?

Throughout the essay, it is clear that Walker and her family view her eye injury differently. Her mother, for example, does not believe that her daughter changed as a result of the shooting, whereas Walker sees a significant alteration in her own behavior and attitudes. An essay could assess how perception affects judgment. In what ways do our knowledge and experience of people and situations affect the way we respond to that person or that situation? There are several instances in the essay where people make judgments of one another with consequences either for themselves or for the other person.

3. **Acceptance:** Why does Walker come to feel rejected as a result of her eye injury? How does the author finally reach self-acceptance?

   An essay on the theme of acceptance could consider the interplay between acceptance and rejection in terms of Walker's family members or in terms of Walker herself. Why does young Alice feel that her classmates do not accept her? Why does the young girl feel rejected by her family after the injury? Eventually, through surgery and a comment from her own daughter, Walker reaches a point where she can accept herself and what has happened to her. How does Walker employ dance and music imagery to describe this moment of self-acceptance?

4. **Difference:** In what ways does Walker feel alienated from her family, from her peers, and from her society? How does perception of difference affect Walker's behavior throughout her life?

   The theme of difference, although intersecting to some degree with the themes of relationships, acceptance, and perception, could provide an alternative approach for an analysis. How does Walker feel that she deviates from the norm? How does that assertion of difference affect her relationships with others?

# Philosophy and Ideas

Beauty is in the eye of the beholder. This saying has validity when it comes to the different perceptions of Alice Walker before and after her eye injury. The concept of beauty presupposes a standard of acceptability, and failure to conform to those standards may lead to ostracism within a community. This is exactly what happens to the schoolgirl Alice, whose peers taunt her about her damaged eye and fight her when she fails to offer up an easy explanation as to the circumstances of the injury. Little girls are often praised for being beautiful, and Walker feels that she lost this sense of being appreciated by everyone after she no longer conformed to the standards of beauty for femininity. Walker's belief in her external ugliness is accompanied by a belief in her internal undesirability. In other words, the girl Alice feels that she is rejected as a person because of the ugliness of her external appearance. Sadly, the impact of this childhood trauma haunts Walker even after she has become a mother herself. Her eye stands as a symbol of her lack of perfection, of rejection, and of blindness. Other people's blindness in perceiving the truth about the young Alice's feelings ironically juxtaposes the girl's own literal blindness. In this essay, it is unclear who is affected the most by blindness. Throughout the essay, the idea of blindness is explored both literally and figuratively, and its analysis could become the focus of an essay.

## *Sample Topics:*

1. **Beauty**: What objects and people are defined as beautiful by Walker or by other people? How does belief in having, or not having, beauty affect the way Walker interacts with others?

   When Walker is 12, she prays for beauty, not for restored vision. Since girls are routinely judged by their physical beauty, losing this precious and tenuous quality affects Walker's self-esteem and self-love. It takes her young daughter's innocent observation that her mother has a "world" in her eye to bring back Walker's confidence in her appearance. An essay could examine the idea of beauty as explored by Walker and show how she ties it to a girl's sense of self-worth, her relationships with others, and her perception of the natural world. Additionally, Walker's perception of beauty transforms as she matures. How does her understanding of beauty change? Another angle to this topic could consider Walker's insinuation of a link between female beauty and male violence. Why would men want to destroy beauty deliberately?

2. **Blindness:** How does Walker's partial blindness affect the way she conducts her life? Which other people are characterized by their inability to see things clearly?

Blindness can be defined as a lack of visual perception due to physical factors. However, the essay also suggests that blindness is a lack of perception due to psychological factors. This conclusion is implied by the doctor's observation that, "Eyes are sympathetic. If one is blind, the other will likely become blind too." An essay on this topic could investigate all the different manifestations of blindness that "Beauty: When the Other Dancer Is the Self" explores. How do people react to the condition of blindness?

## Form and Genre

Similarly to "In Search of Our Mothers' Gardens," this essay mixes in elements from other genres within its framework. It includes a poem entitled "On Sight," which evokes the beauty of the desert and its stark, untarnished remoteness. In addition, Walker structures the essay around personal anecdotes and autobiographical memories of her family, thus making the essay essentially a memoir. Arguably, however, the personal memories are used to substantiate the essay's thesis, rather than to relay the author's life. "Beauty: When the Other Dancer Is the Self" could be analyzed for its combination of genres, analyzing the function and effect of its unconventional form. Why does Walker seem to favor nontraditional forms of essay writing?

### *Sample Topics:*

1. **A blend of genres:** Why does Walker describe her epiphany at the desert in poetic form? With what goal does Walker combine the genres of the memoir, the essay, and the poem in "Beauty: When the Other Dancer Is the Self"?

A paper on this topic could analyze the mixture of genres that the essay exploits. How does the mix of different genres bolster the text's themes of difference and acceptance? The final paragraph of the essay confounds generic conventions because Walker describes a dreamlike moment where she dances with her self and that leads to inner transformation. How does this musical, dance ending to the essay add to Walker's destabilization of genre?

## Language, Symbols, and Imagery

Since the essay charts Walker's changing feelings on the meaning of beauty, a key symbol is Walker's actual eye. The author includes graphic descriptions detailing the nature of her injury and how it affects her overall appearance. Beyond the physical damage, Walker explains how the physical destruction of her eye triggers psychological problems. The young, extrovert Alice brimming with self-confidence, changes into a girl who no longer looks up. Walker claims that she does not raise her head and look someone in the eye for six years because her self-assurance has been shattered. The act of looking extends beyond her physical capacity for vision. After all, Walker still has one good eye. It is the welter of negative emotions inside that causes her to hang her head. Walker is not able to come to terms with her injury until 30 years after the event. Her epiphany at the desert, with her appreciation of her capacity to see its beauty, starts the journey toward healing and restored wholeness. Her daughter's observation that her mother has a "world" in her eye allows Walker to look at her self clearly in the mirror and accept what she sees. A technique that the essay deploys to underscore this slow journey to self-acceptance is repetition. By repeating the same phrases in different contexts, Walker is able to add weight to the depiction of her emotions and to add an overall sense of unity to the essay. Several different phrases and sentences are repeated for effect throughout the essay. Similarly, some images, symbols, and the overall structure of the essay rely on repetition to add to their effect.

### *Sample Topics:*

1. **The eye:** How does Walker's perception of her eye affect her behavior? How does Walker's capacity to look and see change as a result of her injury? How does an act of looking finally allow Walker to accept herself?

   An essay on the symbolism of the eye and the motif of looking and vision will likely link to the idea of blindness discussed in the "Philosophy and Ideas" section. How does Walker use the appearance of her eye to explore the themes of difference, acceptance, and relationships? Interestingly, even her growing fame as a writer is not able to quell her insecurities about her eye. What ultimately facilitates her self-acceptance, and how does this allow Walker to redefine her eye's appearance?

2. **The use of repetition:** Which phrases and sentences does Walker repeat throughout the essay? How does the structure of the essay use the technique of repetition to reinforce its thematic and philosophical goals?

An analysis of the topic of repetition could evaluate how Walker applies this technique and to what effect. The essay uses a variety of different types of repetition. Some repeated sentences are quotations from other people; others are sentences that emanate from Walker herself. The essay presents comparable images and actions in different contexts. What are the differences and similarities in the effects of these various types of repetition? Why does Walker rely on the technique of repetition to accentuate the essay's messages?

## Bibliography and Online Sources

*Anniina's Alice Walker Page.* December 30, 2007. <http://www.luminarium.org/contemporary/alicew.htm>.

Lauret, Maria. "Alice Walker's Life and Work: The Essays." *Modern Novelists: Alice Walker.* New York: St. Martin's, 2000. 1–29.

Waxman, Barbara Frey. "Dancing out of form, dancing into self: genre and metaphor in Marshall, Shange, and Walker—Paule Marshall, Ntozake Shange, Alice Walker—Intertextualities." *MELUS.* Fall 1994. FindArticles.com. 16 Sept. 2007. http://findarticles.com/p/articles/mi_m2278/is_n3_v19/ai_18583122

White, Evelyn C. *Alice Walker: A Life.* New York: Norton, 2004.

# "FOR MY SISTER MOLLY WHO IN THE FIFTIES"

## READING TO WRITE

WRITTEN IN 1972, Alice Walker's poem "For My Sister Molly Who in the Fifties" is addressed to the poet's older sister. Similar to Dee in the short story "Everyday Use," Molly left the family home in Eatonton in order to pursue an education. Carving out a life for herself that would offer more lucrative opportunities than the sharecropping lifestyle of her parents, Molly was obliged to tread a pioneering path that ultimately caused a rift in understanding between members of her family and herself. However, the process of disconnection with her family is gradual. At first, Molly seems intent on sharing the knowledge she has learned with her family, even if the knowledge is of questionable practical use given their farming lifestyle:

> FOR MY SISTER MOLLY WHO IN THE FIFTIES
> Knew Hamlet well and read into the night
> And coached me in my songs of Africa
> A continent I never knew
> But learned to love
> Because "they" she said could carry
> A tune
> And spoke in accents never heard
> In Eatonton
> Who read from *Prose and Poetry*

And loved to read "Sam McGee from Tennessee"
On nights the fire was burning low
And Christmas wrapped in angel hair
And I for one prayed for snow.

This is the second stanza of the poem and describes Molly's early optimism that she could educate her siblings and re-create them in her own, changed image. The idea of education that is explored in the poem is one that Walker discusses in other works, such as "Everyday Use," and assessing education's advantages and disadvantages could be the starting point for an essay. Such an essay could either compare Molly with Dee or evaluate the negative and positive consequences of education on someone who is the first in their family to be formally educated. Molly must have been fairly unique in Eatonton in the 1950s as an African-American woman leaving her family in pursuit of self-improvement and advancement. In this time period, the social norm for women was to get married and raise children, although dire economic straits obliged many African-American women to work inside and outside of the family home throughout their married lives.

The excerpt touches on a variety of themes that could form the basis for an essay. The theme of family relationships is of paramount importance in the poem, as it is in much of Walker's work. When the educated daughter returns home, there is tension and misunderstanding on both sides. For Molly, education has changed her perception of the way her family speaks and behaves. She understands that the outside world would judge her family harshly for their incorrect grammar usage and limited grasp of literature, geography, and history. From her family's perspective, Molly wants to change them—which implies that they are not good enough the way they are. Although both sides of this divide are acting from a position of love, a chasm opens up when a child's values are altered and become different from that of her parents. Molly, according to the stanza above, now speaks differently, "in accents never heard/in Eatonton." How do Molly and her family negotiate this clash of values? Another theme that emerges from this scenario of the return home of the educated daughter and her compulsion to inform her family of things they know nothing about is transformation. How does Molly change, and how does she try to make her family adjust their behavior and attitudes?

The gulf between Molly and her family is illustrated in the excerpt by the types of information that Molly attempts to impart to them. She has become familiar with Shakespeare's *Hamlet* and has become interested in poetry. Her awareness of the significance of Africa to black Americans is information she shares with her younger siblings. However, in their current situation, the information she gives them is not particularly useful. The irony of her situation is not lost on Molly, as is indicated by her repeated readings of Robert Service's "The Cremation of Sam McGee." This poem narrates the story of a man from the South who dies of cold in his search for fortune in the extreme North. When he is cremated, the warmth of the flames causes his resurrection. At this point, he remarks that it is the first time he has been warm since he left the South. This implies that Molly is aware of the contrast between her new lifestyle and the one she has left behind. Since Sam McGee's adventures take place in the snow, the speaker's comment that as a child she "prayed for snow" hints at the possibility that Molly's barrage of new information sowed the seeds of a desire for education and change in young Alice's life.

Snow can obviously be bright and white, and throughout the poem Molly is described as bringing light where there is darkness. In the excerpt, the snow (or the desire to pursue a life that is perceived as better) is contrasted with the dying fire around which Walker's family sit. Thus, the family becomes associated with a lack of light, whereas Molly and all the knowledge that she has accrued act as beacons of light in this darkness. Light and dark imagery is used extensively throughout the poem, and tracing its usage and effects could make a valid topic for an essay. However, light is not automatically associated with positive values. In a later stanza, the speaker of the poem describes Molly's light as "blinding." However, the last lines of the poem admit that the family, on the whole, was "[g]roping after light," with variable amounts of success.

When writing about this poem, it is important to pay attention to the ambivalence that Walker has toward her sister's transformation. Sympathy for her sister's plight is undercut by resentment and feelings of rejection. Empathy is marred by an acknowledged lack of full understanding of what Molly felt and experienced because of the time the two sisters spent apart. By paying close attention to the tone, the subtleties of feeling in this poem will become apparent.

# TOPICS AND STRATEGIES

The rest of this chapter will present possible essay topics for "For My Sister Molly Who in the Fifties." The suggested approaches should help inspire you to develop fresh ways to write about the poem.

## Themes

Although Walker's family is depicted as providing support and love, conflicts and tension develop as Molly becomes educated and has different values from other family members. In order to pursue her education, Molly is obliged to make choices that take her away from her family, literally and psychologically. Molly's transformation is gradual; thus her family's changing response also happens incrementally. The first time Molly is described coming home, her young sister finds something magical in everything that Molly does. Through her eyes, Molly is able to transform the ordinary into the special, as is symbolized by her mashed potato rooster. Molly readily answers all her siblings' questions, but the price they have to pay is to remove certain "vulgar" words from their vocabulary. Molly is now aware of how her family's English does not conform to standard white English. As time passes, Molly tries to improve not only her siblings, but also the appearance of their house, their cleanliness, and their knowledge of the world. As she grows older, Molly has the opportunity to travel, and this physical distance between her and her family is paralleled by their increasing psychological gap. Her parents are concerned with crops, church, and the weather. Molly becomes concerned with world issues rather than her family's local focus. Eventually, young Alice feels that her sister is looking at her family's behavior from a critical perspective. Not everyone in the family is able or willing to make the changes necessary for their self-improvement, according to Molly's standards. Thus, when one member of a family changes, this can have both positive and negative consequences on relationships within the family unit. The themes of change and family relationships, as presented in this poem, could both become the focus of an essay.

## Sample Topics:

1. **Family relationships:** How does Walker portray the interaction between Molly and her family in the poem? How does Walker present Molly's effect on her?

   An essay could analyze Walker's presentation of family relationships, looking at both its positive and negative aspects. How well does the family understand Molly? How well does Molly understand her family? This paper could also examine the sibling relationship between Molly and young Alice. How does this relationship help mold Walker's perspective on life?

2. **Change:** How does Molly's education transform her? What is the rest of the family's attitude toward change?

   A discussion of this theme could examine Molly's, Alice's, and the rest of the family's response to transformation in their lives. Similarly to the theme of family relationships, Walker presents both the positive and negative consequences of change in the lives of her family. Why are some family members unable to make changes in the way that Molly suggests? How sympathetic is Molly to her family's circumstances? How does Molly's changed perspective on life affect her and her relationships?

## Philosophy and Ideas

The reason why Molly's outlook on life differs so radically from her family's is because of the formal education she is receiving. This education allows her to view her family's behavior and lifestyle through the eyes of an outsider. She has become aware of how the rest of society critically judges incorrectly spoken English and attributes of the sharecropper lifestyle. However, it is unclear whether she is ashamed of her family, whether she wants to try and shield them from other people's critical assessments, or whether she sees her suggestions simply as self-improvements.

Eventually, Molly's educational journey causes the gap between her and some members of her family to become wide to the point of rupture. Thus, education has allowed Molly to escape a life of ignorance and poverty, but it is also responsible for divisions within the family. Other Walker texts, such as "Everyday Use" and *Meridian,* similarly describe how education can cause a person to become alienated from the community in which she or he were raised. Leaving in search of an education and returning home a stranger is portrayed as a distressing experience that affects both the one who leaves and those who get left behind.

### Sample Topics:

1. **Education:** What are the advantages and disadvantages of Molly becoming educated? How does the family respond toward Molly's new ideas, behavior, and attitudes?

A potential approach to this essay topic would be to consider Molly's relationship with her family as a result of being educated. Are Molly's suggestions for change within her family appropriate for the family's situation? Does she show any insensitivity to them? Additionally, the essay could examine the effect on Molly of her education. How does the knowledge she acquires drive a wedge between her and her past?

## Language, Symbols, and Imagery

When someone learns something that transforms their perspective on a certain issue, we might refer to that person as having been illuminated. The words *illuminate* and *illumination* describe the process of knowledge acquisition using imagery that conjures up the transition from a state of darkness to a state of light. Molly is compared to a "blinding" light, and Walker's use of light imagery in connection to Molly has both positive and negative connotations. Molly is bringing knowledge to her family, enlightening them about many different aspects of their world. Prior to her education, they were pretty much in the dark about anything unrelated to farming, church, and Eatonton. On the other hand, Molly's light is described as being an "overhead" light, which shines a spotlight on her family's limitations. Her light's brightness makes her mother's remoteness and her father's constant tiredness stand out. "For My Sister Molly Who in the Fifties" uses contrasting light and dark imagery throughout the poem, and analysis of its functions and effects could make a legitimate essay topic. Similarly, Walker's unconventional use of syntax could be discussed in a paper. The use of broken, syncopated sentences and capitalization creates contrasts and ruptures, which mirror the differences and divisions within the family.

## Sample Topics:

1. **Dark and light imagery:** How does Walker link light imagery to a state of knowledge and dark imagery to a state of ignorance? How does Walker use the contrast between light and dark to reveal differences within the family?

   An essay writer exploring Walker's use of light and dark imagery could trace its effects within each stanza and analyze how its meanings shift from the beginning to the end of the poem. If the family is associated with darkness and Molly with light, how does the family respond to light and how does darkness affect Molly?

2. **The poem's punctuation and syntax:** How does Walker use syntax to emphasize division and difference within the family? How does Walker use capitalization to reflect hierarchies within the family?

   An essay could evaluate how Walker uses syntax and capitalization to accentuate some of her poem's messages. Molly's deeds and accomplishments are frequently described in sentences that are completely capitalized. How does this use of capitalization serve to differentiate Molly from the rest of her family? The syntax of the poem is also characterized by gaps and unusual spacing. How do these spaces support the poem's focus on the clash of values and interests between Molly and her family? Finally, Walker uses enjambment, resulting in sentences that stop in the middle of lines and lines containing only a few words; this gives a choppy, syncopated rhythm to the poem. How does this rhythm further reinforce the idea of Molly's disturbing influence on the family?

## Compare and Contrast Essays

When Dee returns home to her family in "Everyday Use," her mother and sister prepare themselves for her arrival, experiencing a gamut of mixed emotions. On the one hand, Mama thinks of her daughter as some kind of celebrity, who must be treated differently from other family members. On the other hand, Dee's arrogant, superior attitude toward her sister and mother now that she has been educated provokes fear and resentment. Similarly, Molly sets herself apart from her family by demonstrating her newly acquired knowledge and trying to get others to adapt to her new ways. Despite her transformation, Molly is still a family member who shares the same roots and memories as everyone else. Thus, for Molly and Dee, there remain feelings of love and affection, which are complicated by the fact that each woman has been influenced by the world outside of the small southern community from which she hails. Each woman is equally an outsider and an insider.

### Sample Topics:

1. **Molly and Dee:** In what ways has each woman changed as a result of her education? How does each woman clash with her family on her return home? How does each family respond to their educated family member?

   An essay comparing and contrasting Molly and Dee could look at how the return home is perceived by each woman and her respective family. Dee has been influenced by the Black Power movement of the 1960s and 1970s, whereas Molly received her education in the 1950s. How does the historical context contribute to each woman's behavior on her return home? Does the poem present Molly more sympathetically than the short story does Dee? This topic could be expanded to compare and contrast the different families' reactions to the return of their educated family member. What effect does the older sister have on the younger sister in each case? How do the parents feel about their transformed child?

## Bibliography and Online Sources

*Anniina's Alice Walker Page.* December 30, 2007. <http://www.luminarium.org/contemporary/alicew.htm>.

Christian, Barbara T., ed. *Everyday Use: Women's Writers Texts and Contexts.* New Brunswick, NJ: Rutgers, 1994.

Washington, Mary Helen. "An Essay on Alice Walker." *Alice Walker: Critical Perspectives Past and Present.* Eds. Henry Louis Gates, Jr. and K. A. Appiah. New York: Amistad, 1993. 37–49.

# "I SAID TO POETRY"

## READING TO WRITE

FROM THE collection *Horses Make a Landscape Look More Beautiful* (1985), "I Said to Poetry" presents a spirited argument between a writer and her creative impulse over the writer's reluctance to put pen to paper. In the introduction to the collection, Walker writes how the move from New York to Northern California in 1978 allowed her spirit "which had felt so cramped on the East Coast [to expand] fully, and [she] found as many presences to explore within [her] psyche as [she] was beginning to recognize in the world." This poem discloses one of those presences. Her creative impulse urges her to wake up and start writing, while Walker herself fights the intrusion of inspirational images and memories because she feels that they will cause her so much pain to bring to artistic fruition:

> Poetry said: "You remember
> the desert, and how glad you were
> that you have an eye
> to see it with? You remember
> that, if ever so slightly?"
> I said: "I didn't hear that.
> Besides, it's five o' clock in the a.m.
> I'm not getting up
> in the dark
> to talk to you."

This stanza illustrates the intensity of the battle between the writer and her Muse. The creative process is connected to images of vision, life, and openness, whereas the writer's refusal to give in to the creative urge is linked to darkness, sleep, and denial. In the first stanza of the poem, Walker personifies this inspirational force as "Creation," and throughout the poem, as the excerpt above shows, this Muse talks in a persuasive, almost seductive, tone. Furthermore, the Muse is persistent, never relenting in its prodding of the writer to start composing. Since the Muse has access to the writer's store of fondest memories and images, it can titillate the writer by evoking emotions that are harnessed to specific memories. The personified Creation is a manipulator and resorts to guilt-tripping the writer in order to make her start writing poetry. Creation is aware that the writer only has one good eye and that this makes her feel more compelled to respond to the beauty that she is still able to see in the world. An essay could explore Walker's use of personification, or analyze her presentation of artistic inspiration, or consider the nature of the creative writing process as described in the poem.

The excerpted stanza alludes to Walker's essay, "Beauty: When the Other Dancer Is the Self," where she discusses the loss of vision in one of her eyes and how she battled to reach acceptance of her diminished vision and the resultant diminished sense of self through appreciation of the spectacular beauty of the desert. In "I Said to Poetry," Creation reminds the writer of her epiphany in the desert, invoking the positive things in her life as opposed to the pain. Additionally, the beauty of nature that the writer witnessed in the desert, with its unexpected colors and surprising discoveries, connects the writer to a sense of divinity in the world. Thus, to shut out the beauty of nature is to shut out the divine spirit. It is obvious from this stanza that Poetry is going to win the battle with the reluctant writer since this stanza (and the one following it) starts with the two words, "Poetry said." This shows the powerful, authoritative voice of Poetry when addressing the writer. Poetry's power over the writer takes on an almost godlike, omnipotent status. In this way, the link between the creative impulse and the divine is reinforced. The writer's desperate attempt later in the poem to shun poetry by saying she will turn to religion and prayer is not taken seriously by Poetry because the divine, the beauty of nature, and the creative impulse are all manifestations of the same force of the universe. An essay could examine Walker's vision of the divine and could draw on other of her works, such as "Beauty: When the Other Dancer Is the Self" for additional supporting evidence.

## TOPICS AND STRATEGIES

Suggested topics and approaches for essays on "I Said to Poetry" will be the focus of the remainder of this chapter. Ideally, these proposals will help you to generate your own topics and approaches to writing on the poem.

## Philosophy and Ideas

Two interconnected, but nevertheless distinct, ideas that offer themselves as essay topics are artistic inspiration and the writing process, and these topics could be explored together or in isolation. The process of creative writing is something that many writers examine at some point in their careers. Where do original ideas come from? Why do writers feel a compulsion to transform mental stimuli into words on paper? "I Said to Poetry" describes the process of writing as a torturous one. The speaker asserts that, "Having to almost die/before some weird light/comes creeping through/Is no fun." Nevertheless, trying to resist the creative impulse is ultimately impossible. If someone feels compelled to write, resisting the impulse is essentially fighting a losing battle. In this poem, Walker personifies the creative impulse, naming it "Creation" and "Poetry." Walker's Muse is insidious and employs ruses designed to entice Walker into responding to the urge to create. The Muse, although ironically a component of herself, is portrayed as an external force that has tyrannical power over her.

### Sample Topics:

1. **The writing process and artistic inspiration:** How does Walker depict the creative impulse? Why does she present the writing process as a battle that rages within?

   A potential approach to this essay topic would be to consider how the battle between the writer and her creative impulse plays out. Why does the speaker initially stave off the urge to create and write? How does her Muse retaliate and gain the upper hand in this battle? Ultimately, how does the fight between the writer and her creative impulse resolve itself?

## Language, Symbols, and Imagery

"I Said to Poetry" is written largely as a dialogue between the speaker and the figure of Creation/Poetry. Evidently, in order for this imagined dialogue to occur, Creation/Poetry must be personified to allow it to think and speak. At the start of the poem, Poetry is silenced by the speaker's aggressive denunciation of the creative process. However, this silence is only temporary and, by the fourth stanza, Poetry has found its voice and utters most of the words of the dialogue, while the writer attempts to ignore and shut out its insistent voice. However, Poetry cajoles and tempts the speaker with alluring memories and images from her past. The speaker tries to thwart Creation as she claims that she will take up religion again, but the confrontation concludes with the brutal recognition that she cannot deny the urge to write forever.

### Sample Topics:

1. **The personification of Poetry:** What characteristics does Walker assign to Creation/Poetry? How does the dialogue between Poetry and the writer unfold?

   An essay could examine Walker's use of personification when describing the creative impulse. What human attributes does she give to Poetry? These attributes may include emotions, desires, and powers of speech, among others. The dialogue between the writer and her writing is described as a battle of wills. Who wins this battle and how do they win? What effect does the humor of the last two lines of the poem have on an understanding of the personified Poetry?

### Bibliography and Online Sources

*Anniina's Alice Walker Page.* December 30, 2007. <http://www.luminarium.org/contemporary/alicew.htm>.

Walker, Alice. *Horses Make a Landscape Look More Beautiful.* San Diego: Harcourt Brace Jovanovich, 1984.

# INDEX